Organizing for Foreign Policy Crises

Organizing for
Foreign Policy Crises

Presidents, Advisers, and the
Management of Decision Making

Patrick J. Haney

Ann Arbor

THE UNIVERSITY OF MICHIGAN PRESS

2000   1999   1998   1997   4   3   2   1

A CIP catalog record for this book is available from the British Library.

Library of Congress Cataloging-in-Publication Data

Haney, Patrick Jude.
    Organizing for foreign policy crises : presidents, advisers, and the management of decision making / Patrick J. Haney.
        p.   cm.
    Includes bibliographical references and index.
    ISBN 0-472-10704-6 (acid-free paper)
    1. United States—Foreign relations—1945–1989—Case studies.
    2. United States—Foreign relations—1989–1993—Case studies.
    3. Presidents—United States—Decision making—Case studies.
    4. Crisis management in government—United States—History—20th century—Case studies.   I. Title.
    E840.H36   1997
    327.73—dc21   97-4582
                                                                        CIP

To Mom and Dad, who keep loving me,
and to John Lovell, who keeps teaching us

Contents

Tables

Preface

This book examines the ways that five modern American presidents organized and managed advisory groups during foreign policy crises. It focuses on the ways that crisis decision-making groups were managed and how they performed the tasks of providing information, advice, and analysis. The project keeps an eye toward links that might be seen between presidents' crisis management structures and the decision-making processes that emerged during nine U.S. foreign policy crises. The goal of the study is to increase our understanding of the organization, management, and behavior of the decision-making groups that presidents assemble during foreign policy crises.

I come to this project with an institutional and management perspective on foreign policy analysis, and I use a case-survey methodology to explore nine cases of crisis decision making in the Truman, Eisenhower, Johnson, Nixon, and Bush administrations. I examine the groups that were organized and managed, sometimes with greater success than others, in crises in Berlin (1948), in Korea (1950), in Indochina (1954), in Suez (1956), in the Tonkin Gulf (1964), at Tet (1968), in the Middle East (1970 and 1973), and in Panama (1989). The book highlights the organizational approaches to crisis decision-making management in these cases and evaluates the performance of the tasks of decision making in each crisis and across the crises. The evidence also provides broader lessons about the nature of crises and crisis management.

This book started as a dissertation at Indiana University (Haney 1992). In that form I examined six crises. To reach its expanded form I added the cases from the Truman and Bush administrations. From the start the project was energized by the work on presidential management by Alexander George (1980) and the provocative article by Herek, Janis, and Huth (1987) about the relationship between decision-making process quality and the quality of outcomes in crises. It seemed to me that these items must be linked in important ways. Herek, Janis, and Huth, who also used a case-survey method, found reason to believe that there is some connection between high-quality decision-making processes and crisis policy successes. My attention has been focused since on the origins, especially the structural origins, of decision-making process quality. Decision-making groups perform the tasks of decision well sometimes, and poorly others, it would seem. Why? This question is not going to be answered overnight, though we already have lots of good hypotheses on the table from the work of Irving Janis and others. I wished to enter this issue in a preliminary way by extending the type of analysis Alexander George performed on presidential foreign policy advisory systems into the realm of crisis decision making. I have thus tried to build on his abstract management models and on his methodological focus on case-based research. I hope this book contributes a small part to the process of answering important scholarly and practical questions about crisis decision-making management.

As with most books, some of the research reported in this book has appeared in earlier forms. Some of the literature discussed in chapter 1 is reviewed in "Structure and Process in the Analysis of Foreign Policy Crises," which appears in *Foreign Policy Analysis* (1995). Some of the Nixon material from throughout the study appeared in an earlier form in "The Nixon Administration and Middle East Crises: Theory and Evidence of Presidential Management of Foreign Policy Decision-Making," *Political Research Quarterly* 47 (1994): 939–59. Finally, some of the findings that I discuss and compare in chapter 4 appear in "Decision-Making During International Crises: A Reexamination," *International Interactions* 19 (1994): 177–91. These are each earlier and partial versions of the evidence and argument presented in this book. The progression of this project has also been tracked in a variety of conference papers, far too many to name here.

I am in debt to many who have helped and supported me along the path from dissertation to book. It is with great respect that I thank the members of my dissertation committee at Indiana University for their assistance and insight. From the time that I arrived in Bloomington, Professor John Lovell, my chair, has always been a friend, has always treated me as a colleague, and has always been most helpful. Professors Mike McGinnis, Lin Ostrom, and Jim Perry have similarly always been helpful and available (and prompt!). I would also like to thank Professor Leroy Rieselbach, graduate secretary Sharon LaRoche and the rest of the faculty and staff in Bloomington. I am much richer for the association. I would also like to recognize the financial support of the Indiana University Department of Political Science, the Indiana Center on Global Change and World Peace, the John D. and Catherine T. MacArthur Foundation.

I also thank the Department of Political Science at Miami University and the Committee for Faculty Research for their support, as well as my many friends and colleagues in Oxford and in the profession. My thanks especially to my research assistant, Erin Carriere, and to Larry Berman, Alexander George, Jeanne Hey, Lynn Kuzma, John Lovell, Bill Mandel, Mike Pagano, Jerel Rosati, Keith Shimko, Phil Williams, and a number of anonymous reviewers who have helped make my work better. This book probably still reads too much like a dissertation, but that is due to my failings, not theirs. I wish to also recognize the group at the University of Michigan Press who have been very helpful. Chuck Myers, and Malcolm Litchfield before him, Mike Landauer, Kevin Rennells, Lori Meek Schuldt, and Jillian Downey. (They have made this process as painless as could be expected for a good Buckeye publishing his first book with the Press Up North.) I would also like to thank Maureen Rada for preparing the index.

I deeply appreciate the people who helped not only in my professional development and debt relief, but also in the maintenance of my sanity. I owe much personal gratitude to John Lovell, Mike McGinnis, John Champlin, and Al Kuhn. I also want to thank old Bloomington friends Carl, Bob, Jim, Eric, Mark, Keith, Roger and Denise, and the City Hall softball team. I would like to thank Oxford friends Jeanne, Bill, Sheila, Sherry, Doug, Sherrie, Walt, Jerry, and the YankCanucks hockey team. Thanks also to friends and supporters across locations: Mabel, Dave, Tony, Marshall and Lisa, Elizabeth, Tommy and Karen, Amy, Betty, and Bud. Thanks to Maureen for putting up with me. I know this list is getting long, but I have been lucky to have great colleagues and friends. Thanks to my students who ask good questions and challenge me. Finally, I wish to thank my mom, dad, and family, who have always stood with me. Because of all of you this book is better; its certain weaknesses remain mine.

CHAPTER 1

Organizing for Foreign Policy Crises

The purpose of this study is to examine the ways that U.S. presidents since World War II have organized and managed advisory groups during foreign policy crises and the ways that these groups, so structured, performed the tasks of providing information, advice, and analysis. The goal of the project is to further our understanding of how presidents try to organize and manage decision making and with what effects. In the chapters that follow, I use a case-survey method to examine structures and processes of U.S. foreign policy crisis decision making and to explore how presidents try to cope with crises and how they build on their own and each other's experience with crisis decision making.

Nine crises in U.S. foreign policy provide empirical windows into the organization of crisis decision making: the 1948 Berlin airlift and the decision to intervene in Korea in 1950 for the Truman administration; crises over Dien Bien Phu in 1954 and the Suez Canal in 1956 for the Eisenhower administration; the events in the Tonkin Gulf in 1964 and the 1968 Tet Offensive for the Johnson administration; the 1970 civil war in Jordan and the 1973 October War for the Nixon administration; and the decision to invade Panama in 1989 for the Bush administration. Each crisis provides a historical example of the strategies that presidents use to organize and manage a group of advisers and an empirical record of how the advisory groups do the work of making decisions. Ultimately, we would like to build a body of policy-relevant theory about what works and does not work in the organization and management of crisis decision-making groups and about the links between structure and process in crisis decision making. I try to move in this direction by exploring the record of crisis decision-making management in a number of crises and presidencies.

This project is rooted in foreign policy analysis and the study of U.S. foreign policy crisis decision making. It builds on research on the management of the White House and of foreign policy-making by Richard Johnson (1974), Alexander George (1980), and Stephen Hess (1988; cf. Walcott and Hult 1995) by extending their approach into the study of structures and processes of crisis decision making. The project also builds upon the research on crisis decision making by Burke and Greenstein (1989), Janis (1989, 1982), and Herek, Janis, and Huth (1987) by trying to understand the organizational genesis of the processes of decision making. This study is particularly energized by the theoretical focus on "institutions." The link between institutions and crisis behavior may seem unusual, since traditional foreign policy analysis has largely not drawn on this perspective. This project explores the ways that the organizational structure and management of crisis advisory groups may have an important influence on the processes of decision making during crises.

Much of the foreign policy research that has focused on organizational management during crises points to the Cuban missile crisis as the birth of crisis management (e.g., Lebow 1983; Nathan 1975; Perlmutter 1975). Here is a clear case of a president learning from a fiasco (the failed Bay of Pigs invasion) and applying lessons to the management of a decision-making group in a future crisis. But this case was perhaps more unusual than representative for a variety of reasons (E. Cohen 1986), and while it does provide an example of a president consciously managing a decision-making group, we ought not presume that it was the first time a president sought to control crisis decision making by managing its structure. Part of the empirical purpose of this project is to explore the level of attention to the management of the structures of crisis decision-making groups that has been paid by U.S. presidents before and after this famous crisis.

Crises are, by definition, unexpected events. They are ambiguous situations that require a response; they are "critical points" for states (Roberts 1988, 10). Yet, perhaps paradoxically, a key purpose of crisis management is to make crises more like routine situations. One goal of crisis management is to construct mechanisms for controlling crises and to therefore treat them like "normal" situations, rather than like "novel" situations. Perhaps the most important ways that organization helps the president at any time, and certainly during crises, are to process information and to provide analysis and advice. Organizational structures and management techniques have greatly enhanced presidents' ability to make decisions and policy since these reports were issued. We might presume that presidents have similarly sought to control foreign policy crises through the organization and management of crisis decision-making groups and processes. The questions that drive this study are how have they sought to do so and with what effects? The remainder of this chapter reviews previous research that has explored the structures and processes of crisis decision making in U.S. foreign policy in an effort to set the theoretical and intellectual origins of this study.

Research on the Structures and Processes of U.S. Foreign Policy-Making

Structure refers here to the organizational configurations within which foreign policy-making takes place (cf. Haney 1995a). This configuration can include a broad set of formal institutions and how they are organized (e.g., the Department of State, the National Security Council, etc.) and/or may include a focus on how much smaller decision-making groups are structured or configured in a crisis. The suggestion that policy-making structures need to be part of the focus of foreign policy analysis can be found in the early emphasis on the study of foreign policy decision making. Snyder, Bruck, and Sapin, while urging that research attention be focused on the explanation of discrete decisions, remind us of the importance of the context of decision.

> The definition of the situation which we consider to be central to the explanation of state behavior results from decision-making processes in an organizational context . . . To ignore this context omits a range of factors which significantly influence the behavior of decision-makers (and therefore state behavior), including not only the critical problem of how choices are made but also the conditions under which choices are made. (1962, 87)

Robinson and Snyder argue that there are three major clusters of factors that explain decision outcomes: the occasion for decision, the individual, and the organizational context in which the individual operates (1965, 439–40). With respect to organizational factors, they assert that decision-makers not only act in an individual capacity when they make foreign policy decisions, but they also act within an organizational environment. An integral part of the study of policy-making, then, must be the "organization" cluster of variables (cf. de Rivera 1968, 207–44; Frankel 1963).

Government Organization

Research on routine U.S. foreign policy-making, much of which has sought to document the organizational configuration of specific departments or foreign policy organizations or to track the structure of the relationships between various foreign policy organizations in policy-making, has shed considerable light on the structures of policy-making. A long line of research has been performed within the U.S. government, focusing on the organization of the government and on the organization of the foreign policy apparatus of the United States. Concluding its review of the organization of the executive branch of the U.S. government in 1937, the "Brownlow Commission" argued that the president "needs help" for policy-making—more staff, better structures, and better management of those staffs and organizations (see Hess 1988). These recommendations have led over time to the development and expansion of the Executive Office of the President, a large staff that works for the president and vice-president to coordinate and plan policy-making.

The Eberstadt report, issued in 1945, focused specifically on the problem of foreign policy coordination and recommended the establishment of a National Security Council to facilitate such coordination (see Jackson 1965). Former President Hoover directed two commissions (1949 and 1955) that examined the organization of the executive branch of the U.S. government and the policy-making needs and functions of that branch (see Jackson 1965). In 1961, the Jackson subcommittee of the U.S. Senate examined the organization of the executive branch and, like the earlier Eberstadt report, focused attention on the way the National Security Council is organized for policy-making (Jackson 1965; cf. Hunter 1988; Prados 1991). Finally, the Commission on the Organization of Government for the Conduct of Foreign Policy explored the organization and administration of U.S. foreign policy (*Report of the Commission on the Organization of the Government for the Conduct of Foreign Policy* [hereafter *Report of Commission*] 1975). These studies show a consistent emphasis from inside the government on trying to assess the relationships that exist between the structure and management of foreign policy-making and the processes they produce. This focus on structure and process has traditionally been brought to bear on routine foreign policy-making, rather than crisis decision making.

Research on Presidential Advisory Structures

Research on the American presidency as a political institution is diverse and rich in description and provides some background for the present study. Unfortunately, it is often not systematic or amenable to cumulation (see C. Campbell 1993; Pika 1982; Pika and Thomas 1991; Rockman 1986). Research in this area ranges from psychobiographical studies, biographies, and research on personality and personal character to studies of individual presidents' foreign policy approaches and the relationship between Congress and the president in foreign policy. Foreign policy research has also examined American presidents' management of foreign policy bureaucracies, such as Hilsman's (1967) discussion of foreign policy-making within the Kennedy administration, Hammond's (1992) study of the Johnson administration, and the studies by Destler (1972); Destler, Gelb, and Lake (1984); and Allison and Szanton (1976) of the U.S. foreign policy bureaucracy (cf. Barnet 1971; Hunter 1988; McCamy 1964). Research in this tradition has been largely descriptive (and sometimes critical) of the organization and management of the foreign policy bureaucracy by particular presidents and has focused on the difficulties that leaders face in trying to manage foreign policy bureaucracies.

Case studies of crises and biographies and autobiographies provide a wealth of descriptive information about decision-making groups and provide much of the "data" for this study. The recent memoirs of James A. Baker (1995), McGeorge Bundy (1988), Clark Clifford (1991), and Paul Nitze (1989), for example, reflect on the activities of presidents' advisers across a variety of foreign policy issues. Case studies such as Quandt's (1977, 1993) studies of U.S. policy-making in the Middle East provide grist for our theoretical mills. Unfortunately, case studies are rarely written with the expressed purpose of trying to extract lessons about the relationship between decision structures and decision-making processes during crises. Nor have many foreign policy analysts tried to return to case studies and extract from them general lessons about the relationship between structure and process. While discussed in more detail in chapter 2, this study attempts such an analysis: to use existing case material to extract information about the presidential management of crisis decision-making groups.

There has also been a substantial amount of attention in the social science literature paid to the structure and organization of advisory groups in policy-making, such as Cronin's and Greenberg's (1969) review of the U.S. advisory system (cf. Herken 1992; Schilling 1962; Sickels 1974). Kernell and Popkin (1986) focus on the changing nature of presidents' chiefs of staff, noting the increasingly important role of the chief of staff to the president as a manager of, or one who structures, policy-making (cf. Benveniste 1977; George 1980; Meltsner 1990; Plowden 1987). Meltsner (1990) builds on earlier work to develop a set of guidelines and warnings for rulers who must rely on advisory groups (e.g., Benveniste 1977; George 1980; Hess 1988; Plowden 1987; cf. Burke 1984; Hult 1993; Neustadt 1990; Walcott and Hult 1995).

In his study of presidential advising, Barrett (1988) draws on data from appointment logs and other sources to discuss the important role of President Johnson's advisers in the execution of the Vietnam War. From this evidence, he contests the argument that Lyndon Johnson was a victim of groupthink or that he acted nearly alone in running the Vietnam War, showing rather the broad spectrum of advisers and advice that Lyndon Johnson received about U.S. policy in Vietnam (cf. Barrett 1993; Mulcahy

1995). Best (1988a, 1988b) and Best and DesRoches (1991) also use this sort of data to investigate the sources of advice that presidents have received. They focus on how those sources change over time and across issue areas (domestic policy versus foreign policy). Moens (1991) investigates the role of President Carter's advisers leading up to and following the fall of Iran's shah. Maoz (1990) discusses the ways that group settings are ripe for manipulation and explores their implications for policy formulation. He draws attention to the important role played by individuals and institutions in the process of translating preferences into policies (cf. Haney, Herzberg, and Wilson 1992).

Burke argues in *The Institutional Presidency* (1992) that studies of the U.S. presidency need to begin to examine in more depth the nexus between the enduring institutional (structural) features of the presidency and the management strategies and styles of particular presidents, and the implications of each for the other. He attempts to move in this direction by showing how modern U.S. presidents have dealt with these issues. The present study works from the tradition developed in the aforementioned research, in its effort to empirically explore the record of presidential management of advisory groups.

Research on Presidential Management

Many of the studies mentioned up to this point suggest that a link exists between structure, process, and policy performance; that is, they assume a relationship to exist between sound organizational structures and sound policy-making and policy. What they have largely failed to do, however, is to explicate the links between foreign policy structures, policy-making processes, and policy outputs in ways that would allow us to draw even contingent generalizations about the relationships between these variables. For example, what lessons might we draw about the role and impact of advising more generally from the research that examines President Johnson's advisory system? We seem to know a lot, continuing the example, about Johnson and his advisers. But we still have not learned much in a more general way about how leaders might structure an advisory process for decision making and with what effects.

Scholarship that attempts to understand how U.S. presidents have organized the White House for policy-making have at times explored more directly the possible effects of those structures on the processes of policy-making. In *Organizing the Presidency* (1988), Hess tracks the ways that modern U.S. presidents have structured White House operations. Besides describing the organizational styles of each administration, Hess discusses how presidents "learn" from the perceived organizational mistakes of each former president in an effort to fine-tune the structure of policy-making. For example, John F. Kennedy perceived problems in policy-making due to President Eisenhower's formalistic and hierarchical policy-making structures, so President Kennedy designed a less-structured, collegial organization for policy-making, which created its own difficulties (1988, 74–87; cf. Campbell 1986; Henderson 1988; Kessel 1983, 1984; Light 1982; and Porter 1980).

Burke and Greenstein (1989), in an excellent study that has helped inspire this project, examine the importance of advisory groups as well as presidential personality and the political environment during two cases of American decision making about Vietnam—Eisenhower in 1954 and Johnson in 1964–65. They seek to explain why two presidents who were faced with very similar problems responded in such very different ways. Their analysis indicates that the way presidents organize advisory groups may have an important impact on the process of decision making, but that the individual president's style and the political climate also affect the process of decision making.

Richard Johnson (1974) explores how U.S. presidents manage advisory groups that provide information, explore alternatives, and otherwise extend the president's "reach" so that the president can be successful at leadership and policy-making. Johnson focuses on how the White House is organized for general policy-making. He identifies three generic models of organization that presidents have used to organize policy-making—a formalistic, a competitive, and a collegial model of decision making (cf. M. Hermann and Preston 1994; Orbovich and Molnar 1992; Pika 1988). Alexander George (1980) borrows these models from Johnson in an attempt to similarly explore how presidents manage foreign policy-making groups in an attempt to use information and advice effectively.

The models that Johnson and George use to order their inquiry include a formalistic model that seeks to strongly structure the decision process, thus insuring a thorough analysis. It stresses hierarchy and a structured staff system. It allows the president to receive the benefit of information and advice already screened through the bureaucracy. It stresses optimality in decisions and discourages open conflict and bargaining among the advisers (George 1980, 150–57; Johnson 1974, 3–5). The orderly decision process enforces a thorough analysis and conserves the decision maker's time and attention. But the hierarchy that screens information may also distort it. This model may also respond slowly in a crisis (George 1980, 165; Johnson 1974, 238).

The competitive model places the president in the mainstream of the information network and places a premium on open discussion of diverse opinions. It relies on the stimulus of competition among advisers and bureaus to generate creative alternatives. It uses an unstructured kind of information network, open to ideas from outside normal channels. It may encourage overlapping jurisdictions and multiple channels of information. It stresses doability in its decisions (George 1980, 148–50; Johnson 1974, 5–6). This model may generate solutions that are politically feasible and bureaucratically doable, but it places a large demand on the decision maker's time and attention and may expose the leader to partial or biased information, and it may aggravate staff competition (George 1980, 165; Johnson 1974, 238).

The collegial model involves the decision maker in the information network but eases the demands placed upon decision makers in this process by relying more heavily on teamwork over competition. This model attempts to benefit from diversity and competition within the policy-making system, while discouraging parochialism. By stressing teamwork and collegiality, it attempts to avoid the pitfalls of infighting and intragroup bargaining associated with the competitive model. It stresses both doability and optimality (George 1980, 157–59; Johnson 1974, 6–8). This model does, however, place considerable demands on the leader's time and attention, and it requires unusual interpersonal skill in dealing with subordinates and maintaining teamwork. It risks that "teamwork" will degenerate into a closed system of mutual support (George 1980, 165; Johnson 1974, 238).

Much of what we do know about how presidents structure advisory groups is still drawn from the empirical work of Richard Johnson (1974) and Alexander George (1980). Indeed, it is in George's study of foreign policy-making that one can find perhaps the clearest attempt to discuss how modern U.S. presidents structure foreign policy advisory networks and the impact of that on information processing. There have been some recent attempts to refine or go beyond the models that Johnson and George both use in their studies (e.g., Crabb and Mulcahy 1995; Hermann and Preston 1994; Orbovich and Molnar 1992; Pika 1988), but there has been little empirical research on this topic that lends new insights. I try to add to our substantive understanding of how presidents organize and manage advisory groups by using the George and Johnson models as "ideal" types and starting points to organize an empirical study of presidential management of crisis decision making.

Burke and Greenstein (1989) take issue with these models as a useful scheme of classification. They argue that the effort to classify advisory structures misses the complex mix of formal and informal procedures that presidents use and often fails to provide a basis for distinguishing among different advisory models (1989, 21). While their dissent is a useful warning about the pitfalls of using ideal types, this study attempts to identify and compare patterns of advisory and decision processes for each crisis under consideration—an endeavor that Burke and Greenstein themselves recognize as beneficial (275). This strategy allows for more dexterity than simply classifying the management model that a president uses over the course of an entire administration (as George and Johnson do). It is appropriate in an exploratory analysis such as this to begin with simple, abstract models as ideal types to help order the confusing empirical record we are likely to uncover. Furthermore, the research design of the project and the coding form allow for deviations from or hybrids of these abstract models and take into consideration both formal and informal groups that presidents use to help make decisions.

Crisis Studies

Much of the research mentioned thus far has focused on routine foreign policy-making rather than on crisis decision making. Crisis research has largely not focused on organizational and management issues (see Holsti 1979, 1989; and Roberts 1988 for useful reviews of the crisis literature). There is a perception by many in the field that crises are fundamentally different from routine events. Crises are situations characterized by the perceptions of decision makers of (1) a serious threat to national values or interests that may come about as (2) a surprise with (3) relatively little time to respond (see C. Hermann 1972). Crises are situations that include a high likelihood that force will be used (see Brecher 1978). These variables contribute to well-documented phenomena: selective screening of information, enemy-image enhancement, the perception of being at a marked disadvantage, and others (see Milburn 1972; McCalla 1992). This research approach argues that while organizational structures, routines, and bureaucracies are important, crises are ruled by different dynamics. During these situations, the dominant disciplinary view seems to suggest, decision making is controlled by a few elite leaders and is highly personal, driven by individual perceptions of the situation. Structure may cease to be important during these situations as personalities increase in significance in the policy-making process.

Volumes of research explore crisis decision making with little reference to the potential importance of organizational configurations. Much of this literature deals with individual decision making and personality. This emphasis is at the heart of the decision-making framework presented by Snyder, Bruck, and Sapin (1962). It has been extended by research on cognition, operational codes and belief systems (e.g., George 1969; Holsti 1962; Kinder and Weiss 1978; Larson 1985; Mandel 1986; Sylvan and Chan 1984; Shapiro and Bonham 1973; Walker 1977). Research has also emphasized the impact of personality on foreign policy selection (e.g., Etheredge 1978; M. Hermann 1980) and on extending and systematizing a decision-making paradigm (e.g., Hogarth and Reder 1987; Mefford 1987; Rosati 1981; Shlaim and Tanter 1978; Snyder and Diesing 1977; Sylvan, Goel, and Chandrasekarin 1990).

This conventional view is inadequate and misses important components of decision making during crises. If crises heighten the importance of small, ad hoc groups of decision makers, as evidence overwhelmingly suggests that they do (see M. Hermann, C. Hermann, and Hagan 1987; Hagan, C. Hermann, and M. Hermann [forthcoming]; M. Hermann and C. Hermann 1989; Williams 1976, 69), then the structure and organization of these groups ought to continue to have an impact on the way decision making proceeds within those groups during crises. Indeed, if the underlying assumption of the aforementioned research on routine policy-making that management and structures matter in policy-making is on target, and if crisis research is correct that the group of top advisers to a president take on special importance during crises, then I would suggest that management and structures are not only *still* important during crises—*they are a vital component of decision making during crises.* Our focus must be not only on "players," but on "players in position" and on how those positions are constructed and managed during crises.

Bureaucratic Politics, Advocacy Models, and Decision Units

There are some examples of research that tries to make the connection between structure and process in foreign policy-making and focus on crises. One such example is the "bureaucratic politics" approach (Allison 1971; Allison and Halperin 1972; Halperin 1974; Ripley 1995). Research in this area has focused on how organizational structures and bureaucratic games shape the policy-making process and direct policy outputs or outcomes. This approach, or family of approaches, has sought to open the "black box" of decision making to analysis and to explore the ways that internal political processes affect foreign policy-making. An emphasis on the ways that organizational processes and procedures (Allison's Model II) and bureaucratic bargaining and infighting (Allison's Model III) affect the decisions reached by groups is central to this approach. Allison (1971) examines these components in American decision making during the October 1962 Cuban missile crisis. For example, Allison demonstrates that the organizational procedures of the U.S. Navy dictated how the naval blockade of Cuba would proceed and how these routines had to be overcome by the president when the navy's procedures were seen as counterproductive to the Kennedy's political effort in the crisis. Research within this tradition has extended Allison's method of analysis to different decisions and different national settings, though much of the research within this paradigm has studied noncrisis decisions.[1]

There has also been some attention to what have come to be called "advocacy" models in the study of policy-making. In a prescriptive article, Alexander George presents a view of how leaders of complex organizations can rely on "multiple advocacy" for policy-making, rather than centralized management. This policy-making structure "requires management to create the basis for structured, balanced debate among policy advocates drawn from different parts of the organization" (George 1972, 751). These structures would permit adversarial proceedings or provide for the role of a "devil's advocate" whose job it would be to question others and argue in favor of unpopular viewpoints.

In a more recent and extended treatment, Schwenk (1988) elaborates on ways that policy-making structures can be established within complex organizations, such as foreign policy organizations, so as to improve the quality of the processes of policy-making. The goal of these advocacy frameworks is to develop a set of structures that will allow for a thorough performance of the tasks of decision making and problem solving. The underlying assumption of these models is that some structures are more likely to lead to effective decision making than are others. In other words, they assume that structure does affect process in policy-making and that some structures are better suited than others for the tasks of policy-making. This research clearly has implications for crisis decision making, but the exact nature of those implications remains somewhat unclear because foreign policy crises have not been the subject of much "advocacy" research.

Another line of inquiry that examines the potential relationship between decision structures and the processes of policy-making is the research on "decision units" and their impact on foreign policy behavior (Hagan, Hermann, and Hermann [forthcoming]; M. Hermann, C. Hermann, and Hagan 1987; M. Hermann and C. Hermann 1989). Charles Hermann proposes that changes in decision structure should have an effect on the decision process, which in turn should have an effect on foreign policy behavior (1978, 71). The research strategy employed in this perspective seeks to discover the impact of different "decision units" on foreign policy behavior (M. Hermann, C. Hermann, and Hagan 1987). Specifically, research has focused on how different decision units can lead to different types of foreign policy behavior, such as how prone each unit is to the use of force. Theoretical research has focused on the impact of three different types of ultimate decision units: "predominant leaders," "multiple autonomous actors," and "small groups" (M. Hermann, C. Hermann, and Hagan 1987). Empirical support for the theoretical propositions about the different effects of these decision units has been fairly high (see M. Hermann and C. Hermann 1989; Kaarbo, Beasley, and M. Hermann 1990).

Managing Crisis Structures

One notable example of research that looks to the management of policy-making structures during crises, and the implications of that management for decision-making processes, is Irving Janis's *Crucial Decisions* (1989). Janis tries to develop an understanding of how the management of a policy-making group can eliminate "avoidable errors" in decision making. His goal is to examine management strategies that may lead to "vigilant problem solving." While much of Janis's book examines procedures (and thus may fit better in the discussion of process that follows), in his concluding chapter he presents a number of propositions about how leaders can manage or structure the process of decision making to make it more effective.

There are multiple approaches to the study of foreign policy-making that place emphasis on organizational structures and the management thereof, though often this emphasis is not extended to studying decision making during crises. I try to extend this theoretical emphasis into the substantive area of crisis policy-making. The project is particularly energized by research on policy-making structures that begin to show the connections between structure and process. In particular, this project works to extend the focus seen in the work by Johnson (1974), George (1980), and Burke and Greenstein (1989) into crisis decision making. Other research that begins by looking at the processes of decision making also shed some light on the management of those processes.

Studying the Processes of Foreign Policy-Making

Process refers here to the tasks that are performed by a group that lead to a foreign policy decision or choice. These tasks include conceptualizing goals and objectives, searching for information, and developing contingency plans. Anderson has argued that "at least a few individuals should focus on developing theories which describe the process of policy-making in foreign affairs" (1987, 285). His research suggests that decision making is a loosely coordinated activity that requires more attention by scholars on the decision-making processes that occur in group settings. One often-used strategy for studying the processes of policy-making has been the in-depth case study. The goal here is to examine the details of a historical case and from that attention to detail extract lessons about how the process of policy-making works. Comparative case-study designs may be employed as well that seek to "trace" the process of decision making and compare it from one case to another (see George 1979; George and McKeown 1985). Examples of this approach include the comparative research by George and Smoke (1974) on deterrence cases in American foreign policy; by George, Hall, and Simons (1971) and George and Simons (1994) on American attempts to use coercive diplomacy as an instrument of foreign policy; and the studies of Israeli decision making during the 1967 and 1973 wars by Brecher (1980) and Wagner (1974). While research that focuses attention on organizational structures has looked to crises relatively little, research on decision-making processes has focused a large amount of scholarly attention on crisis situations (see Holsti 1979, 1989). There are also many examples of case studies of routine or noncrisis policy-making processes, such as Art's (1968) study of the TFX aircraft and Greenwood's (1975) analysis of the decision to use MIRV technology on American nuclear missiles.

Malfunctions in Group Processes

Probably the most well-known study of the process of decision-making is Janis's study of groupthink (1982). Janis was motivated to explain performance failures, such as the American fiasco at the Bay of Pigs, by examining the internal dynamics or group processes that lead ultimately to group decisions. Groupthink happens when individuals within cohesive groups seek unanimity or concurrence to such an extent that they cease to vigilantly perform the tasks of decision making. Janis hypothesized that the presence of groupthink during the process of decision making might lead to policy failures because decision makers will not vigilantly pursue the tasks of processing information. While a psychological phenomenon that cannot be directly observed, Janis argued that groupthink produces behavioral consequences or symptoms that could be observed. These symptoms of groupthink include the failure to survey objectives, the failure to survey alternatives, the failure to examine risks of the preferred choice, the failure to reappraise initially rejected alternatives, the failure to search for information, a bias in processing information, and the failure to work out contingency plans (175). Janis proposed that the presence of groupthink made it less likely that decision-making groups would perform thoroughly the tasks of decision making; or, in other words, that groupthink made it likely that the decision-making process would include several malfunctions and might therefore lead to policy failures, such as the failure to survey objectives and alternatives and the failure to work out contingency plans (175).[2]

In a manner similar to Janis, George (1980) argues that there are several critical procedural tasks in effective decision making. He argues that decision-making groups must ensure that sufficient information about the situation at hand is obtained and analyzed so that it provides policymakers with an incisive and valid diagnosis of the problem. They must facilitate consideration of all the major values and interests affected by the policy issue at hand. They must assure a search for a relatively wide range of options and a reasonably thorough evaluation of the expected consequences of each option. They must provide for careful consideration of the problems that may arise in implementing the options under consideration. And finally, George asserts that they must maintain receptivity to indications that current policies are not working out well and cultivate the ability to learn from experience (10). Drawing on this concept of decision making, George identifies nine common malfunctions of an advisory process. These include, for example, when the president and advisers agree too readily on the nature of the problem facing them and on a response to it; when advisers and advocates take different positions and debate them before the president but their disagreements do not cover the full range of relevant hypotheses and alternative options; when advisers thrash out their own disagreements over policy without the president's knowledge and confront the president with a unanimous recommendation; and when the president is impressed by the consensus among the advisers but fails to ascertain how firm the consensus is, how it was achieved, and whether it was justified (122–32).

In an effort to build upon Janis's earlier work on groupthink and the research on decision making by Janis and Mann (1977), Herek, Janis, and Huth (1987) use a case-survey methodology to try to study the relationship between decision-making process and crisis outcomes in American foreign policy (cf. Williamson 1979). They draw upon multiple case studies of each of nineteen crisis decision-making instances and attempt to "code" whether the malfunctions in decision making used by Janis are present or absent in each crisis. They also had each crisis examined by a specialist to determine whether the crisis outcome was a success or a failure for U.S. foreign policy. Finally, Herek and his colleagues examine whether a relationship can be seen to exist between those crises with "high-quality" decision-making processes (those with few or no malfunctions present) and successful outcomes, and those with "low-quality" processes (many malfunctions present) and failed outcomes.[3]

This study merits much attention. Herek, Janis, and Huth find support for the notion that the quality of the process of decision making is related to the quality of the outcome, or resolution, of a crisis. They also find that some malfunctions (e.g., failure to reconsider rejected alternatives) occur more regularly than do others (e.g., failure to search for information). They pursue these empirical findings with a case-survey method, using case studies as "data sets" that can be scrutinized and from which additional information can be extracted. Multiple case studies of each crisis are used to obtain as full a picture as possible of the decision-making process.

An Institutional Perspective: Structures, Processes, and Outcomes

While there are a variety of studies that examine the processes of decision making during crises and noncrises, the development of "process theory" does not receive the attention that Anderson (1987) encourages. Nor does the process literature tend to look explicitly to structures and institutions as causal influences on process behavior, even though there have been many calls for foreign policy analysts to take the *group* in *group decision making* more seriously (Gaenslen 1992, 189; cf. Hult 1993). Alexander George argues that "information processing will be affected . . . by the structure, internal processes, and management of (decision-making) groups and relationships" (1980, 82). To address George's insight, analysts must begin to bridge the gap between the study of structure on the one hand and the study of process on the other. To do so, we need a conceptualization of politics and decision making that indicates how these issues may be interrelated. An institutional perspective may provide such a view. The institutional perspective stresses that institutional configurations set the context within which individuals operate. They give incentives and constraints to certain behaviors, and they produce behavioral effects. The institutional setting within which decision making takes place must be part of our analysis, even—and perhaps especially—during crises.

Research in public management and policy analysis has long focused on the importance of organizational configurations for policy-making. Increasing attention has been paid recently to the area of overlap between organization theory and political science (Bacharach 1989; March and Olsen 1989; Palumbo 1975; Rainey 1984). Within this common ground is a renewed emphasis on institutions within political science, international relations, economics, law, and public management (see E. Ostrom 1995). The philosophy that ties these approaches together is the proposition that an understanding of the impact that institutional structures, socialization, norms, expectations, rules, and selection mechanisms have on individual decision makers is vital to understanding political decision making (Crawford and E. Ostrom 1995). Research in this area is diverse, and views on what institutions are and how they affect policy-making vary widely.

Definitions of what constitutes an "institution" abound. March and Olsen define *political institutions* as "collections of interrelated rules and routines that define appropriate actions in terms of relations between roles and situations" (1989, 160). Within the study of international relations, Young defines them as "recognized practices consisting of easily identifiable roles coupled with collections of rules or conventions governing relations among occupants of these roles" (1986, 107). Keohane argues that the term *institution* may refer to "a general pattern or categorization of activity or to a particular human-constructed arrangement, formally or informally organized, that persists over time" (1988, 383).

Kiser and E. Ostrom state that organizations are "composites of participants following rules governing activities and transactions to realize particular outputs" (1982, 193). Rules are institutional arrangements. Ostrom defines rules as "potentially linguistic entities that refer to prescriptions commonly known and used by a set of participants to order repetitive, interdependent relationships." They specify what actions are required, prohibited, and/or permitted (E. Ostrom 1986, 5; Crawford and E. Ostrom 1995).

In summary, political institutions are sets of rules, constructed by men and women, that set the context for political action. "Institutional structures refer both to the organizational characteristics of groups and to the rules and norms that guide the relationships between actors" (Ikenberry 1988, 223). I use this conception of an institution because it focuses on both the formal and informal structures used in decision making. It concentrates attention on the "rules in use" in a decision situation, the rules and norms that are known by members of the group, even if they remain unstated. The existence of the rules of the institution can be inferred from the behavior of members of the institution.

Two characteristics are central to an institutional perspective. First, this approach emphasizes the derivative character of individual behavior. It focuses on how individual action is shaped by institutional settings. This perspective stresses that preferences are not exogenously determined; rather, they are developed through involvement in political activity that is structured by institutional arrangements. Second, in order to be an institution, a set of roles, rules, or behavior patterns must persist. It is through time, by an iterative process, that institutions affect individuals and thus political life.

The most basic feature of an institutional argument, according to Krasner, is that prior institutional choices limit future options.

First, capabilities and preferences, that is, the very nature of the actors, cannot be understood except as part of some larger institutional framework. Second, the possible options available at any given point in time are constrained by available institutional capabilities and these capabilities are themselves a product of choices made during some earlier period. (Krasner 1988, 72)

Keohane notes that political actors develop within the context of more encompassing institutions: "Institutions do not merely reflect the preferences and power of units constituting them; the institutions themselves shape those preferences and that power" (1988, 382). Keohane extends this point and argues that institutions mediate the types of action that will emerge from a process. If political action is to be the object of study, then the links that exist between observable behaviors and identifiable institutional settings must be explored.

Views on what institutions "do" vary as well. March and Olsen argue that institutions affect the flow of political life. They take as their basic assumption that the organization of political life matters, that institutions "define the framework within which politics takes place" (1989, 18). In a precursor to the new emphasis on institutions, March and Simon argue that the organizational environment in which a decision maker functions "determines what consequences he will anticipate, what ones he will not; what alternatives he will consider, what ones he will ignore" (1958, 139). They argue that these institutional factors cannot be treated as unexplained variables but must be subject to examination themselves if we wish to understand and explain decision making in groups.

Ikenberry argues that institutional structures "serve to mediate the interests and capacities of individuals and groups" (1988, 243). He urges increased research effort on the nature of these "constraining and enabling circumstances" as they impact on political processes. Krasner (1988), drawing on the insights of evolutionary biology and epistemology (see Gould 1989; Mayr 1982), states that an institutional perspective regards enduring institutional structures as the building blocks of social and political life. The preferences, capabilities, and basic self-identities of individuals are conditioned by these institutional structures; in this sense, historical developments are path dependent. Future decisions and actions, he argues, are constrained and guided by past decisions and arrangements; institutional settings are the genesis of future perceptions, preferences, and political action.

Methodological approaches used in institutional analysis range from formal game theory to in-depth case studies (E. Ostrom 1991, 1995; W.

Scott 1987; Zucker 1983). Research within this perspective may use a "micro" orientation, such as transaction cost economics and the economics of organization (e.g., Moe 1989; North 1990; Williamson 1975, 1981). A micro approach is also used in studies of committee decision making (e.g., Krehbiel, Shepsle, and Weingast 1987; Shepsle 1979, 1989; Tullock 1981). Institutional studies may alternatively take a "macro" perspective, such as V. Ostrom's (1991) study of American Federalism and Netting's (1972) study of political culture in African communities. Others have tried to craft institutional analyses that explore multiple levels of analysis (e.g., Kiser and E. Ostrom 1982; E. Ostrom 1990)

Within this tradition of institutional analyses are traditional policy-oriented studies that explore the relationship between institutional arrangements and political performance. Much of this research can be traced to Arthur Chandler's (1962) exploration of the relationship between strategy and structure; to the public choice tradition (V. Ostrom and E. Ostrom 1971; V. Ostrom, Tiebout, Warren 1961); and to the design science perspective presented by Herbert Simon (1981) in *Sciences of the Artificial* (see Shangraw and Crow 1989).

For example, Richard Nelson, in *The Moon and the Ghetto* (1977), argues that attention must be paid to exploring the right "fit" between organizational structure, environmental needs, and technical necessities. He urges increased attention to a rich range of organizational alternatives to policy problems and an exploration of the properties that emerge from such arrangements. Maynard-Moody discusses the "major influence" that "the institutional setting for policy-making has on policy ideas, choices, and actions" (1989, 137). Dilulio (1989) reviews recent studies of the effects of different organizational and management arrangements on the performance of schools, prisons, and armies. Chubb and Moe (1990) explore the relationship between institutional arrangements and school performance.

In an exploration of NASA's *Challenger* space shuttle disaster, Vaughan (1990) explores the impact of organizational design and autonomy on monitoring and safety control. She uses an institutional approach to investigate how institutional arrangements can produce behavioral effects. Elinor Ostrom has pursued an institutional analysis of the effects of different institutional arrangements on the management of small-scale common-pool resources (E. Ostrom 1990; Martin 1989).

Much attention has also been paid to the performance of public services by public and private enterprises. While the study of "privatization" by Savas (1987) is perhaps the most well known of these studies, Donahue (1989) presents an excellent analysis of the mixed blessings of privatization (see, e.g., Boardman and Vining 1989; Spann 1977; Wise 1990). Attention has also been given to the public-private distinction. This research explores if and how public and private organizations differ in their organizational characteristics and the outputs that they produce (Allison 1979; Bozeman 1987; Emmert and Crow 1988; Perry and Rainey 1988; Rainey, Backoff, and Levine 1976).

There is also a varied body of research that explores the relationship among structure, process, and outcomes; there is even a two-volume handbook on the topic (Starbuck and Nystrom 1981; see also Fredrickson 1986). This perspective on process management can be found in "private sector" management studies (e.g., Hayes, Wheelwright, and Clark 1988; Melan 1989) as well as public management research (e.g., March and Olsen 1989; Mintzberg, Raisinghani, and Theoret 1976; Oakerson 1987; Pennings and Goodman 1977).

These various studies and research traditions share a common perspective on the study of politics. Research as varied as congressional committee studies, investigations of common pool resources, studies of privatization, and international relations theory reflect a common view of the importance of organizational configurations for political behavior. This research explores the ways that different institutional rules and arrangements produce political processes and outcomes. In an effort to understand and explain political processes, the perspective that underlies this diverse body of research begins by exploring the structures that produce and shape political processes.

Conclusion: Structure and Process in Crisis Decision Making

An institutional perspective, which underlies this project and many of the approaches discussed in this chapter, provides a theoretical basis for exploring empirically the ways that organizational configurations and the management thereof work during foreign policy crises. Research on the presidency and foreign policy recognizes that organization matters for the process of policy-making during routine situations. It also notes that during crises, attention and importance shift to small decision-making groups. My basic premise is that if crises heighten the importance of small decision-making groups and the individuals within those groups, then the structure and management of those groups will be of increased importance for the process of foreign policy decision making during a crisis than is commonly recognized. This project aims to increase our substantive understanding of how these factors work during crises, to take up Hammond's call for more attention to drawing comparisons about how presidents deliberate (1992, 213).

To pursue this empirical link between structure and process, I draw directly from research on the importance of organization in the making and execution of (mostly routine) foreign policy. Research on how presidents organize the White House (e.g., George 1980; Hess 1988; Johnson 1974) and the foreign policy bureaucracy (e.g., Destler 1972; Hunter 1988; Jackson 1965; McCamy 1964) is extended by exploring the importance of organization during foreign policy crises. Most helpful in this effort is the research by Richard Johnson and Alexander George, both of whom draw implicitly on an institutional approach and thus begin the synthesis of institutions and decision making. Johnson (1974) focuses on how the White House is organized for *general policy-making*. George (1980) uses these models to explore how presidents manage *foreign policy-making*. These ideal models are an important starting point for this study to explore *crisis decision making*.

While these models are ideal types, they can be seen as operating in one form or another in the United States's postwar presidential administrations. But this project goes beyond noting that, for example, Eisenhower organized the White House in a "formalistic" manner. It explores what happens inside the White House when a crisis begins. How does Eisenhower structure and manage a group of advisers for decision making during a crisis? This project builds on George 1980 and Johnson 1974 by identifying the organizational models, or variations on the ideal models, used by American presidents for information, advice, and analysis in crisis decision making.

A key concern of this project is what effects these organizational forms have on crisis decision making. Here I draw directly from conventional research on decision making that implicitly uses an institutional approach (Burke and Greenstein 1989; Herek, Janis, and Huth 1987; Janis 1989, 1985; Janis and Mann 1977). These studies explore the relationship between the quality of a decision-making process and the quality of outcomes. They tend to focus on the presence of decision-making malfunctions and performance failures, though they also focus attention on performance successes. They employ an institutional approach in the sense that these studies do focus on the potential organizational sources of decision-making processes. I recast their emphasis on malfunctions and conceptualize decision making as a series of generic tasks that can be performed well or poorly by a decision-making group. Each task may be performed well or poorly by a set of decision makers.

While this study emerges from the aforementioned tradition, it also fits within the conventional focus of crisis studies (see Roberts 1988). It can be seen as part of the "organizational response" approach to studying international crises (Haas 1986), as the project investigates the ways that decision-making groups organized by the president work during crisis situations. There is also a crisis management concern in its emphasis on the ways that decision-making groups are managed during a crisis situation, though this is only one component of the crisis management literature (see, e.g., Gilbert and Lauren 1980; Holsti 1980; Haas 1986; Janis 1989; Milburn 1972; Sagan 1985; Williams 1976).

I also examine the extent to which presidents learn from their own (or their predecessors') experiences so as to improve the process of decision making. The literature on organizational learning varies in focus and perspective (Levitt and March 1988; see also Ventriss and Luke 1988). In the analysis of foreign policy, Etheredge (1985) sees organizational learning as an analogue of individual learning. He focuses on how governments "do better" or fail to do better over time. Neustadt and May (1986) explore the ways that leaders use historical analogies to help make decisions (cf. Vertzberger 1990). Lovell's approach to organizational learning is less value-laden on the part of the researcher and perhaps easier to make operational. I use this version of organizational learning that conceptualizes learning as "organizational change" in response to past experience (Lovell 1987, 1984; cf. Ravenal 1978). This approach focuses attention on organizational change that is brought about because of a "lesson" from past experience.

I also build upon the tradition of governmental studies of executive branch organization, such as the Brownlow report or the report of the Commission on the Organization of the Government for the Conduct of Foreign Policy. The project flows from an institutional perspective that is largely drawn from fields other than foreign policy analysis. It extends this perspective into the study of foreign policy by continuing the focus on structure and process that is evident in some studies of the presidency and the foreign policy bureaucracy. I use this theoretical synthesis to explore the nature of international crises and crisis decision making.

This project examines the nature and form of the decision-making groups that presidents have used during foreign policy crises. It explores the manner in which these groups performed their job of providing information, advice, and analysis during the crises. The broader goal of the project is to begin to identify the links that might exist between presidents' attempts to manage the process of crisis decision making through the use of organizational structures and the processes that were produced by the groups. The project attempts to generate a fuller understanding of the ways that presidents attempt to structure decision-making groups. The link between structure and process in crisis decision making is examined—

a link that is recognized and studied in other fields and subfields, that is explored for routine foreign policy-making, but which has not been systematically explored for crisis decision making.

My fundamental assumption in this project is that there is no perfect model for decision making. Rather, there are a variety of institutional forms that leaders can utilize, each of which has certain potential benefits and costs that may depend upon circumstances and upon presidential leadership style and strength. These tendencies are not deterministic. If a president is cognizant of the potential strengths and pitfalls of the organizational model that is used in a crisis, the possibility exists that the dangers of the model can be avoided. The empirical question of how presidents have tried to organize and manage advisory groups during crises and with what effects is the heart of the project. This empirical goal is joined with a methodological goal: to try to use case-study materials in a systematic way through the case-survey method.

Plan of the Book

Chapter 2 presents the methodology and research design used in this project and includes a full discussion of case selection procedures and coding instruments as well as a general discussion of the use of case-based methods in foreign policy analysis. In chapter 3, I present the empirical evidence of the management models that Presidents Truman, Eisenhower, Johnson, Nixon, and Bush used in the crises studied here. Chapter 4 examines the evidence of the decision-making processes that emerged during the crises. Chapter 5 concludes the study. It pulls these two bodies of evidence together and discusses broader lessons and conclusions that are drawn about the nature of crises and crisis decision making as well as areas for future research that emerge from this study.

CHAPTER 2

Case-Based Methods and Theory Development: Designing an Empirical Inquiry

Alexander George (1979) argued in an influential essay that researchers must begin to employ a more rigorous use of the case method to better allow for theory building in world and comparative politics and in the "bridging discipline" of foreign policy analysis (cf. Haney 1991). He presented a comparative case strategy, called "structured, focused comparison," that may help meet this goal. George argued that while cases are unique events, analysts must find ways to treat these unique events in systematic ways. He urged analysts to see individual cases as classes of events. In essence, he encouraged scholars to ask Rosenau's (1980) famous question of discrete events—"Of what is this an instance?" George was not the first to discuss these issues (e.g., Eckstein 1975; Eulau 1962; Lijphart 1971, 1975; Mill [1843] 1967; Przeworski and Teune 1970). Nor has he been the last. In the time that has passed since George's essay appeared, the case method has continued to be widely used for studying world and comparative politics and the foreign policies of nations. Some improvements in the way that individual cases have been used are evident. There has been an increase in the use of comparative case studies and some applications of George's structured, focused comparison. More attention has been paid to the logic of case selection and inference in qualitative research (King, Keohane, and Verba 1994; Geddes 1992).

However, there continues to be a large amount of case literature that lends little hope to theory cumulation and may actually impede theory development because of a lack of attention to theoretical and methodological concerns at the stage of research design. At this same time, some have continued to develop a case-study methodology that may be valuable for theory development and hypothesis testing. The purposes of this chapter are to extend the discussion about the role of case-based methods in the process of building theory about foreign policy; to discuss the part that the case-survey method can play in this endeavor; and to present the research design used in this study.

Uses and Abuses of Case Studies

There is a long tradition of case-study research in the social sciences and history. Detailed, individual case studies can serve many purposes. They can provide a rich understanding of an event that can be useful at the beginning of theory development by highlighting potentially important factors in a political process that can later be studied in a more systematic way. But individual case studies do not provide general theory. They provide few lessons that can be easily generalized. Eckstein (1975) discusses the many uses that case studies can serve. These uses include configurative-idiographic studies, disciplined-configurative studies, heuristic case studies, plausibility probes, and crucial-case studies. He argues that case studies are valuable at every stage of the theory-building process, and encourages a more theoretical treatment of cases and a more strict logic of case selection. In short, Eckstein argues for theory-driven inquiry.

With this optimistic note having been sounded, we are all nevertheless familiar with the observation that the case study falls victim to the problem of "too few cases, too many variables." But this problem need not be a death knell for case-based methods. Smelser observes that "the crucial factor determining the limitation of the case study lies not in the actual number of cases studied but in the lack of variation in possible causes and effects (1976, 199). D. Campbell (1975) suggests how to increase the theoretical value and validity of case studies. In particular, he argues that strong theory can eliminate the "degrees of freedom" problem (i.e., too few cases that are used to study too many variables). If cases are selected for strong logical and theoretical reasons, and if the research design includes some aspect of variable control through strategic case selection and comparison, then Campbell argues that problems associated with a "small N" relative to the number of variables under investigation can be minimized. He points to other factors that can make case studies a more theoretically useful pursuit, such as including cross-validation of findings, keeping facts that do not "fit" the theory, and paying attention to the potential impact of the researcher's prior knowledge of the cases.

Russett (1970) also discusses the value of case studies for theory building. He asserts that case studies have at least four uses in building cumulated knowledge. First, they can stimulate hypothesis production about regularities. Second, they can test inferences developed from a correlative analysis. Third, they can pursue the causal relationship between two variables of interest identified in a correlative analysis. Finally, they can refine and qualify hypotheses and theories (1970, 428–29). Russett emphasizes the complementary nature of case and correlative studies. He encourages the use of an iterative approach to theory building that may begin with an original case study that leads to the development of tax-onomies of classes of events or processes. A correlative analysis may follow this step. Then a return to case studies for theory refinement and testing would take place, followed by a second stage of correlative analysis.

Singer (1977) extends this emphasis by discussing three strategies for establishing control in a "historical experiment": the comparative case study, statistical manipulation of the variables of interest, and simulation. Concerning comparative case studies, Singer argues in favor of selecting a small number of cases (two or more) whose characteristics are such that they permit the sort of comparison that is desired. These cases must be identical or similar in some specified characteristics and different in others (1977, 10). Singer's point is that validity is not a matter of type of research or number of cases, but a matter of research design (cf. Mohr 1985). If designed according to logical and rigorous criteria, case studies can produce useful, valid theory about variables and processes that are of interest to analysts of world and comparative politics and foreign policy.

Concurrent with this interest in the case method, increased attention has been paid to the comparative method. Haas discusses the comparative method's values and pitfalls but emphasizes comparison as "the basis for creativity . . . in science" (1962, 303). While (single) case analysis is different from comparative analysis, the logic of the comparative method, when merged with case analysis, can provide a powerful tool for theory building. Verba (1967) argues in favor of a "disciplined, configurational approach" to theory building that looks beyond the single case to the comparison of many cases. This approach would search for factors that account for variation across cases, and it would search for rules that explain the relationships between many factors.

Lijphart also discusses the links between single case studies and the comparative method. He notes that the great weakness of the case approach is the problem of the small number of cases with many variables and that especially problematic is the temptation to dismiss a hypothesis on the basis of a nonconfirming case. Generalizations and theory testing are operations not well-performed by single or small-N case studies (Lijphart 1971, 685–86). Lijphart then presents a variety of strategies for comparative inquiry that can improve upon the single-case method: increase the number of cases, reduce the property space of the analysis ("collapse" similar variables), focus on comparative cases (cases that are similar in certain important respects but dissimilar in others), and concentrate on "key" variables (1971, 686–90). In a later essay, Lijphart defines the comparative method as "the method of testing hypothesized empirical relationships among variables on the basis of the same logic that guides the statistical method, but in which the cases are selected in such a way as to maximize the variance of the independent variables and to minimize the variance of the control variables" (1975, 164). This definition places emphasis on the careful selection of cases that fit the research problem (Lijphart 1975, 176). While Lijphart may have been advocating only a comparable case strategy, which is of course not the only viable research strategy (see Frendreis 1983), his emphasis on the role that strategically selected cases in a small-N study can play by allowing a logic of inference to be developed is similar to the arguments of Eckstein, Campbell, Russett, Singer, and those I discuss subsequently who explicitly use the comparative case approach.

Experiments and Quasi Experiments

The logic that underlies the design of experiments and quasi experiments addresses the ability to make general statements from a project's results. These issues are important for case studies as well. Quasi-experimental designs may have especially important implications for case-study designs because they deal with similar research environments and are similarly interested in explaining the nature of the relationship between variables. The way that these designs deal with random assignment and external validity may have important implications for case-study designs. Caporaso notes that "quasi-experimental designs are rooted in conditions where there is no possibility of manipulating the stimulus and no control through matching and randomization over competing stimuli" (1973, 12). Instead of experimental manipulation, control is approximated by attempting to control for confounding variables while probing for causal dependencies.

Campbell and Stanley elucidate the logic of control in experiments and quasi experiments. They discuss both internal validity, that is, issues concerning the treatments in the experiment or quasi experiment, and external validity, or the ability to generalize from the results of a project. They assert that several factors are relevant to internal validity: history, maturation, testing, instrumentation, statistical regression, selection bias, experimental mortality, and selection-maturation interaction (1963, 5). For the purposes of a case-based research strategy, selection bias (e.g., picking cases for nontheoretical reasons and thus drawing conclusions from an unrepresentative sample of processes, selecting on the dependent variable, or not paying sufficient attention to possible confounding effects) is probably most important. However, policy history (time-dependent behavior) is also a potentially confounding problem.

Campbell and Stanley cite as relevant to external validity the reactive/interactive effect of testing, interactive effects of selection bias, and multiple treatment interference (1963, 6). Again, a case-based research strategy should be largely concerned with issues of selection bias and the interactive effects of selection bias and the explanatory variables. In order to build and test theory from case studies, these potential pitfalls of quasi experimentation must be controlled for by carefully selecting cases based on theoretical criteria that are robust and explicit. The comparative case method attempts to do just that. Next I not only will discuss this approach in abstract terms, but also will attempt to illustrate the theoretical usefulness of the approach by drawing on existing research.

The Comparative Case Approach

Perhaps the clearest development and use of a comparative case-study methodology in foreign policy analysis is Alexander George's method of the "structured, focused comparison" (George 1982; George and McKeown 1985), a method whose roots can be seen in the work of Lijphart, Verba, and others. George and his associates review the comparative case method and its links to the traditional comparative method and quasi-experimental design, and they emphasize the importance of theoretically-driven research design and case selection (cf. Fearon 1991). George (1982) discusses four problems with which a comparative case strategy must come to terms: variable controls, the independence of cases, the representativeness of cases, and the prospects for cumulation of case-study knowledge into theory. Concerning the control of case-study variables, George discusses Mill's "method of agreement" and "method of difference." The method of agreement, or positive comparative method, attempts to identify similarities in independent variables associated with a common outcome in two or more cases. The method of difference, or negative comparative method, attempts to identify groups of independent variables associated with different outcomes (George 1982, 7; cf. DeFelice 1986). George (1982) argues that a structured, focused comparison allows the researcher to capitalize on Mill's discussion and the benefits of the case method and to minimize its costs by forcing the analyst's attention on issues of case selection and design.

George and McKeown (1985) recognize that attention to elements of quasi-experimental design helps the researcher avoid making erroneous inferences and conclusions, but that the case approach differs from quasi-experimental design in that case studies focus largely on within-case comparisons. They argue that we can capitalize on the strengths of both quasi experiments and case studies with the method of structured, focused comparison. This approach (George 1979, 1982; George and McKeown 1985; George and Smoke 1974) attempts to compare two or more cases in a "focused" way by dealing selectively with the aspects of the case that are relevant to the study. The approach is "structured" in the sense that it is a controlled comparison in which the researcher "formulates theoretically relevant general questions to guide the examination of each case" (George and McKeown 1985, 41–42).

The design for a structured, focused comparison follows a four-step procedure. First, the research design is constructed and the research problem is specified. This step includes the specification of the elements to be studied, the specification of the requirements for case selection, and the consideration of confounding variables. General questions that are to be asked of each case are developed. The second step is to examine the case materials. In the third step, theoretical implications from the case studies are developed. The fourth and final step is to compare results across cases and draw conclusions based on theoretical and empirical evidence (George and McKeown 1985, 43–54). It should be noted here that George's method relies for explanation on "process tracing," or within case examination and explanation, that can then be compared across cases, rather than on experimental control through random assignment or statistical partial correlations by comparing variables.

There is an important role for a case-based research strategy in the theory-building process. Many problems or processes require the type of extensive research that only a case-based method can afford. Further, many of the problems and processes that we study in world politics and foreign policy are limited in number, and therefore the application of statistical procedures and construction of large-N studies is prohibited. While case-based methods have methodological problems associated with them, it is possible to build theory in a more rigorous way than is usually afforded by a case-based approach. Indeed, if we wish to build theory about many of the events and processes we study in world politics and foreign policy, we must come to terms with case-based comparative inquiry. I argue that we can do so by paying special attention to issues of research design and the logic of scientific inference in order to assure the theoretical validity of the study (King, Keohane, and Verba 1994). Theory development can be further facilitated by utilizing the method of the structured, focused comparison to trace the importance of critical variables in the behavior of nations. Theory development can also be aided by increasing the number of cases included in a survey.

Clarifying the Issues

Huth and Russett (1990) discuss issues of case selection as part of an ongoing debate about deterrence theory (see Achen and Snidal 1989; G. Downs 1989; George and Smoke 1989; Jervis 1989; Lebow and Stein

1989). They stress the importance of selecting cases from a population of the theoretically appropriate cases. Huth and Russett assert that this population or sample must be "sufficiently alike in theoretical terms that they can be validly compared" (1990, 473). They also stress that case selection must be based upon independent variables, not dependent variables. Thus, instances of failures *and* successes (in their substantive area this refers to successes and failures of deterrence) must be included (1990, 472). Similarly, Achen and Snidal recognize that defining the appropriate population from which cases will be selected is a difficult task but that severe problems emerge for theory building when cases are selected in a systematically biased way (1989, 160; cf. Bueno de Mesquita 1990; Stern and Sundelius 1992).

In an important discussion of these issues, Eisenhardt (1989b) argues that the concept of a "population" is vital to case-study research. In order to build theory, one must first identify what we are trying to build theory about. What is the population of behaviors we are trying to explain? The population defines the set of entities from which samples may be drawn (Eisenhardt 1989b, 537). In a more recent discussion of the problems of defining exactly what a "case" is, Ragin discusses the role of "casing" in research as that stage at which ideas and evidence are brought together (1992, 217–25). Asking "What is this a case of?" is the same type of question that Rosenau urges us to ask in the question, "Of what is this an instance?" As will be shown, the "population" studied by George and Smoke (1974) is deterrence; for Paige (1972), the population is crisis decision making; for E. Ostrom (1990), the population of interest is common-pool resources.

Once the population has been defined, a sample of that population is drawn for further study. Unlike statistical methods or experiments, however, case-based approaches do not use a randomization strategy for assigning cases or for drawing a sample. A random assignment or selection process may not be possible or desirable for these studies. In a case-based research approach, cases are strategically selected for theoretical reasons (Eisenhardt 1989b). King, Keohane, and Verba (1994) argue that cases can be selected on explanatory variables. Theoretical sampling, or what Ripley (1988) calls "strategic" sampling, is the goal for case-based approaches. George began this discussion in his 1979 essay when he noted that selecting cases because of their intrinsic interest or because of the analyst's language skills is not good enough when theory building is the goal. Systematic theory must be built upon research designs that treat social and political phenomena in systematic ways.

Lieberson (1992) provides an important warning about the type of theory that can be built with case methods. Lieberson demonstrates that small-N studies that draw on Mill's methods of comparison assume a deterministic perspective toward the relationship between variables in the study, even though the researcher may claim to assume only a probabilistic relationship between the variables. A deterministic statement is made by saying that "if X, then Y." A probabilistic statement is made by saying that "the presence of X increases the likelihood of Y" (Lieberson 1992, 106). While we may wish to develop deterministic theory, such theory cannot be made by small-N studies due to problems such as measurement error, "complex multivariate causal patterns," and the role of chance (106–7). "A deterministic theory has deterministic outcomes, but often we can measure it only in probabilistic terms" (107).

Research using a small number of cases, not being able to build deterministic theory due to these methodological problems, must therefore be geared to build probabilistic theory. Lieberson argues, however, that small-N studies have difficulty operating effectively under probabilistic assumptions because in order to explore probabilistic relationships, these studies would need to incorporate a much larger N to accommodate the necessary indeterminacy of the phenomena under investigation by having an N larger than the number and combination of variables examined (Lieberson 1992, 107–9). Lieberson posits that the logic of Mill's methods assumes no interaction effects because the procedure of comparison and explanation cannot "empirically or logically eliminate interaction effects. Rather, it arbitrarily assumes that they do not operate" (1992, 110–11). Indeed, Mill rejects the use of these methods of comparison "when causality is complex or when more than one cause is operating" (Lieberson 1992, 112–13; cf. Nichols 1986). Lieberson concludes that "multicausal probabilistic statements are simply unmanageable" in small-N comparative studies (1992, 113). My purpose in discussing these issues is to extend the discussion of how theory building can be facilitated by more careful attention to issues of research design, populations, case selection, and control, as well as to the assumptions we incorporate into our designs. Case studies can be a vital part of a theory-building process, but they must be well designed and performed.

A Few Examples

One of the most theoretically useful examples of a comparative case study in foreign policy analysis is Paige's (1972) comparative study of crisis decision making during the Korean and the Cuban missile crises. Paige selects two cases that are similar in important respects (crisis characteristics) and traces out patterns and divergences of crisis decision-making behavior. Through careful selection and control, Paige holds the theory of crisis decision making up to two cases, holds certain confounding effects as constant as possible, and traces the decision process and outcomes within and across the cases.

Burke and Greenstein (1989), in another excellent example of a comparative case study, seek to explain why two very similar crises had such very different outcomes. They track theory against two cases that are similar in important respects (an opportunity to use or not use American force in Vietnam in 1954 and 1964) but dissimilar in outcomes (force is introduced in 1964 but not in 1954). They track three clusters of variables—the personal properties of the president, advisory structures, and political environment—within and across the cases.

These projects move in the direction of a more explicit use of a case-study methodology. These research designs are laudable not only for their substantive contributions to our understanding of decision making. The designs employed in these studies are also praiseworthy because of their (1) comparative dimension, (2) rigorous treatment of theory and evidence, and (3) case selection strategies, based on independent variables that focus on explaining variance in dependent variables. The research by George (1991) and George and Smoke (1974), for example, also represents useful theoretical examinations that are rooted in strong comparative case designs, with logical case-selection procedures, and some attempts to control for confounding effects.

Another example of a useful comparative case design is George's (1990) *Avoiding War,* which explores the dynamics of crisis management. George uses comparative case studies to develop empirical and contingent theory that significantly enhances our understanding of the dynamics that lead to war and those that lead to peace in crises (cf. Stern and Sundelius, 1992). In a study that is quite self-conscious of its application of a structured, focused comparison, Shafer (1988) explores U.S. counterinsurgency policy and focuses on the dominant mind-sets or paradigms that have perpetuated a policy that has, he contends, largely been a failure.

The Case-Survey Approach

Even carefully performed comparative case studies, such as those that use a structured, focused comparison, are plagued by methodological and logical impediments to theory building. Achen and Snidal (1989) argue that case studies fail at the task of theory construction and verification because of the nature of method.

The logic of comparative case studies inherently provides too little logical constraint to generate dependable theory and too little inferential constraint to permit trustworthy theory testing. Only when yoked closely to deductive theory and to statistical inference, and made to serve their ends, can case studies provide genuine theoretical contributions. (1989, 145–46)

They concede that the most rigorous example of comparative case studies is George's method of structured, focused comparison. Still, they argue that the empirical generalizations produced by such an analysis are not equivalent to "theory." "Contingent empirical regularities are not to be confused with confirmed statistical regularities" (Achen and Snidal 1989, 168). Here I would echo George's argument that there is a value to empirically based, contingent theory. The choice should not be posed as being between (a) deductively derived, nomothetic explanation and (b) nothing (George 1992). In the middle ground rests a place for explanation of complicated social and political process that, to date, have escaped deductive, deterministic explanation. There is room here for, and a need for, empirically derived, contingent explanations. Achen and Snidal admit that rigorously performed comparative case studies can produce this type of "theory." Furthermore, King, Keohane, and Verba (1994) argue that the logic of scientific inference that underlies quantitative and qualitative designs makes these approaches different only in degree. While it may be that the more rigorous task of theory building and testing is not well performed by even the best case studies or comparative case studies, there have been recent attempts to develop a case-based comparative method that can contribute to the goal of building theory by incorporating the best of statistical, correlative, deductive designs and case-based designs. One of these attempts, the case-survey method, is growing in use and recognition.

Charles Ragin (1987) outlines the logic behind comparative inquiry (cf. Przeworski and Teune 1970) and the case-survey approach. He notes that social scientists face a special problem: the phenomena we wish to understand rarely have one cause, but rather emerge from what he calls "multiple conjunctural causation" (1987, 26). A research strategy that is appropriate for unraveling these sorts of phenomena must be able to deal with classes of events while retaining the ability to deal with the particular. A strictly statistical approach may be unable to address phenomena of this type at this time. Ragin argues that a case method is a valuable technique for building theory and testing hypotheses about causes of such events. There are at least two tasks at hand, Ragin argues,

interpreting historically significant or decisive social phenomena and determining the causes of important categories of social phenomena. . . . The case-oriented strategy attempts to approximate experimental rigor by identifying comparable instances of a phenomenon of interest and then analyzing the theoretically important similarities and differences among them. This approach provides a basis for establishing modest empirical generalizations concerning historically defined categories of social phenomena. (1987, 31)

Ragin argues that a research strategy that synthesizes the case approach, large-N variable-oriented approaches, and experiments should be able to address a large number of cases and should embody as much of the strict comparative logic of experimental design as possible. Such a strategy, he argues, should include a concern for combinations of conditions and for complex, conjunctural causation. It should allow for parsimonious explanations and should be analytic in nature. Finally, such an approach should allow for the evaluation of competing explanations. In short, it should provide a basis for qualitative analysis and the comparison of wholes as combinations or configurations of parts (Ragin 1987, 82–84). The endeavor is to be both interpretive and causal in explanation. Robert Yin (1981, 1984; Yin and Heald 1975) applies these concerns in his presentation of the case-survey method, which is similar to what others call "meta-analysis" (Wachter and Straf 1990; Rosenthal 1991). Yin and Heald note that the goal of the case-survey approach is to aggregate the characteristics of multiple cases, not to aggregate their conclusions (1975, 371).

The case survey method is mainly concerned with the analysis of qualitative evidence in a reliable manner. The method enables the reviewer to note the various experiences found in each policy study and then to aggregate the frequency of occurrence of these experiences. The frequencies form the basis for simple statements of association and nonassociation of different types of experiences. In this manner, the case survey method gives the reviewer the chance to survey different case studies. Until recently, the main shortcoming of case studies was that the insights from the studies could not be aggregated in any sense. The case survey method thus carries the classic case study method one major step forward; it enables aggregate reviews of individual case studies to be undertaken with scientific rigor. (Yin and Heald 1975, 372)

Research using the case-survey method begins by identifying what one is trying to build theory about or what the population of events or processes that one wishes to explain is by drawing on a sample of that population for comparative examination. Asking "What is this a case of?" or what Ragin calls "casing" (1992) must occur as one strategically selects cases to be included in the study (cf. Eisenhardt 1989b). Yin and Heald (1975) discuss the basic techniques of the case survey once its parameters have been established. The analyst begins by answering the same set of questions of each preperformed case study (though the analyst may, of course, perform original case studies as well). The emphasis here is on closed-ended questions so that answers can be aggregated across cases. The schedule of questions to be asked of each case is designed from theory before case analysis begins. Note the logical similarity here between the case-survey method and George's structured, focused comparison and its emphasis on the interrogation of the cases and cross-case comparisons. The analyst codes the answers on the schedule of questions for each case.

With regard to the reliability of coding, the same technical difficulties exist as exist with content analysis. At a minimum, multiple checks of the researchers' coding schemes should be performed before case analysis begins. Intercoder reliability checks of coding may be performed when possible. We know from content analysis and traditional case studies that some things are "difficult" to discern, especially if available information is fragmentary or contradictory. Yin and Heald (1975) note that as part of the coding of cases, the reader-analyst can and should note the level of confidence in the answer to each question asked of the cases (see Kaarbo, Beasley, and M. Hermann 1990). Some cases may be rejected if they do not have sufficient reliable information.

After all the cases have been coded (the number of cases can range from a half dozen or more—as Singer encourages—to more than one hundred), the codings are assessed for cross-case comparisons. Pattern matching, which was encouraged by George, can then take place. These comparisons may take the form of simple cross-tabulations with a small number of cases, larger statistical manipulation if the number of cases is sufficiently large (or Boolean algebra). The method used for cross-case comparisons should be dictated by the number of cases available, the strength of the evidence presented (we should be careful about drawing conclusions about cases in which our reliability or confidence is not high), and the type of theory that is being pursued. When these cross-case comparisons are complete, the iterative task of theory building to which Russett (1970) refers begins again. Evidence and theory are matched against one another, theory is refined, and investigation is resumed.

The case-survey approach relies on the logic of inference embedded in large-N quantitative and experimental analysis: the logic of control, selection, and comparison. Yet, it also relies on the great strength of case studies: detailed, rich analysis. Case studies are still required and valued for the depth of description they provide, their interpretive analyses, and their attention to the uniqueness of events. The case-survey approach attempts to merge these two sets of advantages by using case studies as sources of knowledge about particular events or processes, from which explicit information is extracted and then compared in a rigorous way. Multiple case studies of the same event or process are used to provide as full and complete a picture of that instance as possible. The reliability of the case survey, then, is derived from both the case studies it examines and the logic of inference that underlies larger-*N,* comparative analysis. This approach seeks to avoid the tendency of variable-oriented approaches to disembody and obscure cases through a case-oriented approach and "places cases, not variables, center stage" (Ragin 1992, 4–5).

While affording much power, there are limitations to this approach. As Yin and Heald (1975) note, the results of the case survey are of no better quality than the quality of the original case studies. The user of the case-survey methodology must remember that the original case studies may have been written with a specific purpose in mind and should be careful not to unwittingly incorporate the original study's biases into the case survey's findings. Moreover, the user of the case-survey method must remember that just because the case study does not report something does not mean that it did not happen. Case studies can and do miss important information. The user of a case-survey method can alleviate these problems to some extent by using multiple case studies of the same event, hoping to drown out any original bias in the case studies and pick up information that may have been left out of some case studies.

Second, although attempting to remain sensitive to within-case uniqueness, this method may not give sufficient attention to the unique factors of an individual case (Yin and Heald 1975, 380). While using case material should keep the analyst close enough to the cases to be sensitive to the particulars of history, such is not automatically the case. For example, Lijphart (1975) discusses the inferential problems that exist because cases are rarely independent events, but rather are sequences of events. It is thus possible to spuriously conclude that a causal process exists between variables when history or learning actually are the cause. By staying close to case materials, Lijphart argues that these problems can be identified, but there is no guarantee.

Finally, as is true with other methods, the validity of the conclusions drawn from such a case survey are only as sound as the design is systematic and appropriate. Validity is essentially a matter of design. A poorly orchestrated case survey will be as theoretically useless as a poorly designed case study, content analysis, or large-*N* statistical study. However, if performed with a focus on theory and the systematic treatment of cases and evidence, the case-survey approach offers a powerful technique to analysts of comparative and world politics and foreign policy. This approach seeks to combine the respective strengths of case, correlative, and experimental analyses and to minimize their weaknesses.

A Few Examples

In a continuing examination of the impact of nations' ultimate "decision unit" on their foreign policy behavior, Margaret Hermann and Charles Hermann (1989) pursue a multicase examination of the relationship between ultimate decision units (predominant leader, small group, or multiple autonomous actor) and foreign policy behavior. They use multiple case studies of each case or event to craft a cross-case-based inquiry. They use case studies for theory building and testing and draw on case materials to measure variables deemed theoretically important. They identify the dependent variables of interest (foreign policy, especially conflict or non-conflict, behavior), the intervening variables (ultimate decision unit), and the independent (crisis and environmental) variables that must be controlled. Their examination blends the logic of statistical analysis, quasi-experimental control, and comparative case studies. As a result, it not only provides a theoretical advance in the analysis and explanation of the foreign policy behavior of nations, it is also a powerful example of how case materials can be used to build theory in the analysis of foreign policy.

In *Governing the Commons* (1990), Elinor Ostrom explores the governance of common-pool resources in multiple settings, drawing on institutional analysis. This book presents part of the research conducted in the Common Pool Resource (CPR) project at the Workshop in Political Theory and Policy Analysis at Indiana University. That larger project has cataloged more than sixteen hundred studies of common-pool resource governance over time, and has fully coded approximately one hundred specific cases (see Martin 1989). Drawing on existing case studies and performing some original analysis, this project codes the variables and conditions of interest in order to compile a data bank that can be manipulated statistically. In other words, the project surveys existing case materials (and creates new ones when necessary) in order to code the variables and conditions that their theory about CPRs indicates as important to successful and nonsuccessful common-pool resource governance.

Ostrom uses fourteen cases of common-pool resource governance, some successful, some not successful, to illustrate the theoretical development that is taking place during this project. She presents a set of institutional arrangements and design principles that are thought to be important for understanding the governance of common-pool resources, which is adapted from her earlier (1986) presentation of an institutional framework for understanding general problems of public choice. Drawing on case evidence, Ostrom presents both coded and detailed information from the cases to highlight a mode of institutional analysis and to explore the degree of fit between the institutional theory and the empirical data in the cases. In the process, she also presents a powerful example of how case studies can be used in a more rigorous and theoretically useful way than is commonly the case.

Another interesting study that uses a meta-analytic technique is Wolf's (1995) study of the bureaucratic effectiveness of agencies in the U.S. federal government. Wolf builds a test of competing theories of bureaucratic effectiveness by using a case survey of existing studies of 170 case studies or 104 different federal agencies. He transforms his coding sheet into a data set that can be statistically explored to examine the effects of different factors on effectiveness.

An example of the case-survey approach that is familiar to foreign policy analysts is the study by Herek, Janis, and Huth (1987) that explores the link between the quality of crisis decision-making processes and the quality of crisis outcomes. They draw on nineteen cases of post–World War II crises in U.S. foreign policy. They use multiple case studies to examine each instance of crisis. For each case, they identify and score characteristics of the decision-making process, according to the procedural attributes that are discussed in Janis and Mann 1977. Herek, Janis, and Huth also code the outcome of each case as a success or failure. After coding each instance of crisis based upon the multiple case studies of each crisis, they tabulate the results and search for correlative patterns across cases. They find support for the hypothesis that "better" processes lead to "better" outcomes. Paying attention to issues of design and case selection, they select cases from a population of crises, not crises that result only in conflict or failures.

These examples demonstrate that the case-survey method is amenable to very-large-N studies as well as smaller-N studies. What separates these smaller-N studies from other comparative case studies is (1) their reliance on multiple existing case studies to code and aggregate variables of theoretical importance, and (2) their emphasis on research design and case selection rooted in the logic of scientific inference found in the comparative method, correlative analyses, and quasi-experimental designs. This approach seeks to blend the strengths of the case approach and the comparative approach of large-N studies. Indeed, the case-survey method may be seen as an extension of the comparative method of "structured, focused comparison" by increasing the number of cases in a study through the use of multiple case studies of each case under scrutiny as the source of information about each case. The analyst is able to increase the number of cases under investigation, acquire some control, take advantage of the design's comparative dimension, and still retain the ability to be sensitive to case-specific variance. The approach thus blends the strengths of what are often referred to as qualitative and quantitative designs.

Four of the advantages of the case-survey method over the comparative case study are related. First, by using existing case studies, we do not duplicate work when good case studies already are available. We can begin to use case studies as "data sets" of a type, ready to be mined for new information. Second, investigators are able to include larger numbers of cases in a design since the time of researching and writing original case studies has been replaced by examining multiple existing case studies. With a larger N, and appropriately rigorous research designs, researchers can make more sound causal inferences with a larger-N study than with a smaller-N one. Third, using multiple case studies of the same instance or case gives a fuller picture of an event or process than does a single report. Each case study of an event or process may not be complete. Furthermore, the existing case studies of an event may not agree with one another. By drawing on multiple reports, the investigator is able to gain a full picture of the instance under scrutiny and is in a more sound position to make judgments of validity from the case studies. That facilitates a more sound process of coding events and process, which may include both "quantitative" and "qualitative" measures.

Fourth, the case-survey approach as presented by Yin, Ragin, and others, offers a way to cope with the problems Lieberson (1992) discusses as inherent in small-N comparative studies. The case-survey method, using a relatively larger N than conventional comparative case studies using one of Mill's methods of comparison, can allow for interaction effects, multiple causes, and can (depending on the quality of the original case studies) address measurement error in the ways that a probabilistic theory would require (Lieberson 1992, 117n). George has argued that the method of structured, focused comparison can deal with the problem of equifinality through process tracing (see George 1992; George and McKeown 1985). The case-survey method offers another way to cope with this problem of sorting out interaction effects that plagues studies with small numbers of cases. The case survey provides a research approach that can incorporate the uniqueness of cases into a relatively larger-N approach, thus giving researchers the opportunity to develop probabilistic theory using a case-based method. The case-survey approach still relies on rich original case studies, but it seeks to use them in a manner that differs from their conventional employment—extraction and comparison based upon the logic of large-N analysis. This approach allows researchers to treat case studies and comparative cases in systematic ways with larger comparative studies. Concluding his 1971 article on the comparative method, Lijphart argued that the challenge for scholars is to apply the comparative method "in such a way as to minimize their weaknesses and to capitalize on their inherent strengths. Thus, they can be highly useful instruments in scientific political inquiry" (1971, 693). The case-survey method offers one way to meet Lijphart's challenge. We can use this tool to help us do our work better. This process begins by recommitting ourselves to theory building—by putting theory first in our designs, in our case selections, and in our problem formulations.

A Research Design for Exploring Decision-Making Structures and Processes

There is no single model for decision making that works at all times, for all crises, for all presidents. This project explores the variety of ways that U.S. presidents have designed and managed decision-making groups during foreign policy crises. Subsequently I present the research design that directs the project. I use a sample of cases from the population of U.S. foreign policy crises since World War II to investigate the crisis management approaches used during different crises by Presidents Truman, Eisenhower, Johnson, Nixon, and Bush.

As part of a case-survey methodology, a coding form directs the examination of as many original, reliable case studies that focus on U.S. decision making in these crises as can be found (see appendix). Using the coding form, I identify the institutional or organizational model that is adopted by the president to structure decision making during the crisis. Here I rely heavily on the abstract models discussed by R. Johnson (1974) and George (1980) as a theoretical starting point. The coding form is also used to help determine the possible effects of these institutional arrangements on the processes of decision making. The coding procedures of Herek, Janis, and Huth (1987) and the discussion of process characteristics in George (1980), as well as Janis (1989 and 1982) and Janis and Mann (1977), serve as a point of departure here. Finally, I search for patterns that may link different institutional configurations and certain procedural characteristics of decision making. The evidence may also lead to other lessons about presidential crisis management and crisis decision making.

Case Selection

I focus on nine strategically selected crises in U.S. foreign policy in this project: the Berlin airlift (1948) and the decision to go to war in Korea (1950) for the Truman administration; Dien Bien Phu (1954) and Suez (1956) for the Eisenhower administration; Tonkin Gulf (1964) and the Tet

Offensive (1968) for the Johnson administration; the civil war in Jordan (1970) and the 1973 October War for the Nixon administration; and the invasion of Panama (1989) for the Bush administration. These presidencies were selected for a variety of reasons. The Truman and Eisenhower administrations provide the opportunity to explore the record of presidential management of crisis decision making before its alleged "birth" during the Cuban missile crisis. Indeed, the Berlin crisis provides a look into crisis management at the beginning of the cold war. The Johnson and Nixon administrations were selected because they were the inhabitants of the White House who followed President Kennedy and the alleged birth of crisis decision-making management. Evidence from their administrations may speak to how crisis decision-making management evolved after the experience of the Kennedy administration. The Ford, Carter, and Reagan administrations were not selected so as to keep the number of cases in this investigation tractable and because of concerns that evidence of the structures and processes in these administrations would not be as complete as the earlier administrations. I have, however, included an examination of the Bush crisis management approach in the case of the invasion of Panama. The examination of this case uses less-reliable sources of evidence than the other cases, but it provides a window into crisis management at the end of the cold war and thus provides some possibility to review the evolution of crisis management during this period of U.S. foreign policy.

The Truman, Eisenhower, Johnson, and Nixon administrations are also attractive candidates for research because they have each been identified as using a formalistic model to organize the White House for policy-making—domestic and foreign—by previous research (George 1980; R. Johnson 1974). That allows the formalistic model to serve as a baseline against which to measure organizational change when a crisis develops. These presidents share, in routine times, a rough set of preferences for how decisions should be made. The project can then explore how a president changes the model of decision making when a crisis emerges, if he does; and it can examine whether these presidents—who are otherwise fairly similar—respond in the same way or in different ways to a crisis. This formalistic baseline should help sort out how crisis decision making is (or is not) different from routine decision making.

A series of six criteria helps narrow the population of U.S. foreign policy crises to a workable sample from these administrations. First, the cases must be instances of unilateral U.S. foreign policy decision making, as opposed to a multilateral process that may center on NATO or the United Nations, for example. It may be important to distinguish between these two types of decision making because coordination with another body such as the UN could trigger different processes from unilateral (or at least mostly unilateral) decision making.

Second, the cases should be roughly commensurable with respect to being an instance of crisis. Because it is the link between organizational structures and decision-making processes that is examined here, rather than processes that different types of crises might produce, the cases should be roughly commensurable with respect to the type of crisis situation. This criterion is important because different types of crises may trigger different types of structures or processes. Charles Hermann (1972, 1969) defines a crisis as a situation characterized by three situational variables: threat, decision time, and surprise. He constructs a model of crises as they vary along three dimensions. He proposes that "decision making varies with perceived changes in the amount of threat in combination with the amount of decision time and/or the amount of surprise" (1969, 36). This approach to international crises is not the only one in the crisis literature, but it is mainstream and perhaps dominant in its focus on situational characteristics that affect behavior.[1] The sample of cases should control for the situational characteristics of a crisis. Where the cases differ along these dimensions, it must be noted and taken into account at the stage of cross-case comparison and entertained as a possible confounding effect.

Third, the cases should involve roughly commensurable opponents. Symmetrical crises and crisis management may differ in important (though largely unknown at this time) ways from asymmetrical crises and crisis management (Stern and Sundelius 1992). Instances of a U.S. direct crisis with the Soviet Union should not be compared directly with a crisis that involves, for example, a smaller developing state. Therefore, the cases that are selected should include a Soviet or communist component but should not be instances of direct confrontation between the United States and the Soviet Union. Where this factor cannot be controlled for, the same caveats apply as mentioned earlier.

Fourth, in order to control for potentially confounding variables, the state of the larger political context, including the state of the cold war, relations with allies, and geopolitics, should be roughly commensurable across cases. When such is not the case, it must be taken into account as indicated previously. This criterion is important so that the advisory structures and processes are the center of attention and comparison, rather than the conditions under which a crisis takes place.

Fifth, the cases must have some temporal variance within administrations (early-late) so that "learning" can be evaluated. A temporal range of crises across administrations will allow for the comparison of structure and process through time. A temporal range of crises within an administrations will allow for the exploration of learning within an administration.

Sixth, the cases must be instances in which the decision-making group is called to serve the cognitive needs of the president (i.e., the need for information and advice). Instances of crises that involve groups that primarily serve other needs, such as affective or political needs, will not be considered here. Also, as a practical matter, reliable case material—preferably multiple case studies of each crisis—must be available.

I have tried to select nine instances of crisis that roughly fit these criteria. All the crises involve U.S. foreign policy decision making after World War II. They have all been used as "crises" by other researchers. With the exception of Panama, they all include a Soviet or communist component in the opponent, but none (except Berlin) includes—at least at the outset of the crisis—a direct confrontation between the United States and the Soviet Union. The Soviet-American relationship sets the context for each of the crises, however. The crises occur early and late in each administration (as much as possible). Each crisis does provide an example of an identifiable decision-making group that is assembled to serve the cognitive needs of the president. Their job is to provide information, advice, and analysis. Sufficient reliable case material is available. Indeed, seven of these nine cases were used in the research by Herek, Janis, and Huth (1987) that used a similar method of examining existing case studies (the Tet Offensive and invasion of Panama were not included in their study).

The state of the political environment and the type of crisis are the two criteria that are the most difficult to satisfy. One of the ways I have tried to control for these contextual or situational variables is to focus on crises in two regions for much of the analysis: the Middle East and Southeast Asia. These areas have been selected because three of the administrations dealt with crises in these areas on numerous occasions, and the crises contained a Soviet or communist component, but not a direct U.S.-Soviet confrontation. I hope to restrict the range of situational variables that could confound the empirical results by restricting the crises to these substantive and geographical areas. While the 1968 crisis in Vietnam is not identical to the 1954 crisis, at least the contextual variables in them are restricted to the Vietnam area, rather than comparing crises from six different geographical regions. All the crises afforded use-of-force options to American decision makers and required some form of response in a short-to-medium amount of time. Each of them threatened (perceived) U.S. interests abroad and included a component of Soviet or communist threat.

I conceptualize system-level variables, balance-of-power concerns, relations with allies, the nature of the opponent, and the situational characteristics of the crisis, and so forth as independent variables. These variables trigger a set of routines (decision making) that lead to decisions, actions, and outcomes. They serve to constrain the menu of feasible policy options. For purposes of comparison, and because these variables are not the object of study in this project, these variables should be held as constant as possible across the cases. Obviously, these variables do differ across cases that range from the beginning of the cold war to after its end. When there is variance in these variables, that variance must be entertained as a competing explanation for decisional outcomes. The coding form includes questions that address the state of these variables in the crises.

The models used by the president to structure a decision-making process are seen as a configuration of intervening variables in decision making.[2] These models are artificial constructs designed by the president for the purpose of managing a group of advisers whose job it is to provide information, advice, and analysis. They may be established previous to the crisis and thus be triggered by the crisis, or they may be constructed in an ad hoc manner during a crisis. The dependent variables in this project are the effects of the institutional model employed in the crisis, commonly thought of as characteristics of the decision-making process that may be performed well or poorly. One should note that the "success" or "failure" of a policy outcome is not the dependent variable in this study. Rather, this analysis focuses on the structures and processes that produce decisions. American policy decisions combine with many other factors to produce outcomes. The evaluation of outcomes as successes or failures, a subjective task, is beyond the scope of this project.

I have examined the case studies available for each of these cases by using a coding form as prescribed in George's method of structured, focused comparison and in Yin's case-survey approach. The coding form includes questions that seek to identify the management model used by the president (question set 1 in appendix) and the procedural effects that may follow from that structuring process (question set 2 in appendix). The coding form also includes questions that explore other potentially explanatory variables such as group composition, expertise, and presidential preferences. I will discuss the coding form here as it pertains to each cluster of variables examined in this study.

Identifying Models of Presidential Management

This present study draws on the models of crisis management presented by George (1980) and R. Johnson (1974). These three abstract models try to capture the nature of the interaction between the president and the group of advisers that the president assembles to aid in crisis decision making. The major drawback to these models is that they overlap, they share certain characteristics. The major benefit of the models is their record of use in the field and their ability to order the range of organizational patterns we might see in a crisis. While George and Johnson discuss these models in terms of long-term patterns within presidential administrations, the models are used here to organize our thinking about how a decision-making group is structured, for what purposes, and with what effects, in a crisis. The models give us insights, in other words, into how presidents try to make crises "routine." For the purposes of this project, the model of decision making that the president uses to organize an advisory group refers to patterned relationships among the president and his advisers that structures and focuses the interaction between these political actors. The formalistic, competitive, and collegial model of decision-making management presented by R. Johnson (1974) and George (1980) serve as ideal types or a baseline here against which the empirical record will be interpreted.

The questions on the coding form seek to ascertain the form of the advisory structure that the presidents use for decision making during a crisis. The questions allow for sensitivity to how presidents use variations on these three ideal types (table 1) to structure decision making. Question set 1 on the coding form addresses the nature of the presidents' organizational structure. The model that corresponds with each response is included on the coding form in parentheses next to possible answers as a guide for identifying the models. The questions asked of the case studies try to capture the essence of these models' characteristics as they are presented in George 1980 and R. Johnson 1974.

By noting the appropriate responses on the coding form, one can see that the formalistic model employs clearly defined and hierarchical channels of communication—a highly structured staff system whose members have assigned or recognized jurisdictions. The president is clearly at the top of this decision-making group, assuming full responsibility for decisions that are made. The group's procedures are clear, formal, and structured, and open debate or disagreement is usually discouraged. The president rarely reaches down for information and advice, relying instead on the screening process of the bureaucracy to present "clean" views.

The competitive model uses multiple and open channels of communication and by a staff system that is fairly open and ambiguous, in a relative sense. Members of the group tend to serve as generalists, rather than specialists with recognized jurisdictions, though they will still often represent a suborganizational perspective or specialty (e.g., intelligence, state). The president does assume responsibility for decisions that the groups reaches and is at the top of the group. This group's routines are clear, formal, and structured, but the president incorporates an encouragement of open debate and disagreement into this formal structure. The president may "reach down" into the bureaucracy for information.

The collegial model also uses multiple and open lines of communication and organizational ambiguity. Group members tend to serve general roles, rather than having specific jurisdictions. This model parts company with the other two, however, in its emphasis on teamwork and shared responsibility for decision making. The president is at the center of this decision-making team, and decision-making procedures tend to be informal and unstructured. The president encourages a diversity of views, though not necessarily the open conflict upon which the competitive model places a premium.

I ask each case study of each crisis this schedule of questions to ascer-

TABLE 1.   Characteristics of Ideal Management Models

Formalistic Model
President at the top
Orderly policy-making with well-defined procedures
Emphasis on hierarchy to screen information
Specialized information and advice
Emphasis on functional expertise
President rarely "reaches down" for information
Discouragement of bargaining and conflict in group

Competitive Model
President at the top
Organizational ambiguity
President may assign overlapping jurisdictions
Multiple channels of communication to the president
Promotion and even encouragement of debate
President manages conflict in the group
President may "reach down" for information

Collegial Model
President at the center
Informal procedures
Decision-making team led by president
President an active member of the group
President may assign overlapping jurisdictions
Shared responsibility for decisions
Advisers do not serve as information filters
Emphasis on synthesizing perspectives in the group
Emphasis on generalists
President may "reach down" for information

tain the nature of the management model used by the president. These questions focus on the nature of communication channels, staff systems, and jurisdictions. The questions also focus on the nature and division of decision-making responsibility and the place of the president in the group. The role and use of procedures and debate are considered, as is the importance of expertise. The timing and effect of the president's indication of a preference is to be noted. The questions also probe the extent to which there is explicit evidence of the president structuring the advisory group, perhaps in response to some previous experience. The most appropriate response to each question is drawn from the reporting in the case studies, or by inference from the case studies when no explicit mention of these variables is made by the case-study authors. A brief, generic example may be helpful here. Rarely does a case-study author explicitly report, "President X used a 'formalistic' crisis management model in the Z crisis." Instead, the authors may consistently refer to the members of the decision-making group by their title or jurisdiction or refer to the orderliness of the decision-making process during meetings, the structured nature of the group's interaction. These types of references, in a pattern, would lead me to infer that the style of crisis decision-making management adopted by the president most closely approximated a formalistic model. After coding each case study of each crisis, the codings are reviewed for each crisis so that a determination of the type of management model that was used can be assigned.

Also included on the coding form are questions that attempt to identify nonorganizational variables that may be important during a crisis. These factors include such things as expertise (Is expertise salient?) or presidential dominance (When does the president voice an opinion?). The coding form asks for a typology of participant, and includes questions about whether or not explicit attention to the structuring of a decision-making process can be found. The research design seeks to take advantage of the ability of a case-survey approach to stay close to case materials and uniqueness while pursuing an ordered and systematic investigation.

Identifying Processes in Crisis Decision Making

An institutional perspective expects that there will be an impact on political life by the institutional forms that are used to structure political processes. Parks argues that organizational structures provide opportunities, incentives, and constraints for the actors in them (1982, 1). He suggests that research on the effects of structure should focus on how different structural forms perform differently. I propose that the institutional model adopted by the president in a crisis ought to have empirically discernible effects on the political process of decision making. In so doing, I follow the strategy discussed by King, Keohane, and Verba (1994) of identifying and pursuing one plausible causal linkage in this small-N study.

I conceptualize decision making as a series of tasks that the president and an advisory group must perform. These tasks may be performed well or poorly by the decision-making group. I compiled a list of the generic tasks that groups must perform when they make decisions by drawing on the discussion of decision-making processes found in George 1980; Herek, Janis, and Huth 1987; Janis 1982 and 1989; and Janis and Mann 1977 and discussed in chapter 1. To produce this list, the decision-making characteristics discussed by these other authors has been collapsed, reduced to their common features, and presented in a generic form, rather than a positive or negative form. I leave it to the empirical evidence to assign them positive or negative values. The generic procedural tasks of decision making that must be performed by an advisory group in a crisis are presented in table 2. The items in question set 2 of the coding form explore the state of each task as reported in the case studies of each crisis. I conceptualize these tasks as being performed by the decision-making group along a continuum. The group process may demonstrate a high, medium, or low level of attention to each task.

When all the case studies of each crisis have been coded, the evidence for each crisis is compared so that a value for each process characteristic can be assigned. In other words, the evidence of the decision-making process from N number of case studies of crisis X is brought together so that a value can be assigned for each task performed in that crisis. We can then say that, in crisis X, the decision-making group performed Task 1 "well," Task 2 "poorly," and so on. This approach directly builds on the study by Herek, Janis, and Huth (1987), who explore crisis decision-making processes and outcomes in five of the cases that are used here. They used a case-survey method to explore crisis decision making, and they coded the state of decision-making process characteristics along a continuum of being performed well to being performed poorly. However, they only report the presence or absence of negative characteristics of the decision-making process (Herek, Janis, and Huth 1987, 211n).

I use thresholds to evaluate the state of decision-making process characteristics that are similar to those used by Herek, Janis, and Huth (1987). Tasks of decision making are coded along a continuum where two or three recognitions of the task correspond with the task being performed well, and four or more recognitions of the task correspond with the task being performed very well. Conversely, two or three omissions of the task correspond with the task being performed poorly, and four or more omissions of the task correspond with the task being performed very poorly. These thresholds are used to differentiate between a process that demonstrates a very high level of attention (or inattention) to a task from one that demonstrates a mild level of attention (or some inattention) to a task. If the case studies report only one omission or recognition of the task, a neutral coding is assigned for that task. No code may be assigned to the task if the information in the case studies is insufficient to credibly draw inferences about the decision-making process. Confidence values are also assigned to each coding, ranging from low to moderate to high confidence. They reflect the level of confidence I have in being able to assign a code to the task based upon the type of evidence presented in the case study that is examined. These confidence ratings are intended to aid the evaluation of different values for a task that may be assigned from different case studies. I attempt to identify the procedural tendencies that emerge from certain

TABLE 2.   Procedural Tasks of Crisis Decision Making

1. Survey objectives to be fulfilled by policy response
    This includes to what extent the group surveys a full or restricted range of objectives and whether the full range that is considered is presented to the president.

2. Canvass alternative policy responses
    This includes to what extent the group considers a full or restricted range of policy alternatives, to what extent it reconsiders rejected alternatives, and whether the group quickly accepts a consensus, if it forms.

3. Search for information
    This includes to what extent the group attempts to obtain available information so as to critically evaluate the pros and cons of the preferred course of action and other alternatives. It includes the extent to which the group relies on a single source or multiple sources of information.

4. Assimilate and process new (and perhaps discrepant) information
    This includes the openness and closedness of the group to new and perhaps discrepant information from experts, the mass media, and outside critics.

5. Evaluate the costs, risks, and implications of the preferred choice

6. Develop implementation, monitoring, and contingency plans

Tasks are coded along a continuum for each category, ranging from performing the task "very well" to "very poorly."

Very Poorly	Poorly	Neutral	Well	Very Well
4+	2 or 3	1	2 or 3	4+
omissions	omissions	omission or recognition	recognitions	recognitions

In addition, each coding is given a confidence rating: Low, Moderate, or High.

decision-making configurations. While the project seeks to further our understanding of these tendencies, the tendencies may not be present in the crises if decision makers are careful to avoid pitfalls of the model that is used. That implies a learning process, where decision makers incorporate lessons about structure and process from previous experience. To pick up such learning, the coding form includes questions about learning and the conscious attention to the management of decision-making groups.

A Note on Sources and Coding

Table 3 presents the case studies of each of the nine crises examined here and from which evidence about crisis decision-making structures and processes was extracted. The process by which inferences are made from these case studies is fairly straightforward. Inferences about the management structure that a president uses in the crisis and the nature of the decision-making process evident in the crisis are drawn from the existing case studies. In the Dien Bien Phu crisis, for example, ten case studies are interrogated. These case studies serve as a quasi database from which the variables of interest in this project are extracted. Inferences about decision-making structures and processes in the Dien Bien Phu crisis are made from these case studies.

Inferences about patterns within, for example, the Eisenhower administration, can be drawn by comparing and contrasting the evidence and inferences drawn from the case studies of both Eisenhower crises— Dien Bien Phu and Suez. Multiple sources of information inform inferences about each crisis. Two crises inform the inferences about each administration's structures and processes. Larger inferences about the nature of presidents' attempts to manage crisis decision making and about the nature of international crises can be drawn from the full set of crises under examination. This inferential process can be represented as:

1. N existing case studies $\rightarrow$ inferences about crisis 1 where question set 1 explores decision-making structures; question set 2 explores decision-making processes; and the coding form interrogates each of N case studies of the crisis
2. evidence from crises 1–2 $\rightarrow$ inferences about Administration A
3. evidence from Administrations A–E $\rightarrow$ broader lessons about presidents, crisis management, and international crises

The case-survey methodology focused on the development and execution of step one. The crisis cases were selected by design criteria in order to facilitate the making of inferences at steps two and three.

Empirical evidence from the case studies and conclusions are presented throughout the book. Citations from the case studies are included in the presentation of the evidence. I have tried to be as specific as possible in this presentation, without being overly burdensome on the reader. The citations are of two kinds, based upon the nature of the case-study evidence. Some citations are very specific, noting the author, year, and page number to support a specific point or inference. Other citations are more general, noting only the case study from which a point or inference was

TABLE 3.   Case-Study Sources

Truman Administration
  Berlin Airlift, 1948
    Davison 1958; Shlaim 1983; Smith 1963
  Korean Intervention, 1950
    Bernstein, 1977a, 1977b, 1989; Donovan 1982; George 1956; Gosnell 1980; Paige 1968

Eisenhower Administration
  Dien Bien Phu, 1954
    Burke and Greenstein 1989; Gelb and Betts 1979; George and Smoke 1974; Gerson 1967; Gurtov 1967; Gravel 1971; Immerman 1989; Kalicki 1975; Parmet 1972; Randle 1969
  Suez, 1956
    Bowie 1974; Gerson 1967; Guhin 1972; Hoopes 1973; Kingseed 1995; Kunz 1991; Kyle 1991; Love 1969; Neff 1981; Neustadt 1970; Parmet 1972; Thomas 1970

Johnson Administration
  Tonkin Gulf, 1964
    Austin 1971; Galloway 1970; Goulden 1969; Gelb and Betts 1979; Gravel 1971; Halberstam 1972; Hoopes 1969; L. Johnson 1971; Windchy 1971
  Tet, 1968
    Berman 1989; Clifford 1991; Gelb and Betts 1979; Gravel 1971; Hammond 1992; Hoopes 1969; Isaacson and Thomas 1986; L. Johnson 1971; Oberdorfter 1971; Schandler 1977

Nixon Administration
  Jordan's Civil War, 1970
    Dowty 1984, 1978; Evans and Novak 1971; Garthoff 1994; Kissinger 1979; Nixon 1978; Quandt 1978, 1977
  October War, 1973
    Ambrose 1991; Dowty 1984; Garthoff 1994; Kissinger 1982; Lebow and Stein 1994; Morris 1977; Nixon 1978; Perlmutter 1975; Quandt 1977

Bush Administration
  Panama Invasion, 1989
    Baker 1995; Buckley 1991; DeFrank and McDaniel 1990; Dinges 1990; Donnelly et al. 1991; Hoffman 1990; Kempe 1990; Flanagan 1993; Powell 1995; Scranton 1991; Woodward 1991

drawn (or perhaps a chapter of the case study). These more general citations represent when the case study evidence gave a general impression about the variable of interest but made no specific claim to which I might refer.

For example, I will argue in chapter 4 that the case-study evidence shows that the Johnson decision-making group in the Tonkin Gulf crisis largely ignored discrepant information about the events in the gulf. I can make a specific reference to Austin (among others) to support this claim (e.g., Austin 1971, 343). But on this same point, I can make no such specific reference to the case study in the Pentagon Papers (Gravel 1971, vol. 3). Rather, it is the general tenor of reporting in this massive case study that leads to such an inference. I try to be as specific as possible in the chapters that follow about citations, but the nature of the case studies is such that in some areas the best that can be discerned is an educated guess. When multiple case studies point in the same general direction, however, such an educated guess moves in the direction of a sound inference.[3]

As this discussion suggests, some case studies are more helpful, complete, and specific than others. This fact is important not only because of the sort of citations that the case studies afford, but also because of the nature of inferences they support. The inferences made in a case survey are only as good as the case studies upon which the survey draws. The case studies of the Truman crises are fairly complete and well known to students of U.S. foreign policy by now. Studies of the Berlin airlift by Shlaim (1983), Smith (1963), and Davison (1958) are rich and in general agreement. Studies of the decision to go to war in Korea by Paige (1968) and many others paint a fairly complete picture of decision making in this crisis.

For the Dien Bien Phu crisis, the case studies by Burke and Greenstein (1989) and Immerman (1989) are particularly useful. They are both based upon recently declassified evidence and are quite complete and detailed. However, no such authoritative case studies of American decision making during the crisis in the Suez canal exist. Several are useful, though none are as detailed and complete as the Burke and Greenstein study, for example. Robert Bowie's (1974) case study is useful. Bowie had served as the director of the State Department's Policy Planning Staff in the Eisenhower administration. Neff's (1981) study is insightful, as are the case studies by Love (1969), Neustadt (1970), Parmet (1972), and Kingseed (1995). Even with solid new studies of the Suez crisis (e.g., Kingseed 1995), there is a real gap in our understanding of American decision making in this crisis that future research should address.

The case studies of the incidents in the Gulf of Tonkin are generally complete. The case studies by Austin (1971), Galloway (1970), Goulden (1969), and Windchy (1971) combine to provide a full picture of the events in this crisis. Their reports are very consistent, and while none of these case studies completely covers the material, they cover it well as a group. I am not concerned about the independence of these case studies, which were all written during the same time period. While their tone and conclusions are essentially the same, the evidence used to support those conclusions is often very different. There is a new study of the events in the Gulf of Tonkin in 1964 by Edwin Moïse (1996). His historical study is extremely detailed and well-documented and provides the most definitive account to date of the events leading up to and including August 1964. The study by Moïse became available too late to be included in the list of case studies that was coded here, but I have been able to draw on the book's findings to round-out the discussion of the Tonkin Gulf episode. While the Moïse study differs on some details and interpretations from earlier studies of the Tonkin Gulf crisis, it does not do so in important ways on the points relevant for this study.[4]

The case studies of decision making leading up to and following the Tet Offensive are generally not very useful, with two strong exceptions. Clark Clifford's recently published memoirs (1991) are very helpful. Clifford had directed the task force that evaluated American policy in Southeast Asia after Tet; shortly thereafter he became secretary of defense. Schandler's (1977) study of the Johnson decision-making process is very reliable and authoritative. Schandler had been on the inside of the Johnson machinery and served on the Clifford task force. It is usually recognized as the most complete and reliable case study of decision making in this period (Gelb and Betts 1979, 171n).

The case studies of Nixon decision making are generally useful. Dowty's case studies (1984, 1978) of both the civil war in Jordan and the October War are very detailed, as are Quandt's (1978, 1977). Their reports are in general agreement, though I note where they disagree in the chapters that follow. Quandt served in the Nixon administration and was present at many of the meetings of the Washington Special Action Group. The memoirs of Henry Kissinger (1979, 1982) and Richard Nixon (1978) are worthwhile, if a bit self-serving, for both crises. The more detached studies by Dowty and Quandt help put these self-reports into perspective. The discussions of decision making during the October War in the third volume of Stephen Ambrose's biography of Richard Nixon (1991) and in Lebow and Stein (1994) are also very valuable and bring some new evidence to light.

There has not been enough time to provide for a careful examination of the classified record of the U.S. invasion of Panama. This record will no doubt be addressed in time, but for now I rely on what is available. Studies by Kempe (1990), Flanagan (1993), and Buckley (1991) provide some useful sketches with some documentation, while *The Commanders* by Bob Woodward (1991) provides much more detail but no real documentation. While I do not prefer to rely on such devices, the recent memoirs by Dan Quayle, James Baker, and Colin Powell do tend to reinforce the picture presented by Woodward, and I am at least not too uncomfortable drawing some inferences from this body of evidence in order to broaden the scope of inquiry in this project.

Conclusion

The ultimate goal of the project is to build better theory about how presidents organize decision-making groups in crisis situations and what the effects of that structuring and managing are on the way those groups do their work. It is a conceptual goal. As a step toward this goal I pursue a substantive goal of exploring the dynamics of presidential management of crisis decision-making groups during nine crises. These crises serve as windows into the broader set of crises that have emerged for U.S. foreign policy. The project seeks to track the way presidents have organizationally responded to these crises and how decision making, so structured, has worked. The methodological component of the project is to utilize a case-survey method in the analysis of U.S. foreign policy in order to see how well it works in this area and what insights it might afford. I have tried, as Alexander George urged, to treat these unique events in a systematic way.

CHAPTER 3

Presidential Management of Decision-Making Groups during Foreign Policy Crises

This chapter presents an analysis of the structures and strategies of presidential crisis decision-making management. It begins with a brief sketch of the crises studied here and then presents the evidence derived from the case studies of how Presidents Truman, Eisenhower, Johnson, Nixon, and Bush structured and managed crisis decision-making groups. This evidence has been gathered from the case studies of each crisis listed previously in table 1 with the items in question set 1 of the coding form (see appendix), according to the design discussed in the previous chapter. The chapter concludes with an initial assessment of the utility of the Johnson-George framework used here for understanding crisis decision-making management.

Truman Administration

Berlin Airlift, 1948

The crisis for the United States and the West began in Berlin on March 20, 1948, when Soviet Marshal Sokolovsky walked out of the Allied Control Council, the four-power body established after World War II to administer Germany. This action effectively ended the period of cooperation over Germany and left the future of Western access to Berlin in a precarious position. Tensions grew by April 1, 1948, as the Soviets imposed a partial blockade of traffic into Berlin. It was followed by a full blockade that was imposed on June 24, 1948. Soviet moves in Berlin should not have come as a total surprise. As early as October 1947, General Lucius Clay, the American military governor for Germany, had warned the National Security Council to be prepared for Soviet action designed to force Western withdrawal from Berlin (Shlaim 1983, 110). This warning was followed by a Soviet coup in Czechoslovakia in February 1948 and a warning cable from General Clay on March 5, 1948, about the possibility of war over Berlin

(Smith 1963, 101–2; Davison 1958, 73). There was no consensus among Western leaders, however, about whether the Soviets would attempt a full blockade of Berlin or whether the West could remain in Berlin if the Soviets did attempt such an action. No high-level decision had been made about these possibilities as of June 1948 (Davison 1958, 75).

In response to the announcement of increased scrutiny of travel into West Berlin on April 1, 1948, General Clay sent trains to Berlin to test the Soviet policy. One train was boarded and then went forward, two others refused to allow a Soviet inspection and were thus side-tracked (Shlaim 1983, 128). General Clay proposed in early April to send a convoy of trucks through Soviet checkpoints on the highway to Berlin, but this proposal was vetoed by Army Chief of Staff General Omar Bradley (131). No consensus had yet emerged about how to proceed in Berlin, and American decision makers, except Clay, were reluctant to specify plans for the use of force. In lieu of a firm decision from Washington, Clay began to formulate a way to supply the people of West Berlin through an American garrison and initiated a "baby airlift" on April 2 to this end (133).

The crisis in Berlin reached its height on June 24, when Soviet authorities severed all land communications between Berlin and the Western zones. This move brought President Truman into the decision-making process. Truman was concerned about the risk of war and the legal issues involved and was preoccupied with the 1948 U.S. political campaign, but he was determined to keep the United States presence in Berlin (Davison 1958, 110; Shlaim 1983, 174–82). The three imperatives for U.S. policy that emerged—maintain the U.S. position in Berlin, avoid war, and implement the currency reform program under way—were difficult to reconcile. With the use of an armed convoy to supply the city having been blocked in Washington and the idea of compromising with the Soviets on the currency reform program and the Western presence in West Berlin unpalatable, General Clay began plans to increase the scope of the airlift. Truman fully supported Clay's plan to supply the city by air and sent B-29s to Britain to help (Shlaim 1983, 196–208; Smith 1963, 107–8; Davison 1958, 110–20). At a White House meeting on June 28, 1948, with his advisers in disagreement about the course of U.S. policy in Berlin, President Truman made his intention to stay in Berlin clear (Shlaim 1983, 220). While some consideration of more forceful options took place and some diplomatic efforts were pursued, the situation in Berlin became less tense as the airlift succeeded for months in resupplying the city. An accord was reached on May 5, 1949, between Philip Jessup, deputy chief of the U.S. mission to the United Nations, and the Soviet representative to the UN, Jacob Malik, that ended the blockade and thus the airlift.

Korean Intervention, 1950

On June 24, 1950, armed forces from the Democratic People's Republic of Korea (DPRK), or North Korea, invaded the Republic of Korea (ROK), or South Korea, in a move that came as a great surprise to the ROK and to the United States. U.S. Ambassador to South Korea John Muccio reported the invasion to Washington, D.C. as an all-out offensive. President Truman was in Independence, Missouri, and was notified by Secretary of State Dean Acheson. The president and Secretary Acheson agreed that the United States should go to the United Nations about the invasion and that the State Department would take the lead in formulating a plan. On June 25, Truman returned to Washington to discuss the U.S. response to the invasion, and the first conference of the president and his advisers was held at Blair House that evening. President Truman, Secretary Acheson, Undersecretary of State Webb, Assistant Secretaries of State Hickerson and Rusk, Secretary of Defense Johnson, the service secretaries and joint chiefs, and Ambassador-at-large Jessup discussed U.S. options after dinner. There was general agreement in the group that the United States should work through the UN and that the forces of the ROK could contain the invasion unless the North had assistance from the Soviets. Truman decided that the United States should help supply ROK forces and evacuate U.S. citizens from South Korea (Paige 1968, 125–37).

In a second conference at Blair House on June 26, a number of military assessments were presented, and discussion focused on how to respond without being provocative to China or the Soviets. President Truman accepted Acheson's proposals to use naval and air power to support ROK forces. The UN Security Council was working on a resolution calling for the invasion to be repelled. General MacArthur, after visiting Korea, reported to Washington on June 29 that ROK forces were being routed and that U.S. ground forces would be required (Donovan 1982, 214–15). It was on this day that Truman agreed with a reporter's question that U.S. action under the UN was a "police action" (Paige 1968, 243). Also that day, Truman approved the use of some infantry forces to maintain supply lines and aid in evacuations. The following day, June 30, Truman approved General MacArthur's request to use ground troops in Korea to stop the invasion.

Truman and Formalistic Decision Making

Stephen Hess has argued that Truman believed government should be an orderly business and that loyalty should be a unifying principle for an administration (1988, 40). These assumptions led Truman to design a formal, hierarchical system for policy-making. George argues that Truman employed a very formalistic model for foreign policy-making (1980, 151–52). The pattern of decision-making management seen in both the Berlin crisis and the decision to intervene in Korea show how Truman continued to use a formalistic model in crisis decision making.

The evidence from the Berlin crisis of 1948 shows all the characteristics of the formalistic model. Shlaim argues that Truman used a variant of the formalistic model that relied heavily on staff to acquire information (1983, 70). Truman left the formulation and execution of U.S. policy in Germany to the functional experts rather than to his White House aides (Shlaim 1983, 71). Truman would bring information to the cabinet but not as a voting body. He welcomed advice, but decisions would be his (Shlaim 1983, 72). Truman, not his advisers, made key decisions (McCullough 1992, 631; Davison 1958; Smith 1963). He was the decision maker of last resort (Shlaim 1983, 69).

Channels of communication to and from the president were clearly defined and hierarchical, with the president at the top. This formalism was bolstered by the formalistic managerial style of both Secretary Marshall and General Clay (Shlaim 1983, 90, 97). One of the main lines of communication from Truman to General Clay was through the secretary of the army, Kenneth Royall (Truman 1956, 123; Smith 1963, 99–117). Truman largely did not use the newly formed National Security Council to aid in decision making, though he drew upon its members' expertise (Shlaim 1983, 74). The NSC was used as a forum for recommendations to be discussed, but it was not a decision-making body and operated within clearly prescribed limits (Shlaim 1983, 74). Key U.S. decision makers in the crisis included Truman, Secretary of State George Marshall, General Clay, Undersecretary of State Robert Lovett, Secretary of Defense James Forrestal, Army Secretary Royall, Army Chief of Staff Omar Bradley, and the State Department adviser in Germany, Robert Murphy. Truman, Marshall, and Clay were the central and fundamental decision makers (Shlaim 1983, 43).

During the genesis of the Berlin crisis, Truman's attention was largely devoted to the 1948 presidential campaign, the decision to recognize Israel, and the U.S. budget (Shlaim 1983, 174–75; Davison 1958, 76; Smith 1963, 103–7). Without direct presidential attention, General Clay exercised wide latitude with the support of the president. When the matter of the U.S. position in Berlin was brought to Truman's attention June 28, 1948, Truman clarified the U.S. policy to stay in Berlin (Davison 1958, 110; McCullough 1992, 630). After having done so, Truman again deferred to General Clay in the field to administer policy. Truman dis-

couraged debate among his advisers about the U.S. policy, allowing Clay
to direct the airlift. He did, however, veto Clay's proposal to use force,
preferring instead to use diplomatic measures to resolve the crisis (McCullough 1992, 630, 648). When Truman met with advisers in Washington,
D.C., he used clear, formal, structured procedures that afforded him much
latitude. Truman made wide use of teleconferences to develop institutional
forms of cooperation and to communicate with General Clay. He did not
go outside the institutional forms for information (Shlaim 1983, 165), but
he did make extensive use of ad hoc forums for decision making, rather
than use the formal NSC or cabinet (Shlaim 1983, 276–8). These ad hoc
groups, however, operated very formalistically, with Truman at the top
reserving decisions for himself (Shlaim 1983, 278). As the crisis unfolded
and Truman became more engaged, policy-making became even more
centralized and hierarchical (Shlaim 1983, 414).

Truman's managerial formalism and reliance on expertise and hierarchy allowed General Clay much latitude when no decision was forthcoming from Truman. For example, when the Soviets imposed the initial
blockade, Truman agreed to send test trains to Berlin on March 31–April
1, but that decision still afforded Clay much latitude in implementing the
decision. While Truman's advisers were divided on their view of Soviet
intentions, Clay was free to pursue his course within the confines established by Truman (Shlaim 1983, 44, 171, 195). Three U.S. imperatives in
Berlin were difficult to reconcile: to maintain the U.S. position in Berlin, to
avoid war with the Soviets, and to implement currency reform. While no
coherent strategy emerged from Truman, Clay pursued the airlift option in
a way that forced Truman's hand (196–206). Truman then supported and
expanded the airlift on June 26 (207–8).

A meeting on June 28 about Truman's decision took place in another
ad hoc forum in the White House, with Truman announcing that the
United States would stay in Berlin at all costs; there would be no discussion (Shlaim 1983, 218–21). Another ad hoc group was created in the crisis by Secretary Marshall between July 16 and 19 and headed by Charles
Bohlen to monitor and keep under constant review the situation in Berlin
(246). On July 22, Truman told Clay that the airlift would be continued
and that no ground convoy would be attempted, following an NSC meeting that dealt with U.S. options in Berlin, showing again Truman's use of
ad hoc forums for making formalistic decisions (260–65, 275–78).

The evidence from the Korea case shows a very similar pattern of
presidential leadership and managerial formalism and the use of ad hoc
forums, and where Clay played a key role in the Berlin crisis, Secretary of
State Acheson would play a central role in the Korean decision (Bernstein
1989, 421; Gosnell 1980, 463). Again the formal NSC would not be used as

a decision-making body (Gosnell 1980, 463). When North Korea invaded the South, President Truman was in Missouri, where he would stay, on Secretary Acheson's advice. The flow of information to the president from that point onward was clearly defined and hierarchical, flowing through Acheson to Truman (Paige 1968, 93; Bernstein 1977a, 1977b; Gosnell 1980). Truman did not reach down into the bureaucracy or outside channels for information or advice. Paige notes that Truman was a stickler for "channels" (1968, 24). Truman's advisers knew of his preference to reverse the invasion from very early on, at least by June 25 or 26. His preference set the agenda for the group (Bernstein 1989, 426; Paige 1968, 124).

Truman's advisers worked within recognized jurisdictions and areas of expertise. Acheson was designated as the head of the process in Washington, with MacArthur sending status reports and military recommendations to Truman through Army Secretary Frank Pace, Jr. and Defense Secretary Louis Johnson. Truman again did not encourage debate or conflict among his advisers and even excluded some who held differing opinions, such as George Kennan (Gosnell 1980, 463; Bernstein 1989, 426). The expertise of MacArthur and Acheson was central to the machinery (Gosnell 1980; Bernstein 1977a, 1977b, 33; Donovan 1982, 192–3).

The key forum for the Korea decision was Blair House. These meetings were formal in their procedures, led by Truman and Acheson, with Truman at the top as the ultimate decision maker (Paige 1968; Bernstein 1977a, 1977b; Donovan 1982, 192–3). The first Blair House conference was held June 25 and included Truman, Acheson, Johnson, Pace, Bradley, Undersecretary of State James E. Webb, Assistant Secretaries of State John D. Hickerson and Dean Rusk, Ambassador-at-large Philip Jessup, Navy Secretary Francis P. Matthews, Secretary of the Air Force Thomas K. Finletter, Army Chief of Staff General J. Lawton Collins, Chief of Naval Operations Admiral Forrest P. Sherman, and Air Force Chief of Staff General Hoyt S. Vandenburg. After dinner, and a warning from Secretary Webb not to move too fast, Acheson spoke. Truman then asked those assembled for their views, including asking Secretary Johnson for the views of the Defense Department, showing his respect for jurisdictions (Paige 1968, 125–37). After listening and asking some questions, Truman announced his decision to supply the ROK and evacuate U.S. citizens (Paige 1968, 137; Bernstein 1977a, 33).

A second meeting at Blair House the next day dealt with some implementation problems with the orders given to General MacArthur and reviewed the military situation. Acheson led the discussion, and ultimately Truman supported each of his proposals, including moving the Seventh Fleet and increasing U.S. aid to Formosa and the Philippines (Paige 1968,

161–62, 178; Bernstein 1977a, 35). In this period Truman was taking much heat from Republicans in Congress for doing too little, and he was working on the resolution in the UN Security Council calling for an end of hostilities and the return to the status quo antebellum, including the authorization to use force to repel the attack (Paige 1968, 188–204). This resolution would move more easily with Soviet Representative Jacob Malik absent over a dispute over the China seat on the council.

Truman convened a meeting of the NSC on June 28, the third major conference in the crisis, that opened with a survey of the situation in Korea by Truman himself. Major General John H. Church presented a overview of the situation as well, following his survey that was ordered by MacArthur. He reported that ground troops could be required to repel the attack (Paige 1968, 224). Truman ended the meeting with an order for all departments to perform a complete restudy of areas adjacent to the Soviet Union, searching for points of weakness and opportunity (Paige 1968, 224). Also on June 28, MacArthur visited Korea personally and ordered air strikes north of the Thirty-eighth Parallel (Paige 1968, 230).

The fourth major conference on the crisis in Korea was held June 29 at a meeting of the NSC called by Secretary Johnson to discuss MacArthur's recommendation to use ground troops (Paige 1968, 244). Truman approved the request for a limited use of ground forces to maintain order and help with evacuations and secure supply lines (Paige 1968, 246). The following day, June 30, General MacArthur requested the use in the battlefield of ground troops that were under his command in the Pacific theater, and he wanted a quick reply. Collins and Bradley conferred with Secretary Pace, who called Truman around 5:00 A.M. Truman immediately approved the use of one regimental combat team but delayed the broader request until he could discuss is with his advisers. Later that day, after such a meeting, Truman approved the request for the use of two divisions of U.S. ground forces, again showing his formalistic traits and use of ad hoc advisory groups (Paige 1968, 253–260, 283).

In the Berlin and Korean crises, Truman used a strikingly similar management strategy to control information and make decisions. He relied extensively on jurisdictions and expertise, including the commanders in the field. He maintained and sat atop tidy channels of communication and information. He reserved to himself ultimate decision authority, using advisers for advice, not votes. He used ad hoc groups rather than the institutionalized mechanisms of government, though those ad hoc groups operated very formally. He set the agenda by being determined at the outset to reverse the invasion. His was a classic example of top-down, formalistic management.

Eisenhower Administration

Dien Bien Phu, 1954

The American crisis in Indochina began as the French lost hold on the colony they had only recently regained from Japan after World War II. The French position in Indochina was weakening by 1952–53. The loss of Indochina to communist forces (the Vietminh) seemed certain. The United States was ending its experience in Korea—also an attempt to stop the spread of communism in Asia. Now the question was whether the United States should step in to fill the void left by the French in Indochina. The question of American intervention could not be avoided as the French position came to hinge upon their garrison at Dien Bien Phu. An ally was in trouble and communist forces were advancing. The Eisenhower administration had to determine what American interests were in the region, whether U.S. troops should be sent to Southeast Asia, or if the United States should intervene in some other way.

Eisenhower had begun to support the French endeavor in Indochina financially in 1953, but that was little help in stemming communist advances. A peace conference was set for April 1954 in Geneva. Vietminh forces launched an offensive in the spring of 1954, ostensibly to enhance their bargaining position at the Geneva conference. The French were losing badly and had retreated to the garrison at Dien Bien Phu. The Vietminh laid siege to this garrison on March 13, 1954. The garrison was falling quickly by mid-April. The French requested direct American military intervention three times during 1954.

Eisenhower's principal advisers were split between those who favored unilateral intervention and those who opposed it. A split also emerged between those who were anticommunist in their orientation and those who were anticolonialist in their thinking (Kalicki 1975, 91–120). These two cleavages led one camp to favor American unilateral intervention and another to oppose it. Some in the latter group were interested in a unified response, as anticolonialism was not a high priority for them in this event. Vice President Nixon and Chairman of the Joint Chiefs of Staff Admiral Radford were in favor of a unilateral intervention plan known as "Operation Vulture," which largely centered on air power. President Eisenhower, Army Chief of Staff Ridgway, Secretary of State John Foster Dulles, and Treasury Secretary George Humphrey were opposed to unilateral intervention, as were the members of Congress who were briefed on April 3, 1954 (Burke and Greenstein 1989, 28–115; Gelb and Betts 1979, 50–63).

While the United States did help fortify the garrison on February 6, 1954, by sending forty B-26 bombers and two hundred technicians, no

American bombing raids or ground forces were ever introduced. Eisenhower was unable to get allied (British) or congressional support for intervention. He could not be assured that a Chinese counterintervention would not take place if large numbers of American ground troops were introduced in the region. He was unable to receive guarantees from the French of eventual Indochinese independence and of a continued French presence in Indochina if allied intervention were forthcoming. The garrison fell May 7, 1954, on the eve of the Geneva conference (Gerson 1967, 157).

Suez, 1956

In many ways the crisis in the Suez began as early as when the Eisenhower administration came to power. In a 1953 memo, Secretary Dulles argued that the United States must deal with the Middle East in a way that would not make it choose between NATO and the Third World. Dulles sought a delicate middle role between the interests of the Arab nations in the Middle East and the interests of the United States's European allies and Israel. Relations between Israel and Egypt were increasingly strained by 1955. In February, Israel raided Egypt deep into the Sinai peninsula.

During this period, the United States had supported a hydroelectric project to help stimulate the Egyptian economy—President Nasser's plan for the Aswan Dam. As tension between Israel and Egypt increased, French arms began flowing to Israel as Soviet arms flowed to Egypt. An increase in Egyptian nationalism and radicalism followed. The United States soon began to see Nasser's ascendancy to a role of leadership in the Arab world as a threat. Eisenhower wished to weaken Nasser and to use the Aswan Dam as leverage over him (Neff 1981, 253–72). Eisenhower suspended financial assistance for the Aswan Dam.

The penultimate state of the crisis was reached when Nasser nationalized the Suez Canal on July 26, 1956, seizing ownership and operations of the canal from the West. Britain and France were incensed; Israel was prepared for war. Intelligence reports in the autumn indicated that France and Britain were preparing for war. There were unusually high amounts of activity and cable traffic between Paris and Tel Aviv. The American ambassador in Paris, C. Douglas Dillon, received information in mid-October that an attempt to topple Nasser would be made. Intelligence reports of October 25 indicated that Israel was mobilizing for war (see Parmet 1972, 470–73). Decision makers in the United States were greatly concerned, though Eisenhower still held out hope for a peaceful resolution.

A revolt in Hungary broke out simultaneous with these developments. Soviet tanks smashed resistance forces across that nation. Eisenhower was concerned that any further outbreak of fighting, particularly in the Middle East, could escalate to World War III (Parmet 1972, 472). In September, an initiative for peace that sought to satisfy the needs of all parties—the Suez Canal Users Association—was rejected (Neustadt 1970, 16–22). The ultimate state of the crisis was reached on October 29 when Israel invaded Egypt. Britain and France militarily supported this operation in a coordinated attack. The crisis had peaked and the United States had to decide how (or whether) to respond.

On October 31, 1956, Eisenhower dispatched John Foster Dulles to the United Nations Security Council to demand a cease-fire. Great Britain and France vetoed the resolution. Eisenhower was furious that his allies had kept him in the dark about the invasion plans. He had been against a military option from the beginning of the period (Love 1969, 368). Eisenhower firmly opposed the use of force in this case. He used instead diplomatic and economic pressure to force the withdrawal of British, French, and Israeli troops. The attack on Egypt ceased largely because of a promised U.S. war on the British pound.

Eisenhower and a Competitive-Formalistic Hybrid

The Eisenhower crisis decision-making management model was a hybrid that contained important elements of both a formalistic and a competitive approach. On the formalistic side, the case studies show that Eisenhower was clearly at the top of a well-structured, hierarchical decision-making group (Gurtov 1967; cf. Parmet 1972, 353–72). The president clearly accepted responsibility for final decision making (as opposed to stressing a decision-making team where responsibility is shared). Further, all the case studies of the Dien Bien Phu crisis indicate that early in the discussion Eisenhower revealed his preference against unilateral intervention. Such a revelation, just as the aforementioned characteristics, is indicative of a formalistic model where the president assumes a strong leadership position over the group. Army Chief of Staff Ridgway's opposition to the introduction of ground troops at Dien Bien Phu seemed to be very important to Eisenhower. This position prevailed in the end over Joint Chiefs of Staff Chairman Admiral Radford's preference for at least aerial intervention to save the French garrison. This reliance on expertise is another hallmark of a formalistic approach. Information clearly percolated up through the bureaucracy to authoritative department heads in Eisenhower's decision-making structure.

There is evidence of important elements of a competitive model as well. Gelb and Betts (1979, 50–63) report that Eisenhower encouraged debate and even conflict among his advisers during the Dien Bien Phu episode. Kalicki reports that broad-ranging and open debate took place, even after Eisenhower's preference was known (1975, 91–120). Eisenhower argued against sending American ground troops into Indochina. He stated that "the jungles of Indochina would swallow up division after division of U.S. troops" (quoted in Immerman 1989, 123). Immerman notes that "rather than stifle expressions of alternate viewpoints, Eisenhower's forceful statement [against unilateral intervention] sparked a wide-ranging yet detailed debate" (1989, 123; cf. Foyle 1996). Burke and Greenstein report that "one of the most conspicuous qualities of the Eisenhower administration's meetings was the spirited, no-holds-barred debate that marked them. The participants did not appear to hold back out of deference to the president or to tailor their advice to him" (1989, 54).

Burke and Greenstein argue that Eisenhower's advisers were comfortable challenging Eisenhower, even when he was emphatic about his own views (1989, 55). Moreover, they state that Eisenhower drew on an extensive informal network of opinions and information (1989, 57). This finding indicates that the channels of communication to the president were multiple and open during the Dien Bien Phu crisis—another hallmark of a competitive model. Important elements of both the formalistic and competitive models are evident in the Eisenhower advisory structure. Eisenhower had constructed a well-organized, tightly structured staff of experts who briefed him and over whom he exerted control and authority. Meetings between Eisenhower and his advisers had both a procedural focus and a structured staff apparatus. Intermingled with these qualities were open debate, give-and-take, and a willingness—even encouragement—to challenge each other and the president.

This evidence can be found in all the case studies of Dien Bien Phu, but most clearly in the more recent studies by Burke and Greenstein (1989) and Richard Immerman (1989). These studies of Eisenhower decision making are highly credible. They have the luxury of drawing on recently declassified archival materials that include minutes and notes of the meetings over Dien Bien Phu. The evidence and assessments they present do not contradict the reports in the other case studies; rather, they enhance and augment these other studies.

Before discussing decision making in the Suez crisis, I should mention an interesting use of structure by Eisenhower to affect process; it is also an example of how Eisenhower blended formalistic and competitive elements in his decision-making groups. It also reflects a self-conscious attention to the organizational requirements of crisis management by Eisenhower. Eisenhower was increasingly unsatisfied with the quality of advice and analysis he was receiving by mid-January 1954 (Burke and Greenstein 1989, 37). The debates had gotten stale and the options familiar. Eisenhower selected a subgroup of individuals to form a separate working group on the Dien Bien Phu problem. This group was diverse in its opinions about the situation in Indochina. Eisenhower directed the "Smith group," under the direction of Undersecretary of State Walter Bedell Smith and Undersecretary of Defense Roger Kyes, to form its own staff and reevaluate policy over Dien Bien Phu. Smith and Kyes were to develop new options for the United States. They were not to share their information or analysis with other members of the administration. Their group was to be "self-contained" (Burke and Greenstein 1989, 37).

This group eventually formed its own subgroup, which was directed by General Graves B. Erskine, director of the Defense Department's Office of Special Operations. The "Erskine group" worked in tandem with the Smith group and helped produce an "area plan" for the United States in Southeast Asia. The contents of this plan were not as significant for our purposes as the fact that Eisenhower consciously selected a structural response to a procedural problem. He was unhappy with the advice he was getting, so he created a new structure to take a fresh look. This is an example of the conscious management of structure to affect process. Furthermore, this example predates the Kennedy administration and the beginning of crisis management that is conventionally associated with it.

The case studies of the crisis at Suez are not as helpful as those of Dien Bien Phu. They tend to be historical accounts of the crisis, rather than analyses of decision making during the crisis. There are no appraisals of decision making during Suez that are analogous to the study by Burke and Greenstein (1989) on Dien Bien Phu, though the recent historical study by Kingseed is helpful. Nevertheless, there is evidence that Eisenhower used many of the same management techniques here as he had in the earlier crisis. On the formalistic side, Eisenhower again was clearly at the top of a well-structured decision-making process that he dominated (Kingseed 1995, 148; Bowie 1974; Hoopes 1973, 340–95; Neustadt 1970). Contrary to the belief that John Foster Dulles was the primary player in Eisenhower foreign policy or in this crisis (e.g., Finer 1964), Parmet (1972, 470–87) clearly shows that Dulles reported to Eisenhower at each step of the crisis (this could be contrasted with the autonomy that Kissinger enjoyed during the October War, discussed later in this chapter). Kingseed also shows that Dulles worked within the parameters set by Eisenhower (1995, 109, 153).

Eisenhower's preferences in the crisis were known by his advisers, but this did not stifle debate. Neff (1981) and Parmet (1972, 470–87) report that much debate and discussion took place over the courses of action that the United States might take in response to Nasser's nationalization of the Suez Canal and of Israel's, Britain's, and France's military intervention. Kingseed also records that Eisenhower fostered lively debate among his advisers about different contingencies, though he had already decided on the broad outlines of policy (1995, 106). In this crisis there is evidence of a similar mix of formalistic and competitive elements in Eisenhower decision-making structure. The competitive elements may be more latent in this crisis, however. Their presence can be inferred from the nature of the advisers' interaction with each other and with Eisenhower, but the formalistic characteristics are more immediately noticeable. Eisenhower relied more on legal advisers from the State Department in this crisis than in the 1954 crisis, especially Roger Murphy and Herman Phleger, the State Department's legal adviser. Still, Kingseed (1995) shows that Eisenhower was intensely engaged in this crisis and reserved power to himself.

There was considerable consensus in the administration over the appropriate response to this crisis. I would speculate that if there were more disagreement over American policy in this crisis, then the competitive aspects of Eisenhower's advisory structure would become more visible. The evidence in this crisis of open channels of communication and open debate (albeit at a lower level than during the 1954 crisis) that existed alongside structured arrangement for decision making with the president clearly at the top of established lines of authority (Kingseed 1995, 19) show this model to be an instance of a competitive-formalistic hybrid, rather than an instance of a formalistic model.

Johnson Administration

Tonkin Gulf, 1964

The events in the Gulf of Tonkin on August 2 and August 4, 1964, continue to be controversial today. In March 1964, National Security Action Memorandum (NSAM) 288 laid out the broad objectives of the United States in Vietnam and Southeast Asia. It noted that the situation in the region was deteriorating for American interests and argued for an increased role for the United States within Vietnam. As part of this stepped-up level of activity, the United States had been operating electronic surveillance patrols (code-named De Soto patrols) in the Gulf of Tonkin throughout the summer of 1964. The destroyer USS *Maddox* began its tour on July 31, 1964. The mission of the *Maddox* was to use electronic measures to measure the radar capabilities of North Vietnam and China (Galloway 1970; Windchy 1971; Moïse 1996, 50–55).

South Vietnamese patrol boats shelled several North Vietnamese islands on the evening of July 30–31. On August 2, the *Maddox* and North Vietnamese patrol boats exchanged fire. Reports of the exchange of fire reached Washington, D.C., during the evening of August 2. The next morning, President Johnson and his key advisers discussed the events of the past evening. This group included Secretary of State Dean Rusk, Secretary of Defense Robert McNamara, Undersecretary of State George Ball, Undersecretary of Defense Cyrus Vance, Chairman of the Joint Chiefs of Staff Earl Wheeler, and Special Assistant for National Security Affairs McGeorge Bundy. Johnson decided not to retaliate, largely because no injuries were reported from the Tonkin Gulf. He did decide to continue the De Soto patrols with orders to retaliate to destroy if attacked again. The destroyer USS *C. Turner Joy* joined the *Maddox*.

Units from the South Vietnamese Navy raided the mainland of North Vietnam on August 3–4, 1964. On August 4, under extraordinary weather conditions, the *Maddox* and the *Turner Joy* reported to be under attack once again. Reports of this attack reached the White House at 11:00 A.M. An NSC meeting had been scheduled for 12:00 noon to deal with other matters. During the Tuesday lunch meeting that followed the NSC meeting, Johnson announced to Rusk, McNamara, and Bundy that retaliation must follow. Johnson said that "Hanoi must be punished" for the incidents (Goulden 1969, 35). After lunch, Bundy reported to Ball, Wheeler, CIA Director Helms, and others that air strikes would commence that evening. These directions were given to the CINCPAC in Honolulu, Admiral Ulysses S. Grant Sharp Jr. Sixty-four air attack sorties targeted four boat bases and one oil storage depot. Two U.S. aircraft were lost and two more damaged.

While preparing to retaliate for the August 4 incident, Washington received a cable from Captain Herrick in the Pacific. Herrick asserted that the August 4 contacts were doubtful because the weather conditions made the radar sightings questionable. The very existence of the attack was called into question. Herrick urged a complete examination before moving forward (Windchy 1971, 211). Regardless of Herrick's message, the retaliation was carried out (and in fact publicly announced while the planes were still in the air). Afterward, the Tonkin Gulf Resolution was signed into law by Johnson on August 11, 1964. The resolution authorized the president to take actions necessary to protect U.S. interests in the region. The administration formally argued (through Nicholas Katzenbach from the office of the attorney general) that this resolution was a functional equivalent of a declaration of war on August 17 (Galloway 1970). Whether or not the second attack took place (Moïse demonstrates that it did not), an important firebreak had been breached. The American base at Pleiku was attacked by the Vietcong on February 7, 1965. Aerial bombardment of the North—Operation Rolling Thunder—commenced March 2, 1965. U.S. ground troops followed as marines landed at Da Nang on March 8. American activity in Vietnam continued to escalate until the Tet Offensive in 1968.

Tet Offensive, 1968

The war in Vietnam was at its peak, and intelligence reports indicated that a massive attack on U.S. forces by the Vietcong and the North Vietnamese Army (NVA) was being planned to commence sometime around (but not during) Tet, the lunar new year, at the end of January 1968. General Westmoreland, the commander of American forces in Southeast Asia, believed the object of the attack to be the U.S. Marine base at Khe Sanh. American military planners expected the attack on Khe Sanh to be much like the siege of the French garrison at Dien Bien Phu. In fact, the 304th Infantry Division of the NVA, the division that laid siege to the French garrison, was thought to be surrounding Khe Sanh. Contrary to these expectations, the attacks took place during the traditional cease-fire for the Tet holiday. Nor did it occur in the North at Khe Sanh, as expected. Instead, it included a series of simultaneous and coordinated attacks all across South Vietnam during January 30–31, 1968. Thirty-nine of 44 provincial capitals, 5 of 6 autonomous cities, and 71 of 245 district towns were attacked. Assaults focused on civilian centers of authority and military command installations (Schandler 1977, 74–79). The raids even reached inside the American Embassy in Saigon.

The North suffered a severe defeat in military terms. It lost high numbers of well-trained troops and lost the confidence of many peasants in the South who did not expect such violence to be rained down upon them. But they had scored a decisive psychological victory (Schandler 1977, 79). The Tet Offensive showed most clearly that the progress the Johnson administration had been heralding was illusory (Gravel 1971, 4:604). Bombing to interdict the flow of men and materiel from the North to the South had been a "signal failure" (Gravel 1971, 4:235). As noted by Clark Clifford, a participant in the decision-making process, the most serious casualty of the Tet Offensive was American confidence in its leaders (Clifford 1991, 473–75). The Tet Offensive demonstrated that the Johnson administration had been misleading the public about the progress of the war in Vietnam (Oberdorfer 1971, 174).

The crisis of Tet continued after the attacks were quashed while Johnson and his advisers tried to decide how the United States should respond to these new circumstances. Confusion reigned in early and mid-February, but by the end of the month the Joint Chiefs of Staff asked for more than two hundred thousand more men and fewer restrictions on bombing campaigns. On February 28, 1968, President Johnson appointed Clifford to lead a study group to review U.S. policy in Vietnam. Initially, the Clifford Task Force sought to find a way to fill Westmoreland's request for more troops. Not long into their examination, however, the group began to question the very basis of American involvement in Vietnam (Hoopes 1969, 172; cf. Schandler 1977, 133). Eventually, Johnson would decide to reduce U.S. involvement in the region, to seek a peaceful solution, and to not run for reelection. It would be five more years before the United States would extricate itself from Vietnam's civil war.

Johnson and a Collegial-Formalistic Hybrid

Austin (1971, 32) and Hess (1988, 88–103) argue that Johnson sought to retain some of the Kennedy "collegial" decision-making structures, which Johnson felt were very successful at crisis decision making. Johnson, however, tried to tailor these arrangements with his need for more structure, more control, and fewer advisers. The result was an advisory model that was highly structured, with assigned jurisdictions, and with the president clearly at the top and in charge (Gravel 1971, 5:320–41). This structure followed the president's lead (Goulden 1969, 149). Johnson did not use the full National Security Council, which he thought was too big and included too many untrustworthy people, for crisis decision making. He was also uncomfortable with the variety of views that might be expressed at such a large gathering and preferred more control over proceedings and outcomes (Hammond 1992, 8). Instead, Johnson funneled information through McGeorge Bundy, his special assistant for National Security Affairs (Austin 1971, 32; Hess 1988, 100–101).

The Johnson advisory structure for both routine situations and crises was very formalistic up to the top. Johnson dealt with agency heads and allowed them to handle subordinates (Hammond 1992, 2). But things operated differently at the top. Johnson sought to add Kennedy's collegial aspects of decision making to the top of this formalistic structure below. Johnson was part of a decision-making team at the top that included Bundy, Secretary of State Dean Rusk, and Secretary of Defense Robert McNamara. The group also included Joint Chiefs of Staff Chairman Earl Wheeler and CIA Director John McCone on occasion. Johnson himself recalls in *The Vantage Point* the small number of advisers on whom he relied for advice in the aftermath of the Tonkin Gulf incidents: McNamara, Rusk, Bundy, Cyrus Vance, George Ball, and Earl Wheeler (1971, 113; cf. Halberstam 1972, 556). This group, which came to be known as the "Tuesday lunch group" because of its usual meeting time, made decisions about American involvement in Vietnam.

This "very agreeable group" operated with very informal procedures (Windchy 1971, 211). While the structure that fed into the Tuesday group contained every characteristic of a formalistic model, this group was indicative of a collegial model. Its members operated as a team or unit.

They debated openly. The members of the group did not act as functional specialists with assigned jurisdictions. Johnson wanted consensus in this group. Goulden reports that decisions over the Tonkin Gulf crisis were made very informally by Johnson, Rusk, Bundy, and McNamara, based upon the evidence they received from the structures beneath them (1969, 135–50; cf. Windchy 1971, 8–10, 211). This evidence of decision making concerning the events in the Gulf of Tonkin lead me to infer that the Johnson crisis decision-making structure was formalistic to the top, but collegial at the top. The structured staff system below fed an ambiguously organized ultimate decision-making group at the top. This structure is a hybrid of the formalistic and collegial management models.

This hybrid model is more evident in the crisis at Tet in 1968. As Tet approached, the decision-making group was structured much as it had been in 1964 (though Walt Rostow had replaced McGeorge Bundy as Johnson's special assistant for national security affairs). Paul Nitze and Paul Warnke were increasingly important members of Johnson's deliberative body, and Clark Clifford had begun to emerge as a most important adviser to President Johnson.

Most of the evidence about decision making before, during, and after Tet is drawn from Schandler's (1977) highly credible study *The Unmaking of a President*. Decision making was business as usual until the attacks on the Tet holiday. Once the impact of the Tet Offensive was felt in Washington and around the nation, the Johnson advisory structure became more open and collegial than before. The Johnson structure had been formalistic, with collegial aspects at the top. The structure was opened to include a variety of views from diverse sources. Channels of communication became more open and lines of authority more ambiguous (Gelb and Betts 1979; Hoopes 1969).

Johnson dispatched General Wheeler and Clark Clifford (who was quickly replacing Robert McNamara as Johnson's most important strategist for Vietnam) to feel out Congress in the wake of Tet (Oberdorfer 1971, 289). Johnson felt he needed advice from different sources. He expanded the collegial top of his advisory group. More people were part of Johnson's circle that utilized multiple and open lines of communication, organizational ambiguity, little jurisdictional authority, and informal procedures (Schandler 1977). These are all characteristics of the collegial style. Beneath this level, however, there continued to operate a well-structured, jurisdictionally oriented, bureaucracy (as one would expect). Johnson continued to emphasize consensus among this broadened group of advisers at the top (Schandler 1977, 253).

Generals Wheeler and Westmoreland argued for an increase in American ground forces in Vietnam after the Tet Offensive, a request that

Johnson was in no hurry to fulfill. Wheeler again asked for the troops in a February 27 meeting at the White House. Rostow argued in favor of the request, but suggested that other strategies needed to be examined after this reinforcement. Treasury Secretary Fowler argued that the president must go to the people about the matter. Robert McNamara argued for the examination of alternatives to political and military options (Schandler 1977, 117). The next day, Johnson acted on McNamara's advice. Johnson assigned his trusted adviser Clark Clifford the task of putting together a study group to examine U.S. options in Vietnam. Johnson would be truly open to a group outside his small circle at the top for the first time since 1964.

Clifford saw his primary assignment as to give Johnson a recommendation about the Wheeler-Westmoreland troop request. In the process, Clifford used his "relative ignorance" to ask some basic questions about U.S. strategy in Vietnam (Clifford 1991, 492–93). Clifford's questions included probes about the American plan for victory in Vietnam. He found that there was none, much to his dismay. He wanted to know when the Pentagon expected to defeat the enemy. He got no answer. The Clifford Task Force presented its report to the president on March 4, 1968. It suggested a compromise between filling the military request and seeking political alternatives. The recommendation was not the important part of the task force, however. Its true significance was that an outside group had freshly assessed the situation in Vietnam for the first time and that it would be listened to by the president (Schandler 1977, 176).

Clifford then urged Johnson to meet with another outside group of long-standing foreign policy experts—the Wise Men (see Isaacson and Thomas 1986). The members of this group supported the expansion of American involvement in Vietnam earlier. Their support was important to Johnson. Clifford knew that most of them had turned against the war, and he wanted Johnson to hear their views. Johnson assented and arranged for full briefings for the group. The Wise Men met between March 25 and 26, 1968. The group included George Ball, McGeorge Bundy, Douglas Dillon, Cyrus Vance, Arthur Dean, John McCloy, Omar Bradley, Matthew Ridgway, Maxwell Taylor, Robert Murphy, Henry Cabot Lodge, Abe Fortas, and Arthur Goldberg. The consensus they reached (with Murphy, Fortas, and Taylor dissenting) was that LBJ should get out of Vietnam (Schandler 1977, 256–65).

The collegial layer on top of a formalistically organized crisis decision-making group had always existed in the Johnson administration, but after Tet it began to operate more openly and more effectively. It became a truly "collegial" group, rather than just seeming to be so. Stephen Hess quotes former State Department official and White House staffer James

Thomson as saying that before Tet, dissenters (like George Ball) were made to feel at home (1988, 102). They were permitted to dissent, but their dissent had very little meaning. Many of Johnson's advisers feared him (Halberstam 1972, 555). Others agreed with him. A shock to this system, such as the Tet Offensive, was required to make a collegially organized decision-making group act like colleagues. "After Tet, the decision-making process functioned properly for the first time" (Schandler 1977, 338).

Nixon Administration

Jordan's Civil War, 1970

The American crisis over Jordan's civil war began and ended quickly. The People's Front for the Liberation of Palestine hijacked several planes on September 6, 1970. Its members held the Western and Jewish passengers hostage and threatened to overthrow Jordan's King Hussein. Rescue operations were considered by the Nixon administration, but none seemed practical. The Sixth Fleet in the Mediterranean Sea was moved to support any operation that might take place. King Hussein declared martial law on September 15, 1970. Civil war erupted on September 17, 1970, as Hussein's forces faced off against Palestinian Fedayeen forces. During this period, Soviet involvement in Syria and Egypt had increased. President Nixon issued a firm warning against intervention by outside forces, and efforts to deter a Syrian intervention in Jordan to support the Palestinian forces—the heart of the crisis—were redoubled.

The outcome of this civil war was of interest to many parties. Israel had a particular interest in the outcome, since a loss by King Hussein would likely result in a radical Palestinian state on its border. Israel threatened to intervene on Hussein's behalf against any outside force that sought to support the Fedayeen units. In particular, Israel prepared to attack Syrian tanks that were poised to attack Jordan in support of the Fedayeen. The crisis for the Nixon administration erupted when Syrian tanks invaded Jordan from the north and King Hussein requested assistance. Fear that an Arab-Israeli war would break out should Israel intervene against Syrian forces was probably well founded. American units were not well positioned to fend off the Syrian attack, and it did not seem likely that King Hussein would prevail in the face of Syrian assistance to the Fedayeen units.

Nixon and his advisers had to decide what action the United States should take. The Joint Chiefs of Staff, and their chairman, Admiral Thomas Moorer, were opposed to U.S. ground intervention at a meeting of the Washington Special Action Group. King Hussein renewed his appeal for help on September 21, 1970, as three hundred Syrian tanks invaded Jordan (Nixon 1978, 483). Nixon directed Secretary of State Henry Kissinger to work out a plan with Israeli Ambassador Yitzhak Rabin for a limited Israeli intervention against the Syrian tanks, while American forces in the Mediterranean protected Israel's rear (Kissinger 1979, chap. 15; cf. Evans and Novak 1971, 263–65). The plan was approved for the next day. The United States was committed. Israel was poised to act on King Hussein's behalf against Syrian forces on September 22. However, in a last-ditch effort, Hussein's small air force satisfactorily repelled the Syrian forces. As the tanks withdrew, the need for Israeli intervention faded. King Hussein was firmly in control of Jordan within the next few days. The Fedayeen forces were substantially weakened; the hostages from the hijacked planes were safe. Syria had turned back and the Soviet Union had stayed out. The relationship between the United States and Israel was strong.

October War, 1973

Israel had received credible reports of a pending attack from its Arab neighbors before October 6, 1973. However, Prime Minister Golda Meir assured Washington that she would not preempt an Arab attack. The United States tried to deter the start of a new war in the Middle East. Syria and Egypt attacked Israel in an operation that caught many by surprise at 6:00 A.M. local time, October 6, 1973. "From the first, Nixon assumed that the Soviets were behind the Arab offensive, and from the first he was determined that Soviet arms would not prevail" (Ambrose 1991, 230). The Arab forces experienced early success. Israel was in trouble and asked for help. Nixon promised to resupply Israel's losses, and Kissinger began to work for a cease-fire, which the Soviets also wanted. America tried to prevent the Soviets from resupplying their allies. Kissinger accepted the Soviet proposal for a cease-fire to be in place by October 10. By this time Israel had regained its position, though still having severe difficulties in the field. Egypt had begun to redeploy its troops, and a Soviet airlift was on its way to the Middle East between October 10 and 12. The crisis deepened in Washington. An ally was in trouble and Soviet forces seemed ready to intervene.

On October 13, 1973, Richard Nixon ordered a full-scale, immediate airlift to aid Israel. On October 19, he submitted a bill to Congress for $2.2 billion in aid for Israel. That same day, Nixon dispatched Kissinger to Moscow for peace talks. An Arab oil embargo followed the large and public American resupply of Israel. While a fragile cease-fire was reached, it was short-lived, as Israel broke the agreement on October 22. Israel moved west of the Suez Canal toward the Egyptian Third Army. Soviet Premier Leonid Brezhnev proposed (on October 24) to Nixon that a joint American-Soviet force be used to ensure the cease-fire. He suggested that if the United States did not join the Soviet Union in this endeavor, the Soviets would act unilaterally—anathema to long-standing American interests in the region. There were indications that Soviet troops were already on their way.

Moreover, on October 22, neutron emissions were detected from a Soviet resupply ship, suggesting the presence of nuclear weapons. The United States had known that the Soviets had deployed SCUD missiles in Egypt but had no information about the content of their warheads. The United States responded to this latest discovery by placing American forces around the world at Defense Condition (DEFCON) 3, a heightened state of alert (Dowty 1984, 261). The United States also strongly encouraged Israel to halt its advances and not to crush Egypt's Third Army, which it had encircled. Egypt, the Soviets, and Washington were ready to end to this episode. The UN Security Council passed Resolution 340, which called for a return to the October 22 borders and a cease-fire. All agreed and the cease-fire held. DEFCON 3 was lifted and the crisis quickly faded.

Nixon, Kissinger, and a Formalistic Model

The Nixon-Kissinger model of crisis decision making was centered around the president and his national security assistant, or secretary of state. Kissinger chaired the Washington Special Actions Group (WSAG), the organization charged with crisis management, and the meetings of its principals (George 1980, 156; Haney 1994b). Its members reported to Kissinger, and he reported to Nixon. The case studies of the Jordan crisis and the October War are highly reliable and give consistent reports of the structure of the Nixon advisory system. They corroborate and expand on what Nixon and Kissinger discuss in their memoirs. The case studies by William B. Quandt, a staff member present at most meetings of the WSAG, are firsthand accounts.

Quandt reports that the Nixon-Kissinger model of organization was clearly defined and hierarchical. It mirrored the flowchart where departments reported to department heads, who reported to Kissinger, who reported to Nixon (Quandt 1977; cf. George 1980, 156). The staff system was highly structured and included recognized jurisdictions. In the Jordan crisis, for example, important advisers included Joe Sisco from the State Department, who was responsible for affairs in the Middle East, and Chairman of the Joint Chiefs Admiral Thomas Moorer (Nixon 1978, 477).

The president assumed authority for making decisions, though he did so in close consultation with Kissinger (Evans and Novak 1971, 260–65; Kissinger 1979, 603–25; cf. Quandt 1977, 115, 204). Quandt reports that procedures of WSAG meetings were clear, formal, and well known. There was little in the way of "debate" or "conflict" (Quandt 1977, 200–206).

There is no record of Nixon reaching down or outside the formal information network as part of his decision making (Dowty 1978, 176). Instead, Nixon relied on the structures that he had previously instituted (and on Henry Kissinger) to provide information, advice, and analysis. These structures had much autonomy, especially the WSAG (Kissinger 1982, chap. 15). Kissinger convened and presided over WSAG meetings throughout the crisis and relayed their deliberations to Nixon after the conclusion of their meetings. The decision-making group became more formal and centralized, ultimately leading to dyadic interaction between Nixon and Kissinger as the crisis unfolded (Dowty 1978, 183; 1984, 148). Dowty reports that Nixon purposefully avoided external communication and relied instead on his own internal sources and instincts (1984, 183).

An amusing example of this reporting style occurred when Kissinger needed to relay to the president the recommendations of the WSAG about a U.S. response to the invasion of Jordan by Syrian tanks. This was the peak of the crisis, September 20, 1970. Kissinger eventually found Nixon bowling in the basement of the Old Executive Office Building (Kissinger 1979, 622). As the crisis developed and heightened, the dyadic interaction between Nixon and Kissinger became increasingly important as they stood atop a very formalistically organized crisis decision-making framework (though it sometimes occurred in unconventional venues). The Nixon management model during the Jordan crisis had all the attributes of the formalistic model, with the Nixon-Kissinger dyad at the top.

The evidence from the October War is similar. Kissinger once again presided over the WSAG, which retained great autonomy in the crisis as the organization charged with crisis advising (Kissinger 1982, chap. 11). At the same time, Nixon was deeply involved in the Watergate scandal, the Agnew resignation, and the "Saturday Night Massacre."[1] Nixon retained formal authority over his formalistic decision-making structure, but his attention was divided, and the nature of the Nixon-Kissinger dyad was more problematic.

The decision-making structures that were in place in 1973 were largely identical to the ones used in 1970, and they worked effectively. Quandt reports that the Nixon advisory configuration included a highly structured and jurisdictional staff system that operated in an unambiguous, clearly understood manner—all formalistic traits. The president did not reach down or outside for information. The crisis machinery was largely unchanged from its design for routine decision making. It was simply speeded up during the crisis (Dowty 1984, 304). The interaction between Kissinger and Nixon remained dyadic but was more ambiguous.

The domestic events surrounding this crisis made it difficult for Nixon to concentrate on diplomacy, and Kissinger was eager to take up the slack (Ambrose 1991, 230). Kissinger ran the WSAG during this crisis. Quandt (1977) reports their procedures as unchanged from the Jordan crisis, though the White House chief of staff was an increasingly important player in decision making. Similarly, Dowty (1984) argues that the decision-making structure was mostly identical to the one used in the Jordan crisis, with the Nixon-Kissinger dyad being the key axis of power. This dyad was quite different from before, however. A formalistic model with a dyad at the top still existed, but three events highlight the differences between 1973 and 1970 and the ambiguous nature of this dyad: the resupply of Israel, Kissinger's trip to Moscow, and the nuclear alert.

First, Israel requested that the materiel it lost in the early hours and days of the war be resupplied by the United States. On October 6, 1973, Nixon approved a quiet resupply, but it did not take place. On October 9, Nixon directed Defense Secretary James Schlesinger to resupply Israel. Again, no resupply occurred. On October 13, Nixon vehemently ordered a full-scale and public resupply of Israel. This sequence of events begs the question of who was in charge during the crisis. Nixon states that Kissinger blamed the delay on roadblocks from the Department of Defense, that Kissinger had tried and failed to fulfill the president's order (1978, 924). But Stephen Ambrose draws a different conclusion. Using the notes of Chief of Naval Operations Admiral Zumwalt, Ambrose argues that Kissinger had directly ordered Schlesinger not to resupply Israel. It is Ambrose's contention that Kissinger was pursuing his own agenda for peace after the war and wanted to let the war continue for a time before resupplying Israel (Ambrose 1991, 234). On October 13, Nixon made it abundantly clear to all involved that he wanted Israel to be resupplied (he ordered Schlesinger and Kissinger to put everything the United States had in the air if necessary). Israel finally got its reinforcements (Nixon 1978, 924). This incident shows that Nixon retained final authority, but in a most precarious manner. Garthoff observes the flip side of this conclusion, noting that Kissinger was able to make policy "almost exclusively" in this crisis except for the resupply (1994, 418).

Second, Nixon dispatched Kissinger to Moscow on October 19, 1973, to negotiate a cease-fire agreement. En route, Nixon gave full authority to Kissinger to bind the United States to a cease-fire arrangement (Kissinger

1982, 547). The dyad would no longer be a dyad. Kissinger was in charge, on this issue at least. A cease-fire was agreed to on October 21 and then broken by Israel.[2]

Third, the nuclear alert of October 24–25 demonstrates the precarious nature of the Nixon-Kissinger dyad. As discussed earlier, the United States placed its strategic forces at DEFCON 3 in response to threats of unilateral intervention in the war by the Soviets and indications that the Soviets might have moved nuclear materials into the region. The interesting organizational component of the alert is that it was ordered while Nixon was asleep. He was informed of the alert the next morning. Nixon reports that a group made up of Kissinger, Haig, Moorer, Schlesinger, Brent Scowcroft, and CIA Director William Colby was unanimous in its decision to move to the heightened state of alert and that the alert was flashed in the early hours of the morning (Nixon 1978, 939). He does not mention his own role in this overnight meeting. Kissinger reports that he and the WSAG decided on the alert and reported it to Nixon (1982, 587–91). Kissinger is unclear about whether the alert was flashed before or after reporting to Nixon. Quandt was not present at this meeting and provides little assistance on this question. Dowty reports that Kissinger convened the meeting that led to the alert, and he places Nixon upstairs while the meeting took place (1984, 261). Dowty argues that Kissinger—not Nixon—was in control during this period (cf. Sagan 1979, 172). Others also place Nixon upstairs asleep during the meeting (Morris 1977, 247–49; Garthoff 1994, 425).

Ambrose presents a recent, thorough analysis of this question (as he does of the resupply incident). He draws on CNO Admiral Zumwalt's notes of the meeting that would lead to the alert. The alert was flashed at 12:25 A.M. Eastern Standard Time on October 25. Zumwalt's notes of a meeting between Kissinger and the Joint Chiefs of Staff that took place at 2:00 A.M. October 25 make no mention of President Nixon. Ambrose reports that Kissinger informed Nixon at an 8:00 A.M. meeting on October 25 and that Nixon briefed congressional leaders at 9:00 A.M. Ambrose reports that the president was upstairs asleep throughout (1991, 254–57).

Opinions vary on whether Nixon was in control of the crisis decision-making apparatus during the 1973 October War. It is certainly an unusual instance of presidential activity in a set of important decisions. Ambrose argues that Nixon retained final authority in the crisis (1991, 234–35). He resupplied Israel, albeit belatedly. Diplomatic authority was still his to give to Kissinger when his secretary of state went to Moscow. Nixon probably would have agreed with the nuclear alert, had he been awake. He certainly could have done something about it in the morning, had he wished to do so. Nixon set up an advisory structure, he relied upon it, and it worked—even with him largely out of the process.

The interesting managerial point about this crisis, beyond the normative and constitutional points it raises, is that Nixon relied upon an advisory structure that had previously been established, and this structure worked even with him largely out of the process. Nixon set up a decision-making system that was highly centralized and that afforded a large measure of presidential control. One might expect this system to therefore collapse under the circumstances of presidential inattention. To the contrary, the Nixon advisory system worked even in the president's absence, with the possible exception of the order to resupply Israel—an action that may not have taken place without Nixon's eventual direct intervention. The system had been made robust against the lack of presidential involvement.

Bush Administration

Panama Invasion, 1989

U.S. relations with Panama had been strained for some time, and the quashed election of May 1989 did not help matters. Manuel Noriega had been indicted on drug charges and U.S. attention to Panama was stepped up in the summer of 1989, and the failed coup of October led U.S. decision makers to the brink of a crisis. A full-scale crisis emerged in December when U.S. Marine Corps Captain Richard Haddad's car ran a roadblock of the Panamanian Defense Forces (PDF) and one of the car's passenger's, Lieutenant Robert Paz, was shot and killed as the car sped off. That same weekend a U.S. Navy lieutenant and his wife were detained and questioned in a rather violent and unconventional manner. The costs of inaction had risen intolerably high for President Bush, and a military option had been developed by the commander in chief of the U.S. Southern Command, General Maxwell Thurman, and other planners at the Pentagon.

Three intervention plans were developed. One called for a limited use of U.S. special forces to capture Noriega. This plan had the advantage of keeping casualties low but held little hope for actually finding Noriega. A second plan called for a moderate use of force, about twelve thousand troops, to decapitate the PDF and capture Noriega. This plan had the advantage of keeping casualties low and maintaining secrecy because it would use only forces already stationed in Panama, but it had the potential weakness of leading to prolonged fighting outside Panama City and increasing threats to the security of the Panama Canal. The third plan, which was ultimately selected, was a plan for the use of massive force, about twenty-five thousand troops, to defeat the PDF and capture Noriega quickly. The weakness of the plan was the potential lack of secrecy and the possibility of higher casualties, but the plan held out the hope for a quick success through a massive show of force (Kempe 1990, 11).

On December 17, 1989, President Bush convened a meeting of his advisers to discuss U.S. options in Panama. Present were Secretary of State James A. Baker, Defense Secretary Richard Cheney, Chairman of the Joint Chiefs of Staff General Colin Powell, National Security Adviser Brent Scowcroft, Director of Central Intelligence Robert Gates, Presidential Spokesman Marlin Fitzwater, and Director of Operations for the Joint Chiefs General Thomas Kelly (Buckley 1991, 230). General Powell briefed the group on the plan for massive force that he and General Maxwell Thurman had been developing. He was questioned at length by the president and by Scowcroft. At the end of the meeting the advisers were silent. After one hour and forty minutes, Bush said, "Okay, let's do it" (Powell 1995, 425; Woodward 1991, 147; Baker 1995, 189).

Operation Just Cause (renamed from its previous "Blue Spoon" designation) began at 1:00 A.M. December 20, 1989. By the end of the operation, twenty-five U.S. soldiers had died, as had perhaps one thousand Panamanians, at a cost of about $1.5 billion in damage. Noriega eluded U.S. forces and slipped into the residence of the Papal Nuncio on Christmas eve. Noriega gave himself up to U.S. officials on January 3, 1990. He was later convicted on drug charges and is currently in a federal prison, though he does enjoy prisoner of war status.

Bush and Do-It-Yourself Collegial Formalism

The Bush management style in the Panama crisis would seem to be an interesting hybrid of collegialism and formalism, though a rather different hybrid than that which Johnson employed.[3] On the formalistic side, the case studies of decision making during the 1989 Panama crisis show a clearly defined and hierarchical model of decision-making management. These defined roles existed not only to the top, but at the top, with the president's closest advisers each participating in prescribed ways based on their expertise (Hoffman 1990). The account in Woodward (1991) shows a process led by Bush at the top, with each principal adviser playing his role. Powell and Cheney took care of the military plans and were asked to brief Bush and others within those parameters. The chain of communications between the president, Scowcroft, Cheney, Powell, and Generals Kelly and Thurman and the service chiefs was clearly prescribed and followed (Woodward 1991, 100–152, 133–34; Kempe 1990, 11–12; Powell 1995, 422–25). Scowcroft played the role of the president's adviser and protector, scrutinizing the plans in Panama from a strategic and political perspective (Woodward 1991, 144–48; Flanagan 1993, 52–53; Powell 1995, 422–25).

The Bush team members increased the intensity with which they pursued plans in Panama after the failed coup attempt in October 1989. Scranton argues that the Bush team was united on its key objective—that Noriega must go—before the failed coup, but that the coup led to a greater unity about the means to accomplish this task—the military option (1991, 146). Baker argues that the failed coup "crystallized" the Bush team's "frustrations" and calls it a "watershed" event, after which Bush ordered increased planning activity (1995, 187). Woodward notes that this missed opportunity prompted a reconsideration of the administration's objectives in Panama, and he reports that Bush declared that "amateur hour is over" and wanted more follow-through planning (Woodward 1991, 100–101).

Each part of that team did its work within recognized jurisdictions. Bush and Scowcroft met with members of the Senate Intelligence Committee about the guidelines that exist for intelligence operations (Flanagan 1993, 30). Baker reports that the Deputies' Committee was strengthened to assure greater interagency cooperation and coordination (1995, 186; Flanagan 1993, 30), since the record leading up to October had been one of very poor interagency communication (Kempe 1990, 384). Military planning in the Pentagon and at U.S. Southern Command in Panama City seems to have proceeded without interference from other agencies (Woodward 1991; Powell 1995). General Thurman, who replaced General Fred Woerner as commander in chief of U.S. Southern Command just before the coup, was very active in the development of the operational plans. While Secretary Baker came to support the invasion, during the planning he expressed concern for the legal issues involved (Kempe 1990, 379) and for the diplomatic image of the United States that an intervention would put forward (Woodward 1991, 145–46). The State Department had been very involved with diplomatic efforts to remove Noriega from Panama, including a late mission to Panama by State Department representatives Larry Eagleburger and Paul Wolfowitz, which followed a series of efforts by Michael Kozak. All these efforts were ultimately unsuccessful (Kempe 1990, 275, 323–24, 384, 395; Gilboa 1995–96).

Bush set the agenda for the group of decision makers throughout, though he left the follow-up planning to them with little reaching down for information. Bush began the December 17 meeting that led to the decision to invade Panama by presenting his objectives in Panama; this was followed by Powell's briefing on Operation Blue Spoon and the Bush decision to execute Powell's plan (Buckley 1991, 230). Bush energized the bureaucracy to prepare a military option should Noriega "overstep one day"

(Woodward 1991, 100–101) and (as I mentioned before) replaced General Woerner with General Thurman, who he thought would be more aggressive (Kempe 1990, 363).

There was little or no debate among the Bush team, although there was some infighting during the early negotiations to get Noriega to leave Panama that predated the invasion (Baker 1995, 188–89; Powell 1995, 425; Buckley 1991, 230; Dinges 1990, 313–15; Gilboa 1995–96). At the meeting on December 17, 1989, General Powell told the president that Operation Blue Spoon had the support of the Joint Chiefs, and Secretary Cheney said he supported the plan as well, as did Secretary Baker (Woodward 1991, 145–46). But Bush did not specifically ask his advisers for their opinions (Flanagan 1993, 52–53). "In the end, Bush made the decision alone, without awaiting a consensus among his advisers" (Kempe 1990, 12). This pattern shows what has been called the "do-it-yourself" quality of the Bush style (DeFrank and McDaniel 1990, 27; Hoffman 1990). Bush was a hands-on president who believed in top-down management; he set the agenda and he made the decisions (see Mullins and Wildavksy 1992, 44–45; Hoffman 1990).

There is some evidence of collegialism that is blended with Bush's do-it-yourself formalism. Meetings between Bush and his advisers flowed with rather informal procedures. This was not a chairman-of-the-board system. It was an insular group of experts who interacted like a group of colleagues. The group was small, tight, worked well together, and generally did not leak (Hoffman 1990). Hill and Williams refer to it as a "gathering of friends" (1994, 6). National Security Council meetings ranged widely over topics, including the political end of policy (Woodward 1991, 50). Powell reports that upon his entry to the administration he was surprised at the informality with which critical deliberations proceeded and the lack of follow-up that attended these meetings (1995, 418). In this sense the Bush management strategy departed from a classic formalistic system (see Rockman 1991). Mullins and Wildavsky, reflecting on the Bush presidency as a whole, argue that the Bush strategy could be called "inclusive hierarchy" (1992, 32). They assert that Bush had twin drives for secrecy and consultation (1992, 44–45; cf. Hoffman 1990), which in our terms could be seen as producing a management strategy that incorporated significant elements of both hierarchical and collegial forms. Hill and Williams agree that the Bush approach included a relaxed, informal style that sought to avoid clashes and assert Bush's leadership (1994, 6–7). The downside of this approach was that the emphasis on relaxed decision making could "degenerate into a freewheeling approach that discouraged a systematic consideration and careful scrutiny of options that glossed over differences amongst the advisers" (Hill and Williams 1994, 6).

Bush's mix of hierarchy and collegiality was distinctly different from Lyndon Johnson's. Johnson used informality to create consensus among his advisers, especially in the Tuesday lunch group. Bush's collegiality had no such goal in mind; he wished to minimize personal clashes and maximize his own control (Hill and Williams 1994, 6; Hoffman 1990). He would decide; his advisers' opinions were important but not binding.

Conclusion

The ideal models discussed by R. Johnson (1974) and George (1980) provide a theoretical starting point for the analysis presented in this chapter. The theory behind their presentations was translated into the items on question set 1 of the coding form (see appendix). These ideal models have helped focus this study on the potential forms of interaction that may exist between presidents and advisers during foreign policy crises. The evidence from these nine crises shows the shortcomings of these ideal types. While they are useful starting points, they are not ending points. With each presidency the evidence shows considerable personalization, tailoring, to make a model fit the needs of the president.

The evidence indicates that Truman used a formalistic model to organize his group of advisers and the flow of information and advice to him. Truman's model perhaps most closely approximates the ideal types in its focus on formalism, hierarchy, orderliness, and jurisdictions. The case studies show how Truman brought the ideal formalistic model to life. Eisenhower used a hybrid of two of the ideal types—the competitive and formalistic models. Eisenhower tried to complement formal hierarchical structures with competitive elements that he presumed would aid effective decision making. Johnson also used a hybrid of the formalistic model that built significant aspects of the collegial model. The Johnson model was largely formalistic to the top and collegial at the top. This model underwent important reorganization after the performance failure of Tet in 1968.

The evidence demonstrates that Nixon used a formalistic approach to crisis management. Nixon's formalism was quite different from Truman's, however. His approach placed a dyadic relationship between himself and Henry Kissinger on top of the formalistic structures for crisis decision making that already existed, especially the WSAG. One of the similarities of the Nixon and Truman approaches, however, was the ability of the decision-making machinery to work without much presidential supervision. Bush used a kind of "do-it-yourself" collegial formalism. His style was mostly formalistic, including an emphasis on expertise and jurisdictions, but his procedures lacked the structure usually associated with the formalistic style. We might understand this organizational strategy as an attempt to capitalize on Bush's emphasis on his own expertise. Bush's hybrid of the formalistic and collegial models was very different from Johnson's, however. Johnson sought to use the collegiality to build consensus around policy. Bush used it to strengthen his own position relative to his advisers and to create an atmosphere of teamwork and trust.

The next question to be addressed is what impact the structuring of advisory groups has on decision-making processes. It is interesting to identify how a president manages a decision-making group during a crisis, but it may not be that important if the link between structure and process cannot be demonstrated. The institutional perspective this project draws upon presumes that this link exists. It is another matter, however, to show how it exists. The next chapter presents evidence of the decision-making processes that took place during the nine crises studied here.

CHAPTER 4

Decision-Making Processes during Foreign Policy Crises

This chapter begins to examine the effects of the structural and organizational management seen in the previous chapter on the processes of crisis decision making. I explore how crisis advisory groups assembled in the nine crises studied here performed the generic tasks of crisis decision making. This evidence is summarized in table 4, having been gathered through an examination of the case studies with question set 2 of the coding form (see appendix), though some items from question set 1 focus on the decision-making process as well. I discuss some issues surrounding the reliability of these codings after presenting the empirical findings.

Truman Administration

Berlin Airlift, 1948

The group President Truman constructed and maintained during the crisis over Berlin showed a mixed performance on the tasks of decision making, paying much attention to some tasks but little to others. The group did a reasonably thorough job of exploring a range of U.S. objectives in Berlin during the crisis, or they performed Task 1 "well."[1] Shlaim shows a rather full record of reviewing U.S. goals in the crisis and argues that "throughout April the question of whether America should maintain its position in Berlin was under constant discussion," though there was no consensus on this question among Truman's advisers (1983, 135–38). The cutting of all land communications between the West and Berlin on June 24 led to the height of the crisis and led to more discussions of U.S. goals in the crisis. The advisers grappled with the military logic that dictated withdrawal and the political logic that precluded withdrawal from Berlin (Shlaim 1983, 195). The three "imperatives" of staying in Berlin, avoiding war, and implementing currency reform in West Germany and West Berlin were difficult to square (Shlaim 1983, 196). As the crisis unfolded, a "major reassessment of America's position" was taking place in a variety of departments and levels of the Truman administration (Shlaim 1983, 242), even though Truman had declared that the United States would stay in Berlin (Davison 1958, 157). Between July 17 and 19, these discussions ultimately would lead, through ad hoc meetings, to a consensus that the United States should stay in Berlin (Shlaim 1983, 250).

The Truman group performed Task 2, the search for alternatives, in a "neutral" manner in the Berlin crisis. The group's performance here was mixed, ranging from inattention to the task before the full crisis began to more thorough attention when the full crisis was upon it. Shlaim reports that "the examination of alternative courses of action was conducted at the same time as the search for information and was an equally disjointed and almost random process" at the beginning of April 1948 (1983, 124). Indeed, Shlaim argues that during this period there was no systematic search for alternatives but a tendency to wait for Clay to develop suggestions, which would be examined as they came up (128–29). For example, Clay asked for retaliatory measures that could be taken in Germany against the blockade, so the Departments of Commerce, State, and Army reviewed those options. When Clay asked to send an armed convoy, General Bradley vetoed the idea (130–31). Shlaim concludes that the precrisis

TABLE 4. Performance of Decision-Making Tasks by Crisis

	Task Number					
Crisis Case	1	2	3	4	5	6
Berlin, 1948	W	N	W	N	P	P
Korea, 1950	N	P	W	N	P	P
Dien Bien Phu, 1954	W	VW	W	W	VW	VW
Suez, 1956	W	W	N	N	W	P
Tonkin Gulf, 1964	P	P	N	P	P	W
Tet 1, 1968	P	P	N	P	P	P
Tet 2, 1968	VW	W	W	VW	W	N
Jordan's Civil War, 1970	W	P	N	N	W	W
October War, 1973	W	W	VW	P	W	W
Panama, 1989	N	P	W	N	W	W

VW = task was performed "very well"
W = task was performed "well"
N = task was performed "neutral"
P = task was performed "poorly"
VP = task was performed "very poorly"
Task 1 = survey objectives
Task 2 = canvass alternatives
Task 3 = search for information
Task 4 = assimilate and process new information
Task 5 = evaluate costs, risks, and implications of preferred choice
Task 6 = develop monitoring, implementation, and contingency plans

decision process was noteworthy for its lack of a search for alternatives (167). The crisis period, however, was marked by a more thorough, if sometimes uncoordinated, search for alternatives, including revisiting the idea of an armed convoy and a host of diplomatic options (278). The option of negotiating on the terms established by the Soviets was implicitly rejected at the outset of the crisis (196). Shlaim concludes that stress impaired the evaluation of alternatives at times (209), making the performance of this task not particularly noteworthy for its strengths or weaknesses during the crisis.

The group performed a reasonably thorough search for information, and thus generally performed Task 3 "well." Shlaim reports that the stress of the crisis increased the felt need for information and that multiple channels were used to acquire information, including using the new CIA, the State Department, and frequent teleconferences with General Clay (1983, 164–65). Clay's office was the principal source of information for Truman and his advisers (272). Truman and his advisers frequently pressed for details about the situation in Berlin and the suggestions Clay would make (232).

The group processed new information, Task 4, in a "neutral" manner through the crisis. On the upside, Secretary Marshall set up the "Berlin Group" headed by Charles Bohlen to process incoming information and keep the situation under constant review (Shlaim 1983, 246). On the downside, the group did misinterpret Soviet signals in the crisis and was caught by surprise when it probably should not have been (Davison, 1958, 194, 77). This mixed performance leads me to code this task as having been performed in a "neutral" manner.

The group paid little attention to the evaluation of costs, risks, and implications of the airlift (Task 5) or to the development of contingency plans in the crisis (Task 6), performing both of these tasks "poorly." Concerning the evaluation of risks and consequences, Task 5, Secretary Royall wondered if Truman had adequately thought through the consequences of U.S. actions and of maintaining the U.S. position in Berlin (McCullough 1992, 630). Shlaim reports that Truman was concerned about the risks of war and was thus cautious about the use of force in the crisis (1983, 179–80). In particular, the group was cautious about the use of an armed convoy (Davison 1958, 126; Shlaim 1983, 260–66) and about the use of B-29s to supply Berlin, making sure no atomic weapons were present (Shlaim 1983, 237–39). The idea of turning over the control of atomic weapons to the National Military Establishment was also rejected as unnecessary and dangerous (Shlaim 1983, 254–60). Still, this concern about risks was largely applied only to General Clay's plan for a convoy and not applied to the overall question of the U.S. commitment to Berlin or the risks of the airlift. The group paid little or no attention to the risks of losing planes and thus losing control of the crisis because of accident, like the British plane that was struck by a Soviet fighter plane on April 5, 1948 (Shlaim 1983, 135). Contingency planning, Task 6, was performed in a reactive and ad hoc manner through the crisis and was made more difficult by the need to consult allies (Shlaim 1983, 139). The group had been caught off guard and responded in an incremental way through the crisis, largely responding to the proposals of General Clay.

The decision-making process in this crisis was more intuitive than analytic (Shlaim 1983, 278). As table 4 shows, the Truman group showed mixed performance on the tasks of decision making in this case. They performed "well" on the survey of U.S. objectives (Task 1) in Berlin and in the search for information (Task 3) during the crisis. The group "poorly" performed an examination of the costs, risks, and implications of the decision to proceed with an airlift (Task 5), and its contingency planning (Task 6) was incremental at best. The group performed an adequate survey of alternative responses in the crisis (Task 2) and processed new information (Task 4) in a fairly "neutral" manner as well.

Korean Intervention, 1950

Truman and his advisers did explore a range of U.S. objectives in the crisis in Korea, but not a particularly broad range. The group performed Task 1 in a "neutral" manner. Truman and his advisers quickly defined the stakes for the United States in Korea in symbolic, cold war terms—a test of containment (Bernstein 1989, 414; Bernstein 1977b, 33; Donovan 1982; Gosnell 1980). The overriding objective for the United States, according to Truman and others, was not to appease aggression they saw as similar to that by Japan and Germany before World War II (Paige 1968, 115, 143). The group generally did not, however, revisit the previous decision that Korea was not geopolitically vital to the United States (Paige 1968, 67; Donovan 1982, 200; Gosnell 1980, 463).

The Truman group performed the task of surveying alternative policy responses (Task 2) rather "poorly" in the crisis. In particular, the Truman team did not consider not intervening (Paige 1968, 174; Donovan 1982, 200). It would seem that even before the first Blair House conference, Truman had decided to fight (Paige 1968, 124; Donovan 1982, 203). The group did not address the issues surrounding the U.S. commitment to South Korea, the conditions for expanding that commitment, or the role of ground troops in that equation (Bernstein 1977a, 33–34; 1977b, 8). Because of the lack of exploration of alternatives, Truman was ultimately faced with a decision to either grant MacArthur's request for ground troops or abandon South Korea (Bernstein 1977b, 9). The group focused on single sets of proposals with few conflicting alternatives (Paige 1968, 320).

Truman and his advisers did perform "well" the task of searching for information (Task 3) in the crisis. The group in Washington sought out information from U.S. Ambassador to the Republic of Korea John Muccio and from General MacArthur's headquarters in Tokyo (Bernstein 1977a, 6), as well as from Ambassador John Foster Dulles, who had been in Japan and Korea (Donovan 1982, 194). Truman was bombarded with information and criticism from Congress and the press, though that seemed to have little effect on him (Donovan 1982, 205; Paige 1968, 149–55). At least two surveys of the situation were ordered in course. General MacArthur had General John H. Church head a survey group in Korea to assess the situation and report back to him, and MacArthur would personally go to Korea June 28 (Paige 1968, 224–30; Donovan 1982, 210). Also on June 28, Truman ordered all departments to restudy the situation (Paige 1968, 224). Truman and his advisers cast a significant information net during the crisis.

The group processed the information (Task 4) they received in a "neutral" manner during the crisis. George concludes that the group performed a general analysis of the situation that may have led them to oversimplify the emerging crisis (1956, 216). In this sense they did not always process new information as well as they might have. Paige concludes that the group miscalculated the strength of ROK forces and the efficacy of air power (1968, 343). Bernstein reports some failure to assimilate new information in terms of the group's failure to foresee that ROK forces would fail to hold the line against the invasion (1977a, 9). While the performance on this task was not sterling, it was not particularly deficient either (Bernstein 1977b, 8).

What was deficient was the Truman group's handling of an examination of the costs, risks, and implications of its plans (Task 5) and its development of contingency plans. The group performed each of these tasks "poorly" in the crisis. Donovan notes that "the risks and costs of intervention were taken in stride" by the Truman advisory group, rather than being critically explored (1982, 206). Furthermore, the Joint Chiefs had opposed the use of U.S. ground forces, but their objections were never fully explored—or fully expressed, for that matter (Donovan 1982, 211–15; Bernstein 1977a, 33–34; 1977b, 8, 33; 1989, 426). Gosnell also reports that there was no serious discussion of the consequences of intervention (1980, 463; George 1956, 224). The risks associated with MacArthur's assessment that U.S. ground troops were necessary were never fully explored (Bernstein 1977b, 9).

Contingency and implementation plans were also not well developed. George notes that implementation plans tended to cut against each other, as with the interest in not provoking China through the U.S. response in Korea and yet moving the Seventh Fleet to Formosa in a move that might be seen as provocative (1956, 226–30). Truman and his advisers had some implementation problems because MacArthur was moving faster than Truman; MacArthur had to be constrained (Bernstein 1977b, 9; Paige 1968, 161). The implementation plans for the use of air power or ground troops were not particularly well developed or thought out (Paige 1968, 343). On these crucial occasions, Truman and his advisers failed to develop solid contingency plans.

As in the Berlin crisis, Truman and his advisers show a mixed performance on the tasks of decision making in the Korean crisis. The group searched for information fairly thoroughly (Task 3) and did an adequate job of processing new information (Task 4) and of exploring U.S. objectives in the crisis (Task 1). The search for alternatives (Task 2) in the crisis was performed "poorly," however, as was the examination of costs, risks, and implications of those alternatives (Task 5). Contingency and implementation planning (Task 6) was also flawed in this case. It is perhaps interesting to note that in both of these crises, the group of advisers surrounding President Truman "poorly" performed an examination of the costs and risks of their preferred policy, and it "poorly" developed plans to implement those policies.

Eisenhower Administration

Dien Bien Phu, 1954

The decision-making group that President Eisenhower assembled to deal with the crisis at Dien Bien Phu performed its mission of providing information, advice, and analysis effectively. The group surveyed the objectives and goals of the United States in the crisis (Task 1) in a broad and thorough manner. The group agreed that the main objective for the United States was a noncommunist Southeast Asia, but other objectives were considered and reconsidered throughout the crisis (Immerman 1989, 121–44). The group explored American goals concerning the French (Gelb and Betts 1979, 50–63), and it continuously sought to square "area objectives" with Eisenhower's New Look defense posture (George and Smoke 1974, 246–48). The group explored the competing objectives of anticommunism and anti-imperialism in the region, and it examined whether the United States should fill the vacuum left by the French in Indochina (Gerson 1967, 152–55). Perhaps the only objective the group did not explore was the possibility that Southeast Asia was not important to American or Western interests. I have coded that the Eisenhower advisory group performed Task 1 "well."

The advisory group scored particularly high marks for its performance of Task 2, the examination of alternative policy responses that fit with specific objectives. The Eisenhower apparatus repeatedly reviewed alternative responses that ranged from nonintervention to multilateral, full-scale military intervention (Burke and Greenstein 1989, 28–115). The group explored and reconsidered a wide range of policy options (Kalicki 1975, 104–16). Furthermore, Eisenhower established subgroups to explore the information and construct options that were perhaps missed by the larger group. As the previous chapter discussed, the Smith and Erskine working groups that were established in April 1954 are prime examples of Eisenhower's attention to the decision-making process and its relation to structure. These groups explored policy options that ranged from united action to inaction. As part of this exploration, Eisenhower himself (as well as Senator Stennis) voiced a concern that the introduction of American ground forces could lead to a quagmire for the United States (Burke and Greenstein 1989, 38–39, 106–7). I have coded that the Eisenhower decision-making group performed the task of canvassing policy alternatives "very well" because of its continuous attention to the examination and production of a wide range of alternative policy options.

The Eisenhower group displayed much vigilance in performing Task 3, the search for information, during this crisis as well. Burke and Greenstein suggest that the White House paid especially close attention to ties with the French so as to stay as current as possible on the state of the crisis (1989, 28–115). The decision-making apparatus searched for information from multiple French channels as well as American sources in Indochina. The Eisenhower group sought new lines of communication when it felt too constrained by French intelligence (Gurtov 1967). Admiral Radford was in especially close contact with French military planners. The case studies also indicate a high degree of attention to other channels of communication and sources of information. Members of Congress and people not in the government, such as Milton Eisenhower, were called upon by President Eisenhower (Burke and Greenstein 1989, 28–115).

The group also responded in a sensitive manner to new and discrepant information (Task 4). It certainly remained open to information that was not ideal for American interests or planning. For example, Eisenhower and Congress had several conditions that had to be met for American military intervention to take place. These included a continuing French presence in the region, a plan for independence, and a multilateral intervention force. When Eisenhower realized in April that these conditions would not be met, he accepted this feedback and went "back to the drawing board" (Gerson 1967, 157). The Eisenhower group also responded well to feedback about domestic constraints on its options that came from Congress and from others outside the administration (Parmet 1972, 353–81; Foyle 1996). In short, the president and his advisers processed new information in an unbiased manner. When they received new information that was not ideal, it was nevertheless assimilated and responded to in an appropriate manner.

The evidence indicates that the Eisenhower apparatus was most vigilant in its evaluation of the costs, risks, and implications of its preferred options (Task 5). Burke and Greenstein note that the group was particularly thorough in its evaluation of the costs and risks of American intervention (both unilateral and multilateral) vis-à-vis China, Western allies, the budget, and American prestige (1989, 28–115). Eisenhower and others were openly concerned that a quagmire would develop around American forces should they be introduced to the region. Eisenhower voiced on several occasions the concern that the jungles would swallow American ground forces "by the division." Gelb and Betts also record high marks for the Eisenhower advisory system on this task (1979, 50–68). Comparisons to Korea, worries about China, concerns about the effects of intervention on the budget, and others dangers were voiced continuously (cf. Foyle 1996).

The decision-making task of developing monitoring, implementation, and contingency plans (Task 6) was performed "very well" in this crisis. Burke and Greenstein state that the process included a high level of attention to these issues as contingency planning was "assigned out" to insulated subgroups (1989, 35–42). The National Security Council instructed in January 1954 that the director of Central Intelligence develop a range of contingencies for the United States. This plan came to be identified as NSC 5404 (George and Smoke 1974, 252). Close monitoring of the French position was established and maintained throughout the crisis. The Erskine group was also responsible for developing contingency plans. Plans were developed for unilateral as well as multilateral contingencies (Burke and Greenstein 1989, 28–115; Kalicki 1975, 104–16).

In summary, "the Eisenhower process brought professionally staffed area and contingency plans and a range of policy options before top decision-makers" (Burke and Greenstein 1989, 259). All vital tasks of decision making were performed effectively by the group that was assembled by the president for information, advice, and analysis. Three of the tasks were performed "very well," in fact. The only failing of this otherwise very effective process may have been that the basic, underlying assumption that the fate of Southeast Asia was critical for America's global interests was never fully scrutinized. Randle (1969) and Gerson (1967, 152–74) note that

John Foster Dulles was dubious about whether Dien Bien Phu was important enough to require American intervention. Other case-study authors note the concern held by many (including Dulles and Eisenhower) that American intervention might not be enough to save the eroding French position. Nevertheless, the process kept the United States out of war but left the United States in Vietnam.

Suez, 1956

The evidence of the crisis decision-making process during the Suez crisis is not as complete as the evidence of the Dien Bien Phu crisis. There is no detailed decision analysis of this crisis that is analogous to Burke's and Greenstein's (1989), or Immerman's (1989) treatment of Dien Bien Phu decision making. It is possible to arrive at satisfactory codings of the decision-making process in this crisis, though they are less well supported by case studies and therefore perhaps more tentative and subject to future revelations. I have attempted to work with what is available in the form of case studies of this episode and to make inferences from that available record, rather than to reject the case or perform a decision analysis myself at the Eisenhower Archives. Further analysis of this crisis by new studies, already begun perhaps by the new book by Kingseed (1995), could prove useful, however.

The group assembled by President Eisenhower during the Suez Canal crisis performed "well" the task of surveying American objectives in the crisis, Task 1. Neustadt notes that the group realized that the canal was neither strategically nor symbolically crucial to the United States (1970, 11–16). President Eisenhower was running for reelection on peace and prosperity, which would be an overriding objective for the United States in the crisis (Kunz 1991, 82–83). The group further realized that the United States should not be seen as providing for the continuation of the British Empire. Other objectives were discussed as well, including the wish to avoid a confrontation with the Soviets over Suez but the interest in not allowing them to capitalize upon the crisis either (Kunz 1991, 93). Strengthening the United Nations and promoting anti-imperialism were other objectives discussed by the group (Bowie 1974, 29–35, 99–100; Kingseed 1995, 49, 61, 80–81).

The group also performed "well" the task of canvassing alternative policy responses, Task 2. The group explored a wide range of potential responses to Nasser's nationalization of the canal and to the attack on the canal by Britain, France, and Israel (Kingseed 1995, 107, 149; Bowie 1974, 35–47, 61–77; Parmet 1972, 470–87). An examination of a wide range of alternative responses took place at both stages of the crisis. This discussion especially focused on whether the United States should intervene militarily and also on the overriding goal of how to keep (and later restore) the peace. Bowie (1974, 61–77) and Neustadt (1970, 11–29) note that plans for American intervention were rejected largely because they did not fit the objectives that were discussed and agreed upon by the group (cf. Kunz 1991, 82, 93).

The group performed a "neutral" search for information and assimilation of new information, Tasks 3 and 4. I am tempted to not code these tasks. Information about them is slight, but it is possible to infer from the record that the little reference to them as procedural tasks actually includes useful information, rather than signifying a lack of it. The record demonstrates that Eisenhower and his advisers had open channels of communication to all parties throughout the crisis. They were not particularly concerned about the quality of information they were receiving, however, which stands in stark contrast to Eisenhower's handling of the Dien Bien Phu crisis. Eisenhower was content with the information available in this crisis. He and his advisers remained open and responsive to information throughout the crisis, although they did fail to recognize British, French, and Israeli intentions toward the canal (they mistook Israeli mobilization as being directed against Jordan). They did not systematically ignore information, though, nor did they process and assimilate new information in a biased way.

There was not a particularly thorough search for information, but not a particularly restricted one either. I would argue that Tasks 3 and 4 were performed adequately, or neutrally; they were performed neither particularly "well" nor particularly "poorly." The group's review of objectives (Task 1) and the alternatives that fit with those objectives (Task 2) dictated a course that remained uninterrupted by events in the crisis. They sought a peaceful resolution to the crisis.

The group performed "well" the task of evaluating the costs, risks, and implications of the preferred alternative, Task 5. The evidence indicates that several evaluations of the risks of intervening or not intervening were performed. The Eisenhower group examined the danger to the Western Alliance of not intervening and the costs of nonintervention to the Anglo-American relationship. Eisenhower's advisers explored the risk that general war could begin if the United States intervened while the Soviet Union was involved in a military action in Hungary simultaneously. Implications for Eisenhower's presidential campaign were also explored, as were the potential costs to the United States in terms of a negative domestic and international response to the U.S. use of force (Kunz 1991, 82–93; Kingseed 1995).

The decision-making group did a "poor" job of developing monitoring, implementation, and contingency plans during the crisis, Task 6. The group did not carefully monitor Nasser's moves that led to the takeover of the canal, nor did it carefully monitor British, French, and Israeli actions that preceded their attack on the canal. Alternatives were agreed upon, such as the Suez Canal Users Association, but there is no record that any real implementation plans were constructed. There is no record that contingency plans were officially ordered, though Kingseed reports that the Joint Chiefs of Staff performed some contingency planning (1995, 50). The group failed to perform these jobs, in glaring contrast to the way it performed them in the 1954 crisis. The decision-making process in the Suez crisis proceeded with only one major flaw, the development of contingency and implementation plans (Task 6). The attention of the Eisenhower group to the other tasks was sufficient but not as vigorous as in the crisis at Dien Bien Phu.

Johnson Administration

Tonkin Gulf, 1964

The decision-making process that took place during the crisis of the first week of August 1964 is difficult to evaluate because the process was brief and compact. But it is possible to get a picture of that process and its characteristics from the case studies of the crisis, though no formal decision analyses are available beyond Moïse's (1996) extremely detailed historical account. The Johnson group "poorly" surveyed American objectives in the crisis (Task 1) and "poorly" canvassed alternative policy responses in the crisis (Task 2). All the case reports agree on this point. No real survey of American objectives took place during this crisis. The group used NSAM 288 as a guide for American interests. The group did not question its objectives in the crisis. Gelb and Betts argue that "at no time during the strategy debates was the commitment to the defense of Southeast Asia questioned (1979, 97). There was no survey of American objectives in the region after both the August 2 and alleged August 4 incidents.

Nor did the group explore alternative policy responses during this period. Goulden notes that Johnson made his decision to send the *Maddox* back into the attack area after the August 2 attack almost as a reflex (1969, 135). A consensus about the preferred American response formed quickly (Moïse 1996, 209). No survey of objectives or alternatives was presented. No real choices were presented (Gravel 1971, 3:111). The retaliatory raids that followed the August 4 incident were the only real option discussed or presented in the group. Johnson, Rusk, McNamara, and Bundy all agreed on this course.

The evidence indicates that the Johnson group did a "neutral" job of performing an information search, Task 3. There is mention of a search for information about the events of August 2 and August 4 in all the case reports, especially in Goulden (1969) and Moïse (1996). There is no mention of this search being out carried particularly "well" or "poorly" in the case studies. What is clearly discussed in the case studies is that the information acquired in the search was processed in a systematically biased manner (see Moïse 1996, 208). I therefore code that Task 4, assimilating new information, was performed "poorly." Information that did not fit into the Johnson concept of the situation was rejected, especially information about the alleged second attack. Ambiguous information about the August 4 attack was simply ignored. The Johnson group wished to find the information it needed—that is, the information it needed to confirm the second attack (Austin 1971, 300, 343). The Johnson group ignored information that did not fit into its picture of the events of August 4 (Gravel 1971, vol. 3; Windchy 1971, 212). It ignored Captain Herrick's suggestion that the August 4 attack may not have taken place and that they should therefore refrain from a military response until the events became clearer. Windchy reports that the Johnson group used a cable from Herrick that certified the "original ambush" of August 2 inappropriately as certification of the August 4 attack (1971, 212; cf. Moïse 1996, 143). Halberstam similarly argues that there was tremendous pressure to confirm the second attack (1972, 502; Moïse 1996, 144–47).

The evidence indicates that the Johnson group did a "poor" job of assessing the costs, risks, and implications of its actions, Task 5. There is no report that decision makers considered the implications of becoming directly involved in Vietnam on either August 2 or August 4. There is no evidence that the group considered that it could be heading down a slope to war. The opposite may have been the case, in fact. The only consideration reported in the case studies of the implications of American actions was that this opportunity to step up American involvement could not be missed (Gravel 1971, vol. 3). There was some concern about a Chinese or Soviet response to American armed intervention.

The case studies indicate that the Johnson group performed "well" its task of developing contingency and implementation plans in the Tonkin Gulf crisis, Task 6. The Joint Chiefs of Staff had a contingency plan for retaliation when the August 4 incident occurred that went beyond the contingency plans discussed in NSAM 288 (Goulden 1969, 135–50). The Pentagon Papers record that area contingency plans were continually adopted and modified as the situation developed (Gravel 1971, 5:320). Johnson had a retaliatory plan already prepared at the time of the August 4 incident. He needed only to pick the specific bombing targets. Moïse does report some operational problems with these contingency plans (1996, 224).

The decision process in the Tonkin Gulf crisis was riddled with deficiencies. The only task performed "well" was the development of contingency and implementation plans (Task 6), and even those had some operational problems. The search for information (Task 3) was adequate, but the information was processed in biased ways (Task 4). The group also "poorly" performed a survey of U.S. objectives in Southeast Asia (Task 1) and an examination of alternative policy responses (Task 2) to the events of the first week of August 1964.

Tet Offensive, 1968, Part 1

I have divided the discussion and analysis of decision making during the Tet Offensive into two phases. There is a distinct pattern of organization and behavior that took place before and immediately after the North's offensive. A second pattern occurred in the weeks that followed the attacks as President Johnson tried to decide how to respond to the crisis. The nature of American decision making is markedly different in these two phases. It therefore seems appropriate to distinguish between the two. The Tet Offensive was an important event in many ways. It certainly was a watershed period for the decision-making process inside and around the Johnson administration. The case study by Schandler (1977) is the most thorough analysis of Tet decision making. It should also be noted that Schandler was part of the Clifford Task Force that is discussed subsequently.

The decision-making process in the period before the initiation of the Tet Offensive scored a "poor" rating on each of the six decision-making tasks under scrutiny here. The only exception to this is Task 3 (information search), which I have assigned a "neutral" code. Schandler argues that while American policy in Vietnam was continually reviewed in the Johnson administration, no long-range evaluation of American objectives in the region took place (1977, 3). This is true during the period leading up to the Tet Offensive. At no time were American objectives in Vietnam reexamined, even as information became available that an attack was imminent by the North around Tet. Routine policy-making came to be replaced with an atmosphere of crisis as Tet approached. Nevertheless, at no time were a range of policy responses to the approaching crisis explored (Task 2). American policy responses were motivated "as much because of a lack of other options as the strength of the favoring proposals" (Schandler 1977, 10).

Schandler argues that the search for information about the North's plan of attack was satisfactory, though it was not particularly exhaustive. I have therefore coded that the group performed Task 3 in a "neutral" manner. The group systematically failed to assimilate the information it received in this search, however. It also failed to respond to discrepant information. The Johnson group's performance of Task 4 has thus been coded as "poor." American decision makers seemed unwilling to accept reliable signals that the North's attack would happen on Tet, rather than just after Tet. This did not fit their conceptions of the situation (Schandler 1977, 71–72). They ignored information that indicated the North would not attack at the place the Americans anticipated, Khe Sanh, but rather throughout the South. The time and targets of the North's offensive could have been recognized by American decision makers. Johnson's advisers failed to assimilate the information that indicated these targets and timetables (Hoopes 1969, 81).

Schandler's case study indicates that the Johnson group performed Tasks 5 and 6 "poorly." The group failed to consider the costs and implications of American involvement in Vietnam and the costs of continuing that involvement. There was no attention to these issues whatsoever within Johnson's decision-making circle as Tet approached. Contingency plans and plans for the implementation of American strategy were not developed as Tet neared. In short, there was no search within the consensus that surrounded Johnson for disagreements about the course of American strategy. There was little forward looking or planning, little evaluation of America's situation in Southeast Asia. Schandler argues that the decision-making process had systematically broken down as Tet approached. There was no coherent strategy, no coherent strategy making, no coherent decision making during this period.

> Fundamental assumptions concerning objectives were never questioned. The decision-making process was never engaged to determine ultimate costs and to draw up a balance sheet as to when those costs would become excessive. Alternatives were not examined, and decisions concerning the allocation of American resources to Vietnam were made on the basis of what was the minimum additional that could be done while maintaining public support at home. (Schandler 1977, 337)

Tet Offensive, 1968, Part 2

The decision-making structure and process used by Johnson and his advisers after Tet stands in stark contrast to that which preceded the North's offensive. General Wheeler requested a significant increase in the number of American troops in Vietnam at a February 27, 1968, meeting at the White House about how the United States should respond to the Tet Offensive. Following Wheeler's request, Robert McNamara argued that Johnson must examine other alternatives. Walt Rostow and others agreed with McNamara (Schandler 1977, 117). Decision making about Vietnam would be vigorously examined for perhaps the first time since 1963. The president directed Clark Clifford to establish a task force to review American policy and the Wheeler troop request (Schandler 1977, 120). The Clifford Task Force was born, and with it a new decision-making process.

The decision-making group around Johnson performed the task of surveying American objectives in Vietnam, Task 1, "very well" in the weeks that followed Tet. Members of the Department of Defense began questioning long-assumed objectives. The Clifford group probed deeply into the nature of American objectives in the region (Schandler 1977, 121–76). Clifford reports that he tried to use his "relative ignorance" to ask hard questions about U.S. objectives (Clifford 1991, 493). A consistent pattern emerged, in which American objectives in Vietnam were thoughtfully evaluated.

The group performed the task of canvassing alternative policy responses, Task 2, "well." The Clifford group performed a thorough examination of American options in the wake of Tet—both short-term and long-term options. They paid close attention to whether these options matched stated objectives. The task force provided a full assessment of the situation (Schandler 1977, 121–76; Berman 1989, 160–61).[2]

The Clifford group performed Task 3 "well." It thoroughly searched for information and examined all channels of communication and sources of information. The group performed the task of assimilating new information, Task 4, "very well." Group members were sensitive to new and discrepant information, they were open to feedback from a variety of sources, and they even sought out discrepant information. They did so on multiple occasions.

They performed "well" on the procedural task of examining costs, risks, and implications of U.S. options, Task 5. The group paid special attention to examining the costs of future operations in Vietnam on the United States, not just in budgetary terms, but also in political and moral terms (Schandler 1977, 121–76). I have assigned a "neutral" code to the group's performance of Task 6.

The Clifford group paid relatively little attention to the development of contingency or implementation plans, notwithstanding its exhaustive evaluation and examination of the situation in Vietnam for the United States, which was not the group's charge. Unfortunately, no other source developed these plans either. I have assigned a "neutral" code here, rather than a "poor" code, because it does not seem to me that the group ignored or omitted this task; rather, it was just not an appropriate task at this time. A single omission of this task, even, requires a "neutral" code.

A second review of the situation occurred when the Wise Men examined the U.S. role in Vietnam at Clifford's request (Schandler 1977, 255). They, like the Clifford group, asked tough questions and scrutinized information. The combination of Clifford's reviews and the evaluation by the Wise Men led to codes for the procedural tasks discussed earlier. I agree with Schandler's conclusion that the Johnson decision-making process functioned properly for perhaps the first time after Tet. Objectives were matched with resources, strategy was balanced with costs and benefits, and a full policy debate began (Schandler 1977, 338). The Johnson advisory group began to more vigilantly perform the tasks of decision-making in the period that followed the Tet Offensive.

Nixon Administration

Jordan's Civil War, 1970

The decision-making group formed to deal with the civil war in Jordan was assembled by President Nixon and largely administered by Henry Kissinger (cf. Haney 1994b). It performed the task of surveying American objectives to be fulfilled in the crisis, Task 1, "well." U.S. objectives in the crisis were examined by the Washington Special Actions Group, and they changed after the Syrian intervention. The objectives were narrowed from a large set of goals that had included securing the release of hostages, retaining King Hussein, and deterring Syrian, Soviet, and Israeli intervention. A more restricted objective replaced this list, that of acquiring Soviet support for a Syrian withdrawal and developing of a credible military option (Quandt 1978, 266–68). There is no record of an examination of American goals in the crisis being reviewed beyond this recounting. They were, rather, taken largely for granted. However, this evidence indicates two recognitions of this task by the Nixon group.

The group "poorly" performed Task 2, canvassing alternatives, though there is some disagreement on this point. Evans and Novak report that the group paid attention to options in the sense that it tried to keep open as many options as possible throughout the crisis period (1971, 250–65). Kissinger stresses that as well (1979, chap. 15). Quandt's case study (1978) is ambiguous on this count. Dowty (1978; 1984) makes several points about deficiencies in the canvassing of alternatives by the group. Dowty's general stance is that the option search was colored by the group's misperception of Soviet intentions in the crisis (1978; cf. Garthoff 1994, 321, 740–41). This led, Dowty argues, to a systematic bias in the way the group processed alternative responses (1978, 176–79). He argues that the group did not explore the alternative of going public in the crisis, nor did it explore any options that included dealing directly with the Soviet Union or Syria or going through the United Nations (1978, 182, 195). Dowty argues that the search for political and diplomatic opportunities was diminished by exclusive focus on military alternatives (1978, 186; cf. Dowty 1984, 182–95). No alternatives were developed that would support the Israeli operation that was worked out by Kissinger and Prime Minister Rabin. I find persuasive Dowty's analysis that the search for options in the crisis was limited, biased, and truncated.

I have given "neutral" codings to the group's search for information and its assimilation of that information, Tasks 3 and 4. Quandt and Dowty agree that the search for information in the crisis was adequate but not exhaustive. It focused largely on Israeli and Jordanian intelligence reports (Dowty 1984, 111–80). The group seemed to respond sensitively to changes in the environment and to new information, Task 4. Dowty notes no insensitivity to negative feedback (1984, 182–86).

Task 5, examining costs, risks, and implications, was performed "well" by the Nixon decision-making group. Evans and Novak assert that the group was sensitive to the costs of American action or inaction (1971, 263–65). Dowty reports that Nixon, Kissinger, and other top decision makers paid great attention to the costs and implications of American action. Their attention to costs and implications centered not only on military levels but also on public relations and political levels (1984, 152–56).

The group also performed "well" the task of developing contingency plans, Task 6. Quandt argues that American forces in the region were moved early in the crisis to support a range of American military options (1978, 268). Kissinger echoes this assessment (1979, 610). Quandt, who was present at WSAG meetings, also reports that Nixon directed Kissinger to work out contingency plans with Israeli Prime Minister Rabin (Quandt 1977, 117). These plans were developed and changed as the situation developed in Jordan and Syria. Dowty also argues that much contingency planning took place during the crisis, noting that this planning largely focused on military planning and Israeli operations that could be supported by the United States (1984, 143).

Quandt argues that the Nixon group overlooked the regional implications of the situation by its predominant focus on the superpower implications of the crisis (cf. Garthoff 1994). He argues that the "success" of the United States in this crisis directly contributed to the 1973 war because this crisis failed to resolve important regional problems. These regional problems were instead glazed over by the fortuitous superpower outcome (Quandt 1977, 123–27; cf. Quandt 1978, 285–88). In this sense, the Nixon group may not have performed its tasks of providing information, advice, and analysis "well." In an empirical sense, the group's performance was mixed, though mostly effective. Nixon and Kissinger had to simultaneously deal a number of issues. These included stalled SALT talks, the American invasion of Cambodia, and the revelation of a Soviet nuclear submarine base at Cienfuegos, Cuba. These issues could understandably lead American decision makers to read this crisis as a superpower crisis, as its context was dominated by superpower concerns. Nevertheless, the Nixon group did pay attention to the costs, risks, and implications of action—especially vis-à-vis the Soviet Union. They also developed contingency plans with Israel to help assure a favorable outcome of the crisis for Western interests.

October War, 1973

The evidence from the case studies indicates that the Nixon group performed Task 1, surveying objectives, "well." Quandt concludes that the Nixon-Kissinger group effectively surveyed American objectives during the crisis (1977, 165–204). Stephen Ambrose documents the range of objectives that were discussed and settled upon by the group. These objectives included keeping the Soviets out of the crisis and region, maintaining détente, deterring others (beyond the Soviets) from becoming involved in the crisis, avoiding a superpower confrontation, and using this crisis as an opportunity to begin a comprehensive peace process (Ambrose 1991, 230).

The group also performed Task 2, canvassing policy alternatives, "well." Dowty (1984, 199–319) and Quandt (1977, 165–204) argue that the Nixon-Kissinger group performed well on its task of canvassing alternative policy responses during a very fluid crisis. Dowty argues that the consideration of these alternatives was driven by practical concerns and thus revealed tactical rationality on the part of the Nixon advisory group (1984, 303–19). It tried to identify practical, doable options to fill its needs and objectives.

The evidence indicates that the group performed a very thorough information search (Task 3). On several occasions the group demanded more information and searched alternative channels of communication (Quandt 1977, 165–204). Dowty similarly notes high demands for information throughout the crisis. He argues that the group was particularly interested in battlefield information and in obtaining information from local sources (1984, 303–19). He asserts that the group made efforts to open new lines of communication throughout the crisis. These multiple and consistent demands for information lead me to infer that the group performed this task "very well."

What the Nixon-Kissinger group *did* with this information is another matter. Indeed, the Nixon advisory group performed the task of assimilating new information, Task 4, "poorly." There is some disagreement on this point in the case studies, however. Dowty concludes that the group was sensitive to the information it received from the battlefield (1984, 303–319).[3] I am, however, persuaded to the contrary by the record in Quandt 1977, which is corroborated by Ambrose 1991 and Lebow and Stein 1994. Quandt argues that the group was consistently slow to integrate new information into its dominant outlook on the crisis. He asserts that the Nixon group systematically biased new information with its old lenses and perceptions (1977, 168–70). Quandt argues that the group had particular difficulty processing information about Arab intentions and capabilities and about the course of the war. Lebow and Stein agree with this assessment (1994, 176, 196; Garthoff 1994, 407–12). For example, Quandt reports that the group had great difficulty making sense of Egypt's unwillingness to accept an early cease-fire. Nixon and his advisers had evaluated that Egypt would lose the war and should therefore rationally accept the cease-fire. They would not adapt their mind-sets to see that Egypt was currently winning the war and could expect to continue to do so for some time (Quandt 1977, 165–206). Dowty notes that the Nixon group was very slow to adapt to new and discrepant information (1984, 303–319). The study by Ambrose corroborates this assessment (1991, 229–59). I side with Quandt's evaluation that the group performed this task "poorly" over the course of the crisis, notwithstanding the fact that the group did eventually adapt to new information.

The group performed "well" on the tasks of evaluating costs, risks, and implications of its choices (Task 5) and of developing monitoring, implementation, and contingency plans (Task 6). Ambrose (1991, 229–59), Dowty (1984, 303–19), and Quandt (1977, 165–206) record that the Nixon process was cognizant of these tasks. The Nixon-Kissinger group was particularly concerned with the risks of American action for its relationship with the Soviet Union. The group dealt with this superpower component on multiple occasions. These occasions included the resupply of Israel, the call for a mutual Soviet-American force to assure the cease-fire, and the nuclear alert. Nixon, Kissinger, and their advisers also had to deal with the costs and risks of their actions for the American relationship with Israel.

American concern largely focused on the superpower relationship in this crisis, as it had in the 1970 crisis. There were several calls for the development of contingency and implementation plans by American decision makers. Quandt argues that these plans were initially drawn up at

Kissinger's request in his capacity as the chair of the Washington Special Actions Group (cf. Lebow and Stein 1994, 176; Garthoff 1994, 408). Nixon ordered more contingency plans to be prepared in the event of a Soviet intervention (Quandt 1977, 170–91). The group monitored the battlefield situation and Soviet troop movements.

In short, the decision-making process in this crisis was generally effective. The decision-making group did, however, have to contend with conceptual "baggage" that clouded its ability to assimilate new and discrepant information. It is also interesting to note that this process worked largely *without* the president. Nixon was nearly overwhelmed by other matters in his administration, and he delegated broad authority to Kissinger. The decision-making apparatus worked fairly well in this crisis, even in Nixon's absence. Yet, Nixon retained final authority throughout the crisis (except when he delegated it to Kissinger in Moscow to work out a cease-fire arrangement). The established structures carried out their decision-making tasks fairly well, with Kissinger "filling in" when presidential leadership was required.[4] I shall return to this issue in chapter 5.

Bush Administration

Panama, 1989

It is difficult to evaluate the performance of the Bush group on the tasks of decision making during the 1989 Panama crisis. The case studies of the crisis tend to provide more of a chronology than a decision analysis. Nevertheless, the reports by Woodward (1991), Powell (1995), and Kempe (1990), in particular, provide some reasonable basis to make an evaluation of decision making.

Based upon the evidence presented in the case studies, I have coded that the Bush group performed the task of surveying objectives, Task 1, in a "neutral" manner in the crisis. There was some attention to this issue, but it was rather limited. Bush presented his objectives in Panama at the December 17 meeting: to get Noriega, to install President Guillermo Endara and his vice presidents Arias Calderon and Willy Ford, and to assure the safety of Americans (Buckley 1991, 230). This presentation did not, however, breed any deeper discussion or critical analysis. Woodward reports that after the failed October coup the Bush administration reevaluated its objectives in Panama (1991, 100; Hoffman 1990). The Bush group took part in some review of U.S. objectives in the crisis but not in a manner that was particularly notable for its vigor or deficiencies.

The group performed the task of surveying alternatives, Task 2, rather "poorly" in the crisis. The examination of alternative policy responses was very limited, to discussion of Operation Blue Spoon. Dinges reports that "the decision to force Noriega from power was not the result of any considered policy drafted by expert measuring of the costs, benefits, and alternatives," but, rather, it was improvised as they went along, based on the under-revision Operation Blue Spoon (1990, 313). Dinges reports no real survey of alternative responses, including the lack of attention to a possible Panamanian solution and the possible skewing of policy selection to overcome President Bush's "wimp" factor (1990, 313–15). Scranton reports that the military option was not critically examined for its policy fit (1991, 39). Kempe is fairly critical of the Bush group for selecting the military options without great scrutiny (1990, 11–12), and Woodward's (1991) account also shows a process largely devoid of critical review of U.S. alternatives in the crisis, though Operation Blue Spoon itself received a fair level of scrutiny by Cheney, Powell, and other military leaders throughout the crisis by Bush's team at the December 17 meeting.

The Bush group performed "well" the task of searching for information, Task 3, during the crisis. A net of intelligence gathering was cast widely in Panama City as military planners tried to develop the Blue Spoon operation (Woodward 1991; Kempe 1990; Flanagan 1993). The Bush team processed that information fairly cleanly, accomplishing Task 4 in a "neutral" manner. Bush had been frustrated with the lack of intelligence during the October coup and had ordered more attention to this task (Woodward 1991, 379). In the crisis period between October and December, the group misused the information that Noriega had declared a "state of war" with the United States (when he really had said that U.S. actions were creating a state of war) but otherwise processed information neither particularly "well" or "poorly."

The Bush group, particularly Bush, Scowcroft, and Powell, performed "well" the task of evaluating the costs, risks, and implications of Operation Blue Spoon. Reports by Woodward (1991) and Powell (1995) show much attention to the military plan. The December 17 meeting in particular provided for much scrutiny on the plan itself, which followed weeks of such scrutiny by Powell, Cheney, Thurman, and others at U.S. Southern Command and the Pentagon (Woodward 1991, 138–52; Powell 1995, 422–25). While Dinges concludes that the U.S. invasion did not follow an examination of costs and risks (1990, 313–14), I take this conclusion to really refer to the process of selecting an option that was flawed, rather than the scrutiny to which the selected policy was subjected.

The group also performed "well" the task of developing implementation and contingency plans (Task 6). Reports by Powell (1995), Woodward (1991), and Flanagan (1993) show considerable attention to the development of the operation, though, as Kempe notes, it contained a glaring and costly error of not providing for military police to stop looting in Panama City, which led to huge financial losses (1990, 17). Flanagan notes multiple calls for contingency plans and shows a record of revising plans already prepared (1993, 32–33, 47), and Baker recalls that President Bush ordered new contingency plans after the failed coup (1995, 187; Kempe 1990, 11–13).

The Bush team showed mixed performance on the tasks of crisis decision-making. While it paid significant attention to the costs and risks involved in a U.S. invasion of Panama (Task 5) and to developing implementation plans for the invasion (Task 6), it arrived at the choice to invade (Task 2) in a rather flawed manner. The group searched widely for information (Task 3) and processed that information (Task 4) in satisfactory ways.

Assessing the Reliability of the Findings

I have tried to address concerns about the validity of the findings presented here and in table 4 by documenting the codes in the text in a way that is descriptive but not overly burdensome for the reader. As a way of providing further support for the findings presented here, I have constructed a type of intercoder reliability check from the findings reported by Herek, Janis, and Huth in their 1987 study that examined some of these same cases with a similar methodological approach (cf. Haney 1994a). Herek, Janis, and Huth (1987) examine nineteen crises in American foreign policy since World War II. Their sample includes seven of the nine crises that are investigated in this project (they do not study the Tet Offensive or the invasion of Panama). They use a case-survey method similar to the one used here. I have examined the same case studies for the seven common crises that Herek, Janis, and Huth (1987) examined, plus some that have been published since their study was released.

The list of crisis decision-making characteristics that they explore is similar to the list used in the present study, though they focus on the negative form of each task, or on the presence of malfunctions only. The results of this project can be compared to the results reported in the previous study. It is at least possible to ascertain whether we agree on the presence of a malfunction. The analogue here to the presence of a malfunction in the previous study is a finding that a decision-making task was performed "poorly" or "very poorly." A "neutral" code or the evaluation that a task was performed "well" or "very well" is analogous to the absence of a malfunction. Table 5 presents a summary of their findings and of our level of agreement on the codings of decision-making process characteristics.

The most glaring feature of the comparison of our two studies is their high level of agreement—approximately 88 percent agreement—rather than the marginal level of disagreement. Their findings for each of the seven crises our studies share in common can be summarized in a table with forty-nine cells: seven columns for their seven procedural malfunctions (seven columns, seven rows, forty-nine cells). At first glance we seem

TABLE 5. Comparison of Codings of Crisis Decision-Making Processes from This Project Compared with Herek, Janis, and Huth 1987

	H-J-H Criterion (Analogous to Task)						
	1	2	3	4	5	6	7
Crisis Case	(2)	(1)	(5)	(3, 4)	(4)	(2)	(6)
Berlin, 1948							
H-J-H Code:	0	0	1	0	0	1	1
Agreement:	Yes	Yes	Yes	Yes	Yes	Yes	Yes
Korea, 1950							
H-J-H Code:	1	0	0	0	0	1	0
Agreement:	Yes	Yes	No	Yes	Yes	Yes	No
Dien Bien Phu, 1954							
H-J-H Code:	0	0	0	0	0	0	0
Agreement	Yes	Yes	Yes	Yes	Yes	Yes	Yes
Suez, 1956							
H-J-H Code:	0	0	0	0	0	1	1
Agreement:	Yes	Yes	Yes	Yes	Yes	Yes	Yes
Tonkin Gulf, 1964							
H-J-H Code:	1	1	1	0	0	1	0
Agreement:	Yes	Yes	Yes	Yes	No	Yes	Yes
Jordan, 1970							
H-J-H Code:	0	0	0	1	0	1	0
Agreement:	Yes	No	Yes	Yes	Yes	Yes	Yes
October War, 1973							
H-J-H Code:	0	0	0	0	0	0	1
Agreement:	Yes	Yes	Yes	Yes	No	Yes	No

H-J-H Criterion 1: failure to survey alternatives
H-J-H Criterion 2: failure to survey objectives
H-J-H Criterion 3: failure to consider costs and risks
H-J-H Criterion 4: poor information search
H-J-H Criterion 5: selective bias in processing information
H-J-H Criterion 6: failure to reconsider previously rejected alternatives
H-J-H Criterion 7: failure to develop monitoring or contingency plans
H-J-H Code: 0 = Malfunction Absent; 1 = Malfunction Present
Total number of cells: 49
Cells in agreement: 43
Cells in disagreement: 6
Rate of agreement: 88 percent

to disagree on ten of these forty-nine cells. Upon closer inspection, it is likely that we actually agree on four of these ten questionable cells, leaving six cells of serious disagreement.

We agree completely on the Dien Bien Phu crisis. We also agree on the Suez crises, although we seem to disagree over their Criterion 6. I agree with their conclusion that the Eisenhower group did not reexamine previously rejected alternatives, but this is only one component of Task 2 used in this project. The group performed the other components of this task "well." We also completely agree on the Berlin crisis, although, as in Suez, we seem to disagree over their Criterion 6. I would agree that the group did not reexamine the choice of the airlift once it was under way, but this is only one part of my Task 2—the search for alternatives. I have coded that the Truman group performed this task in a "neutral" manner. It is a close call; I do not think we disagree significantly over this task.

The evaluations of the Tonkin Gulf and Jordan cases differ slightly (on only one procedural task). Our apparent disagreement over the information search in the Gulf of Tonkin crisis is largely contained in the disagreement over their Criterion 5, my Task 4. I discuss this disagreement subsequently. Our apparent disagreement over their Criterion 4 in the Jordan case corresponds to a "neutral" code for my Tasks 3 and 4 and is not a serious dispute. We do disagree over their Criterion 2 in the Jordan case. The evaluations of decision making during the October War and the Korean intervention both differ on two criteria that I discuss shortly.

Herek, Janis, and Huth (1987) do not document their codings, which makes it difficult to identify the source of these few disagreements. We may disagree because our coding forms (operationalizations) are different.[5] The additional sources that were used here could lead to different results as well. For example, Herek, Janis, and Huth (1987) rely extensively on the case studies by Dowty (1984) and Quandt (1977) for the Nixon crises, as do I, but the reports of Dowty and Quandt do not agree on everything. Herek, Janis, and Huth (1989) provide no guidance for the reader as to how they settle these disagreements. I have been able to draw on the recently released biography of Richard Nixon by Ambrose (1991) and the new study of the 1973 October War by Lebow and Stein (1994), as well as the case studies used by Herek and his colleagues. Ambrose's report can help settle disagreements between the case studies and may have led me to settle a dispute differently than did Herek, Janis, and Huth (1987).

There are six items upon which the aforementioned codings and those in Herek, Janis, and Huth (1987) disagree. My reading of the case studies leads me to disagree with the contention by Herek, Janis, and Huth (1) that there was a full examination of the costs and risks of U.S. intervention in Korea; (2) that implementation and contingency plans were well developed in the Korean crisis; (3) that there was no bias in information processing during the Tonkin Gulf crisis; (4) that Nixon's advisory group surveyed a full range of alternative responses in the crisis in Jordan; (5) that there was no bias in information processing during the October War; and (6) that the Nixon administration failed to develop implementation and monitoring plans during the October War.

First, Herek, Janis, and Huth (1987) code no malfunction on the consideration of costs, risks, and implications of U.S. intervention in Korea. As I discussed earlier, my analysis of mostly the same case studies as they used leads me to code that the Truman group did this task "poorly." The risks that military leaders harbored were not seriously considered as it was obvious that Truman had made up his mind. The implications of being in a wider war were not examined. The case reports agree on this.

Second, and similarly, the case reports of the Korea crisis show implementation plans to have been faulty and ad hoc and that no real contingency planning for a limited war in Korea had taken place before the crisis or did take place during the crisis. The case reports agree on this.

Third, multiple case studies of the Tonkin Gulf crisis report that the decision-making group did not perform the task of assimilating new and discrepant information effectively (e.g., Austin 1971, 300, 343; Windchy 1971, 212; Moïse 1996). These reports stand in contradiction to the coding by Herek, Janis, and Huth (1987). Johnson and his advisers ignored information that indicated that the August 4 attack on the *Maddox* and the *Turner Joy* might not have taken place. They disregarded the cable from Captain Herrick indicating that the validity of reports of the attack was doubtful. They failed to consider the provocative nature of the De Soto patrols and the South Vietnamese raids on the North that were ongoing in the same vicinity as the *Maddox*.

Fourth, Herek, Janis, and Huth (1987) report that there was no malfunction present in the survey of alternative responses to the 1970 crisis in Jordan. They must rely on Quandt's case study for this evaluation. I also code a reasonably well-performed task of canvassing alternatives from the Quandt case study. Dowty, to the contrary, persuasively argues that the Nixon group systematically failed to consider a variety of alternative responses to this crisis (1978, 186–8; cf. Dowty 1984, 189–93). I side with Dowty here.

Fifth and sixth, we disagree on two counts in the crisis during the 1973 October War. Herek, Janis, and Huth (1987) code that there was no bias in information processing in this crisis. It is difficult to code this task based upon the evidence in the case studies. Dowty reports that the Nixon-

Kissinger group performed this task effectively (1984, 303–19), but Quandt disagrees with Dowty's assessment. He argues that the Nixon group did a poor job of recognizing that war was imminent, even though information to that effect was available. This information was not assimilated into the Nixon group's existing mind-set about the region. The group did learn as the crisis unfolded and became quite responsive to the situation (Quandt 1977, 165–83, 200–204). I take this failure to assimilate new and discrepant information as an indication that the group was not performing this task well.

Finally, Herek, Janis, and Huth (1987) conclude that the Nixon group failed to develop implementation and monitoring plans during the October War. I cannot explain this evaluation. My reading of Dowty (1984, 199–320) and Quandt (1977, 165–76), the same case studies they used, leads me to conclude that the group performed this task fairly well. There were many contingency plans compiled, and there was a high level of interaction between Washington and Tel Aviv to monitor a very fluid situation. We simply disagree on this task.

It is still the high level of agreement across our two coding enterprises that is most striking. Beyond that, the disagreements—and the ability to explore them—suggest one of the real strengths of the case-survey method. The approach allows the use of multiple cases from which information can be extracted without totally losing the uniqueness of the cases. The coding enterprise still allows the attention to detail that those who prefer case-based methods appreciate, but yet provides a vehicle for treating this case material in systematic ways.

Conclusion

The findings presented here give us a picture of crisis decision making. They depict a range of effectiveness in the decision-making processes. Some crisis processes were particularly effective, such as the Eisenhower process during the Dien Bien Phu crisis. Some were not particularly effective, such as the process that preceded the 1968 Tet Offensive. This evidence shows that some groups paid close attention to the tasks of decision making while others did not. Some were exhaustive in the processes they employed, using what Janis (1989) calls "vigilant" decision making. Others took shortcuts to decisions and took much for granted.

The evidence also demonstrates that the same decision-making group can perform some of the tasks of decision making effectively while, at the same time, it performs others poorly. The Nixon group in Jordan's civil war, for example, performed some tasks quite well and others not as well.

This finding indicates that decision making is not a singular activity. The tasks of decision making are behaviorally separable, to an extent. The findings also highlight the pervasive nature of superpower tensions in these crises. American decision makers were keenly aware of the superpower components of the crises, even when the substantive area of a crisis had little to do with American-Soviet relations or when the crisis had little superpower component to it at all, as in the Korea case.

CHAPTER 5

Presidents, Advisers, and the Management of Crisis Decision Making

The primary goals of this project are to extend our substantive understanding of how presidents organize and manage decision-making groups during foreign policy crises and to explore how these structured groups perform the tasks of providing information, advice, and analysis. The methodological goal of the project has been to apply a case-survey method to this substantive area. In this concluding chapter I review what have we learned about presidents, advisers, and crisis decision making. The chapter begins with a short discussion of how we might expect the models to perform and then presents a synopsis of the empirical findings within and across the nine cases. The chapter continues with a discussion of some of the lessons that can be drawn from these findings about presidential management of advisory groups, about how presidents learn during crises, and about the performance of advisory groups in crises. I also note some of the issues that have emerged from the study that were not a central part of this project but which might be fruitfully pursued in future research (the obligatory "future research" section), and I offer some final thoughts about presidential management of foreign policy-making in times of crisis.

Theoretical Expectations

George (1980) and R. Johnson (1974) provide a theoretical starting point for this research with their presentation of the characteristics of three abstract or ideal models that presidents may use to organize the flow of information and advice, and they discuss the potential benefits and costs of each organizational form. It is possible to conclude from their discussion that each model is designed to help perform the tasks of decision making well, but they bring with them strengths and weaknesses, especially as their dynamics relate to a president's preferred style of management. For example, a president who is not comfortable with conflict and bargaining would be ill advised to use a competitive structure for an advisory group, because such a model does not fit well with the president's personal management style. But if the model matches the president's style, and competent people are placed into the roles prescribed by the model, the structures should help perform the tasks of decision making effectively—or increase the chances that the group will do so. That is what they are supposed to do, in theory: enforce a thorough analysis of objectives and alternatives, provide opportunities and incentives to search for information and to assimilate new information, encourage the examination of costs and risks and implications, and design contingency plans.

But each model contains weaknesses as well. For example, the bureaucracy that is to enforce a thorough analysis of alternatives in the formalistic model may also systematically screen out information and alternatives. The competitive model that is designed to use the spur of competition to force creative problem solving may also force the biased processing of information so as to "win" the game of convincing the president, rather than the game of finding the best solution to a problem.

So two empirical questions emerge. First, are these abstract models useful as starting points for an empirical examination of crisis decision-making management? Second, to what extent is the performance of the tasks of crisis decision making explicable in terms of the organizational model that is utilized in the crisis? Are there any patterns in the performance of the models? I began to answer these questions in the previous two chapters; the discussion that follows brings the findings of these chapters together.

Empirical Evidence

Truman Administration

The Truman management model was highly formalistic, reserving power to the president, who sat above a hierarchical, jurisdictional decision-making framework. The evidence from both the Berlin and Korean crises show this same pattern of Truman using formalistic, ad hoc groups to aid in decision making. Lines of communication to the president were clearly prescribed and orderly. Expertise was important, and Truman was the ultimate decision maker. Debate was not encouraged, and opposing viewpoints were sometimes not heard or explored, as in the case of the military leaders in the Korean case. This is a failure of the formalistic model's expected thorough performance on the presentation of viewpoints.

This model provided mixed results in terms of the performance of the tasks of decision making that emerged from the structures. The formalistic model's emphasis on jurisdictions and expertise is designed to produce a range of views about what the objectives of the United States should be in a crisis (Task 1). On this task the Truman group performed adequately, though better in the Berlin case than the Korean case. Perhaps not surprisingly for a president who loved to make decisions (Shlaim 1983, 77; McCullough 1992), the Truman processes did not survey a particularly wide array of alternative policy responses (Task 2) to either crisis studied here. Truman's reliance on himself as a decision maker may have undermined a formalistic system presumably set up to generate options, as well as be tidy.

On the positive side, the Truman groups did perform well in the search for information (Task 3) and did not significantly mishandle the information they acquired (Task 4). The division of responsibility and reliance on channels that is a hallmark of the formalistic model should produce a thorough information search but holds out the potential for the bureaucracy to screen that information in inappropriate ways. We see some of that in the two cases, especially the wishful thinking about the power of the ROK forces and the efficacy of U.S. air power that accompanied the Korean crisis.

The real procedural weakness in both crises studies here, seen especially in the case study of Berlin by Shlaim (1983) and of Korea by Paige (1968), was the lack of focus on the costs, risks, and implications of the preferred policy (Task 5) and the lack of attention to the development of implementation, contingency, and monitoring plans (Task 6). In both crises, actions were generally taken in an incremental way, with much latitude being left to the theater commanders in lieu of clear direction from Truman and his advisers. Clay in the Berlin case and MacArthur in the Korean case were able to take steps not yet fully prescribed by Truman. It is reasonable to suggest that Truman's reliance on jurisdictions and delegation stretched slightly beyond his grasp in both of these cases.

Eisenhower Administration

The evidence in the case studies of the crises at Dien Bien Phu and Suez for Eisenhower indicate a management approach that could best be called a hybrid of the formalistic and competitive models. This hybrid approach is most clear in the Dien Bien Phu case, though it is also apparent in the Suez crisis. The evidence in both of these crises indicates an approach to advisory group management that sought to build competitive components, often driven by Eisenhower himself, into a formalistic and hierarchical framework. Eisenhower blended multiple, open channels of communication and free-spirited debate—hallmarks of the competitive approach—with the explicit use of formal and bureaucratic (hierarchical) structures and jurisdictions. The president stood clearly at the top of the decision-making apparatus. These components of Eisenhower's advisory system characterize neither the formal nor the competitive model; rather, they blend characteristics of these two models—a hybrid form. This hybridization is most visible in the case studies of Dien Bien Phu by Burke and Greenstein (1989) and Immerman (1989) but can also be seen in the Suez case studies by Neff (1981) and others.[1]

This advisory structure generally served Eisenhower well (see table 4). In both the Dien Bien Phu and Suez crises, the evidence indicates that the Eisenhower advisory group performed the tasks of decision making in a vigilant manner. Eisenhower's approach, in theory, should blend the strengths of the formalistic model with those of the competitive model. Their different benefits would compensate for the weaknesses of the other approach. In theory this hybrid should facilitate the functional execution of decision making. The mix of the structured bureaucracy, which is designed to force a thorough review of objectives, and the open and competitive group at the top of this structure, which is designed to debate and explore objectives, should lead this group to perform Task 1 "well." The evidence in the case studies indicates that the Eisenhower group thoroughly explored objectives on more than one occasion in each crisis.

This hybrid should also facilitate the vigilant review of alternative responses in the crisis (Task 2), and the case studies indicate that the group performed this task on multiple occasions in both crises. The blend of formal structure and structured competition and debate should also lead to a functional information search (Task 3) and the processing and assimilation of new information (Task 4). The evidence is slightly more mixed on these two tasks, though still generally positive (or at least not negative). In the Dien Bien Phu crisis, the Eisenhower advisory group performed a broad search for information, and it performed well the task of assimilating new information into existing frameworks. The case studies, however, show that the advisory group performed these tasks in a "neutral" way during the Suez crisis.

The hybrid that Eisenhower employed in these two crises should also encourage the exploration of the costs, risks, and implications of preferred options (Task 5). The open debate of the competitive model should counteract any tendency on the part of the bureaucracy to screen out and not discuss risks or negative implications. The case studies indicate that the Eisenhower group performed this task quite well. In fact, the case reports indicate that the group performed this task on more than one occasion in the Suez crisis and on multiple occasions during the Dien Bien Phu crisis.

This hybrid should also promote the thorough development of monitoring, contingency, and implementation plans. The competitive components should force such planning by debating and by challenging weak positions. The evidence concerning Task 6 is mixed. The group performed this task vigilantly in the Dien Bien Phu crisis but failed to do so in any thorough way in the Suez Canal crisis.

In summary, the case studies of the Eisenhower decision-making apparatus during crises at Dien Bien Phu in 1954 and the Suez Canal in 1956 indicate that Eisenhower used a management model that was a hybrid of George's (1980) competitive and formalistic types. The decision-making group performed most of the tasks of decision making well in these crises. It performed Tasks 1 through 5 in a positive manner in both crises. However, its record on Task 6—developing implementation, monitoring, and contingency plans—was mixed.

Johnson Administration

The Johnson model of crisis decision-making management used components of both the formalistic and the collegial models—a second hybrid of the three ideal models. The case studies of the crisis in the Tonkin Gulf and the Tet Offensive indicate that Johnson used a small, "collegial," team for decision making that included McGeorge Bundy, Dean Rusk, and Robert McNamara as principal players, and other such as General Wheeler as more ad hoc members. This team sat above a formalistic structure that was hierarchical in nature, operated within clear jurisdictional boundaries, and funneled information to the president only through one of the members of the small unit at the top. The case studies of both crises describe this "collegial-formalistic" hybrid. They also clearly show that this management model did not serve Johnson well in these crises, at least not until after the shock of the Tet Offensive (see table 4).

The collegial model should, by stressing the shared nature of decision making, encourage a thorough review of objectives in a crisis. This tendency should be bolstered, in theory, by Johnson's use of a formalistic bureaucracy to support this small decision-making team. The formal structures should serve to force a full review of objectives and pass them along to the top. The evidence indicates that this advisory structure performed decision-making Task 1 "poorly" during the crisis in the Gulf of Tonkin and during the period leading up to the Tet Offensive. The group failed to explore American objectives in Southeast Asia on either occasion. However, the expanded advisory structure used after the Tet Offensive performed this task with great diligence. It was the very purpose of the Clifford Task Force to explore American objectives in the region.

The aggregated case study evidence indicates that the group performed Task 2 "poorly" in both the Tonkin Gulf crisis and the period leading up to Tet, notwithstanding the fact that the mixture of benefits from the collegial and formalistic structures should force a thorough review of alternative policy responses. A full review of alternatives never took place, according to the case studies. Policy was almost a reflex action (Goulden 1969). However, a fuller examination of alternative policy responses to the problems in Vietnam did take place with the introduction of the Clifford task force.

Task 3 of decision making, the search for information, should also be aided by the blending of the collegial and formalistic models. While the collegial model has the capacity to become closed to outside information, the addition of the formality of bureaucracy should serve to keep discrepant information flowing to the collegial group at the top. The empirical evidence concerning this task is quite mixed. The case studies for both Johnson crises indicate that the Johnson advisory group performed an adequate search for information, but in both instances the decision-making group consistently failed to incorporate new information into policy planning. Perhaps the Tonkin Gulf crisis is the best example of this finding. Johnson sought and received information about the supposed second attack on the *Maddox,* including a report from the field that the second attack could not be confirmed. Johnson and his advisers disregarded this discrepant information. In the period after the Tet Offensive, the Johnson structure performed better on Tasks 3 and 4.

The hybrid model that Johnson used should also further the exploration of the costs, risks, and implications of policy alternatives (Task 5). To the extent that the formal structures may screen out especially risks of preferred options, the collegiality at the top should facilitate such an analysis. Again the empirical evidence is mixed. In both the Tonkin Gulf and pre-Tet crises, the Johnson group failed to perform such a task in any meaningful way. After Tet, however, the group did explore the costs and risks of current and future policy. This decision-making structure should also facilitate the development of monitoring, implementation, and contingency plans. The evidence in the case studies of Task 6 is mixed, however. In the Tonkin Gulf crisis the group did perform this task "well," while in the period leading to Tet the group did not. In the post-Tet period, the Johnson advisory group performed this task in a "neutral" manner.

It is difficult to draw conclusions or generalizations about the effectiveness of the Johnson advisory system across these two crises that include three opportunities for the performance of the tasks of decision making (Tonkin Gulf, the period leading to the Tet Offensive [Tet 1], and the period that followed Tet [Tet 2]) because of the way the system was corrected after Tet. After the "shock" of the Tet Offensive in January 1968 and the establishment of the Clifford Task Force, the Johnson advisory machinery began to perform the tasks of decision making more effectively.

The larger advisory group was encouraged to be more critical and to scrutinize U.S. policies in Vietnam. It still retained, however, the structure of a collegial-formalistic hybrid. The primary difference from before Tet was that the number of players able to directly impact the president increased, and new incentives led to a thorough review and critical analysis of U.S. policies—perhaps for the first time since 1964. The Clifford Task Force was a highly organized group that had clear jurisdictions. It reported to the president directly, as its head was soon to be the secretary of defense. The evidence, drawn especially from Schandler's case study of the period (himself a participant in the Clifford Task Force), shows that this new Johnson machinery—still a collegial-formalistic hybrid—performed the tasks of decision making more effectively than did the old machinery.

Across these three performance opportunities, the Johnson advisory structure was not as effective as the other presidential advisory systems examined here. But it did perform well during one of the three crises—the period after the Tet Offensive. I suggested in chapter 1 that these models could be self-correcting, that presidents and advisers could learn throughout the course of an administration—or even during a crisis. This learning could lead to improved performance without changing the organizational structure. This process is evident in the differences in decision making before and after Tet. A broken system of decision making and advice giving fixed itself, spurred on by the strong stimulus of a performance failure. A more general discussion about learning during crises will return to this point later.

Nixon Administration

The case studies of the two Nixon administration crises clearly show a formalistic approach to crisis decision-making management, though this style differed in important ways from Truman's formalism. The Nixon-Kissinger advisory structure was highly organized and bureaucratized, with specific, recognized jurisdictions. Heads of organizations briefed Kissinger and Nixon in an authoritative way. Ultimate decision making was left to Nixon and his national security adviser and later secretary of state, Henry Kissinger. The evidence of decision making during the Jordan crisis and the October War indicates a decision-making framework that varied little from routine situations. The primary difference was that as the crisis unfolded, information was forced through the existing highly formalized structures at a faster rate. Decision making was centralized at higher levels, containing fewer people. Ultimately, decision making rested in the Nixon-Kissinger dyad. This framework closely approximated the formalistic model George discusses for Nixon and diverged little from the "routine" Nixon-Kissinger model that George discusses (1980, 154–56, chap. 10).

This approach to crisis decision-making management generally served Nixon well, even in his absence during the October War. George (1980) and R. Johnson (1974) both argue that a formalistic approach should allow the tight structure of bureaucracy to force a full and thorough review of information. In both the Jordan and October crises, the Nixon group performed the task of canvassing objectives "well" (Task 1). The Nixon advisory group seemed to pay special attention to this task. The evidence concerning the Nixon group's performance of the task of assessing alternative U.S. responses to the crises (Task 2) is mixed. The group performed this task "well" in the October War, but largely failed to perform this task in the 1970 Jordan crisis.

This management model should also give incentives to the bureaucracy to search out new information (Task 3) and to screen it effectively (Task 4). Here again, the empirical evidence is mixed. The Nixon group did not perform these tasks particularly "well" or "poorly" in the Jordan crisis; a "neutral" coding was assigned. The advisory group thoroughly searched for new information and for new channels of information during the October War. However, the body did not assimilate that information very effectively. Indeed, this crisis is often used as a prime example of misperception caused by firm preexisting mind-sets.

The formalistic system should encourage a full review of the costs and risks of policy options, as well as develop contingency and implementation plans. This is the formal job of subcomponents of the bureaucracy in such a system. The evidence in both crises indicates that the Nixon group effectively evaluated the costs of alternative responses (Task 5) and developed monitoring, implementation, and contingency plans (Task 6).

In general, the case-study evidence of the Nixon formalistic management approach shows that the group performed well the tasks of decision making. The evidence is mixed with regard to the group's handling of Tasks 2 and 4, but it performed the other tasks of decision making quite well.

Bush Administration

In the crisis studied here, the invasion of Panama in 1989, the Bush management strategy might be called a "do-it-yourself" type of collegial formalism, though his hybrid was different in type and intention from Johnson's and his do-it-himself tendencies were different from Truman's. Bush relied on jurisdictions and expertise, used clearly defined routes for information, and wanted information funneled to him in a very hierarchical manner. He blended into this formalism a friendly sense of team among his closest advisers. This sense of team was not intended to produce debates or a shared sense of responsibility at all, but rather a sense of collegiality, esprit de corps, and loyalty to eliminate leaks. Bush reserved to himself ultimate decision-making authority and delegated to his advisers the role of developing the plans for implementing his wishes.

The formalism that should produce a broad survey of objectives (Task 1) and alternatives (Task 2) did not do so in the Panama case. Indeed, the case studies show, particularly the study by Woodward (1991), that the Bush team performed only a minimal review of U.S. goals in Panama and performed the task of exploring options fairly poorly. This record is similar to Truman's record in the Korean case and Johnson's Vietnam cases, where the presidential preference may have precluded a full examination of objectives and alternatives. Also like Truman's record in the Korean and Berlin cases, the formalistic hierarchy that relies on jurisdictions and channels did search for information rather thoroughly (Task 3) and process that information in a rather neutral manner (Task 4).

Most unlike the Truman record in Berlin or Korea, the Bush team performed the task of examining costs, risks, and implications of the invasion vigilantly (Task 5). The units formalistically aligned under Bush did their job of exploring this item, and I would suggest that the collegiality Bush pursued may have contributed to their sense of teamwork in addressing those concerns. Similarly, the Bush team did a thorough job of designing implementation, contingency, and monitoring plans (Task 6). This task fell largely under the purview of Generals Powell, Thurman, and Kelly and Secretary Cheney. The division of responsibility and reliance on expertise paid off for Bush in the form of fully developed plans.

Some Lessons from these Empirical Findings

About Presidents and Advisers

This method of analyzing existing case studies of each crisis has shed light on more than just the form of organizational management that presidents have used during crises and the behavior of the decision-making groups in those crises. It has also provided insights on some interesting questions about these presidents and their advisers, as well as on the nature of these advisory groups, by synthesizing the evidence from across case studies. In the Truman cases, the record bears out the view of Truman as the key decision maker in his administration. The case in the Bush administration shows Bush clearly at the top of a small, well-prepared group of advisers. The record from the Panama crisis supports the view of Bush as his own foreign policy specialist in the sense that he relied on himself more than on advisers to make decisions in this area. The advisers' job was to implement decisions, extend his reach. It also shows a president reacting more out of impulse and instinct than thorough analysis, which does not make Bush much different from Truman or Johnson.

In the Eisenhower administration, the case studies generally support the new revision of Eisenhower as an active, even shrewd, decision maker who liked debate, as long as it was orderly (Greenstein 1982; Melanson and Mayers 1989). It is also apparent that Eisenhower was concerned about the quality of the advisory process. This concern is evident in his construction and use of subgroups during crises (like the Erskine group during the Dien Bien Phu crisis). The case studies show a president who was cognizant of strategy and structure. All of this study supports the new vision of Eisenhower as an active, if "hidden-hand," leader.

The case studies also speak to the nature of the relationship between President Eisenhower and Secretary of State Dulles, if not the nature of Dulles himself. Dulles is often portrayed as a strident anticommunist, a person who saw the world in dichotomous terms—good or bad, right or wrong (see Hoopes 1973). He is often thought of, at least in the old thinking about Eisenhower, as the dominant player in the foreign policy relationship (see Finer 1964). But the case studies, especially the examination by Kingseed (1995), show a different Dulles and a different relationship with the president. They show a secretary of state who was respected by, but subordinate to, the president. When Dulles played a dominant role—with allies, for example—he did so at the behest of Eisenhower. The evidence also shows a Dulles whose thinking was not blindly anticommunist. Dulles did not support unilateral intervention in Indochina. Nor did Dulles support the move against Nasser in the Suez Canal crisis. Dulles saw shades of gray, and he took his orders, at least in these two crises, from the president (cf. Gaddis 1992).

The findings in this project also inform our understanding of the nature of Lyndon Johnson's advisory structure. One of the ongoing controversies about Johnson and Vietnam is the question of whether Johnson was trapped by his advisers, or was a victim of groupthink. Contrary to the conventional wisdom, Barrett (1988, 1993) argues that Johnson was not trapped in Vietnam as a result of his delinquent advisers who overwhelmingly supported U.S. involvement in Vietnam (cf. Mulcahy 1995). In the same vein, Gelb and Betts (1979) argue that the system of decision making was not broken in Vietnam. Rather, it produced exactly what it was intended to produce—one more year without defeat. The case studies of the Tonkin Gulf crisis and the Tet Offensive tend to support these unorthodox views, which may become the new orthodoxy. There were plenty of dissenting voices during the Tonkin Gulf crisis and in the period leading up to Tet in 1968. Johnson faced no unanimous position from his advisers. Moreover, Johnson clearly agonized over what to do after Tet. He was, in that sense, open to dissenting opinions. But on the whole Johnson listened only to what he wanted and disregarded what he did not like. Such was also true of his closest advisers. Johnson and his decision-making team ignored parts of their decision-making apparatus. These parts and the new components like the Clifford Task Force and the Wise Men would, however, would restore the decision-making framework to a functional status after the performance failure at Tet.

The findings also shed light on the relationship between Richard Nixon and Henry Kissinger (see Haney 1994b). They show a pattern of interaction that approaches a decision-making dyad. In foreign policy, the two acted almost as one. Kissinger chaired the meetings of the Washington Special Action Group and reported back to Nixon in both the Jordan crisis and the October War. Kissinger spoke for the president to others in the administration and allies in both crises. But the relationship was not so simple. The evidence shows a divergence in their interests during the 1973 October War. Kissinger's delay of the resupply of Israel against Nixon's wishes showed a dyad in stress. Further, the case studies show a secretary of state who was frustrated with the president while the simultaneous Watergate crisis unfolded and who asserted himself in foreign policy in the president's absence. Kissinger took on more responsibility for himself as Nixon became more removed from the process of decision making. This process reached its pinnacle when the nuclear alert was ordered in the middle of the night, October 25, 1973, without waking the president (though he agreed with the decision in the morning).

Who was in charge in the 1973 crisis? I agree with Ambrose's (1991) position that Nixon retained final authority in this crisis and in his relationship with Kissinger. Nixon retained the right to consent or object to Kissinger's decisions. But that may not be the kind of presidential control that best serves the interests of the nation in a crisis. That normative question notwithstanding, it is interesting to note that the framework Nixon and Kissinger established for crisis management generally worked well in the two crises examined here and that in one of them the machinery worked largely without the president. The advisory process could continue without Nixon's direct attention because of the way that Nixon had placed Kissinger between himself and the rest of the bureaucracy. That may be normatively or constitutionally troublesome, but it is managerially interesting.

Presidents create advisory structures to enhance human decision-making capabilities. They use these groups during crises to deal with information and to help make decisions in a novel environment. Presidents try to control this novel environment as much as possible with these structures—to treat crises as if they were routine. While the president is an important component of these decision-making structures, the president is not the only part of them. Perhaps the president is not even the most important part of a decision-making group. For example, even if crises were random events or shocks (which they are probably not), random events do happen in clusters sometimes. It is to be expected that at some point two or more crises will take place at once at an inconvenient time (e.g., the 1956 Hungarian revolt and Suez crisis) or that a crisis will emerge when the president is otherwise occupied with domestic affairs, such as the reelection campaigns for Truman in the 1948 crisis or Eisenhower in the 1956 crisis. The decision-making structures need to be able to operate in an atmosphere of divided presidential attention, or perhaps lack of presidential attention, if that occurs. These structures need to be able to operate on their own for substantial periods.

This is not intended as a theory of presidential management that includes excluding the president. It is, rather, a suggestion drawn from Nixon's experience that decision-making structures need to be able to operate in times of stress and novelty and to respond with composure, adaptivity, and creativity. They need to be able to work without constant presidential supervision. The Nixon-Kissinger system worked just as it was supposed to work, and it did so largely without the president. While perhaps not to be emulated, this example provides an important lesson about crisis management for the future.

About the Performance of the Tasks of Crisis Decision Making

It is possible to align the evidence from the ten decision processes from nine crises (Tet was divided into two processes), examined here in a way to explore patterns that might exist across time in the performance of the tasks of decision making. This evidence is summarized in table 6. Most apparent from the crises is the lack of extreme performances—few of the tasks of decision making were performed "very well" or "very poorly." There would seem to be a satisficing mentality in crisis decision making, perhaps contributed to by stress and lack of time, that leads groups to not spend too much time on any one task (which may seem odd since it is their job). On the other side, the groups are aware enough of the need to perform the tasks that they seem to pay at least some attention to the tasks so as to avoid severe defects in decision making. It is also interesting to note that few tasks were performed in a "neutral" manner; only the information tasks (Tasks 3 and 4) had many cases load on them. Most of the tasks were performed with some moderate degree of either vigilance or avoidance.

A large majority of the cases included at least minimal attention to the surveying of objectives, Task 1, with eight of the ten crisis processes scoring at least a "neutral" code. In the crises studied here, however, the groups were about as likely to widely search for alternatives as not. This is true for Tasks 5 and 6 as well. From the other side of the coin, only two crises included a particularly thorough job of processing and assimilating new information, Task 4. No doubt the lens of the cold war may have contributed to that, though this excuse would not apply to the Panama invasion. The record of task performance is not all bad, but neither is it that impressive across these nine crises and ten processes. The decision-making systems show some record of breakdown as a result of intelligence failures, of presidential failures, of bureaucratic failures, or some combination thereof.

Another readily noticeable feature of the findings is that there is no obvious, direct relationship between a particular advisory structure and the decision process that results. The management models do not seem to have predictable results; nor do they have inherent advantages. Rather, what does emerge from the evidence is that a president needs to select a management strategy that fits his or her style and work to emphasize the strengths and minimize the weaknesses of that model. For example, Eisenhower liked hierarchy, but he also incorporated competitive elements into his decision-making management to overcome the potential information screening of a hierarchical system. The decision-making process that emerges in each case is a result of more than just the management model—it is a combination of people, structures, and contexts. I have tried to examine here some of the ways that the structures work in crises. This may be seen as a nonfinding, or as a reminder of the complexity of decision making in human systems.[2]

About the National Security Council

The findings from this study also contribute to our understanding of how presidents adapt existing structures to specific needs during foreign policy crises. The evidence concerns the National Security Council most directly. The National Security Council (NSC) was established by the National Security Act of 1947 and was amended in 1949 (see Jackson 1965). The statutory members of the NSC are quite few and include (after the 1949 amendment) the president, the vice president, and the secretaries of state and defense. The director of Central Intelligence and chair of the joint Chiefs of Staff are statutory advisers. Presidents have regularly expanded

TABLE 6. Performance of Crisis Decision-Making Processes by Task

Task 1. Survey objectives

Very Poorly	Poorly	Neutral	Well	Very Well
	Tonkin Gulf	Korea	Dien Bien Phu	Tet 2
	Tet 1	Panama	Suez	
			Jordan	
			October War	
			Berlin	

Task 2. Canvass alternatives

Very Poorly	Poorly	Neutral	Well	Very Well
	Tonkin Gulf	Berlin	Suez	Dien Bien Phu
	Tet 1	Panama	Tet 2	
	Jordan		October War	
	Korea			

Task 3. Search for information

Very Poorly	Poorly	Neutral	Well	Very Well
		Suez	Dien Bien Phu	October War
		Tonkin Gulf	Tet 2	
		Tet 1	Berlin	
		Jordan	Korea	
			Panama	

Task 4. Assimilate and process new information

Very Poorly	Poorly	Neutral	Well	Very Well
	Tonkin Gulf	Suez	Dien Bien Phu	Tet 2
	Tet 1	Jordan		
	October War	Berlin		
		Korea		
		Panama		

Task 5. Evaluate costs, risks, and implications of preferred choice

Very Poorly	Poorly	Neutral	Well	Very Well
	Tonkin Gulf		Suez	Dien Bien Phu
	Tet 1		October War	
	Berlin		Tet 2	
	Korea		Jordan	
			Panama	

Task 6. Develop monitoring, implementation, and contingency plans

Very Poorly	Poorly	Neutral	Well	Very Well
	Suez	Tet 2	Tonkin Gulf	Dien Bien Phu
	Tet 1		Jordan	
	Berlin		October War	
	Korea		Panama	

Very Well = 4 or more recognitions of the task
Well = 2 or 3 recognitions of the task
Neutral = 0 or 1 recognition or omission of the task
Poorly = 2 or 3 omissions of the task
Very Poorly = 4 or more omissions of the task

the size of the NSC to include the director of the Arms Control and Disarmament Agency, the Agency for International Development, and the head of the U.S. Information Agency, among others. The purpose of the NSC is to promote policy coordination among the many actors with responsibility for foreign policy-making.

The NSC would seem to be a likely candidate for a crisis management team. The evidence shows a puzzling record of presidents' uses of the formal NSC to coordinate decision making during crises. In its most basic form the evidence from the nine crises studied here shows that presidents rely on their advisers, who are members of the NSC, and have come increasingly to rely on the national security adviser, but they have tended to avoid the formal NSC as a crisis decision-making body.[3] The record from the Truman crises shows the president careful not to use the NSC as a decision-making body and thus decrease his prerogative. He would use it as a body to be briefed and as a forum for discussion, but he relied on ad hoc forums for key moments of decision. The record is similar for crises in the Eisenhower administration. President Eisenhower used decision-making groups whose membership overlapped with the membership of the NSC. He did consult with the full NSC at times during both crises studied here, but he did not use the NSC as a decision-making body.

President Johnson used a subgroup of the NSC as his decision-making team. This group (the Tuesday lunch group) did contain the statutory members of the NSC, though often not the vice president. It has been widely noted that Johnson liked to inform the full NSC, not deliberate with it. The flow of advice to Johnson, however, came largely from members of the NSC, even if Johnson did not wish to call the group the NSC. The difference between Johnson using the NSC and not using the NSC but using most of its members is largely a semantic distinction. It is interesting to note, however, that Johnson, like Truman, seemed to believe he had more control over the process of decision making if he did not convene the formal National Security Council, but instead relied on its members in other forums.

The Nixon record is similar in this regard. Nixon used the Washington Special Actions Group for crisis decision making. This group was one of six committees chaired by Henry Kissinger and was a subunit of the National Security Council (see George 1980, 156; Prados 1991). The evidence indicates that Nixon, like Johnson, used the NSC framework for decision making but did not call it the NSC. Similarly, President Bush consulted with the NSC, even announced to it that he wanted plans for when Noriega would overstep one day. He also relied heavily on his national security adviser, Brent Scowcroft, to coordinate policy planning and to probe those plans. But when the moment of decision came, it was not at a formal NSC meeting, though the members of the NSC were present (apparently except for Vice President Quayle, whom he had informed earlier of his decision).

This evidence shows that an understanding of the "formal" structures of decision making is only one part of comprehending crisis decision making. Informal (unofficial) networks of decision makers and ad hoc groups of advisers are evident in the crises examined here. The members of these networks cut across formal organizational boundaries. The evidence also suggests that while the NSC may be a useful instrument for routine policy planning and coordination, presidents do not find it a useful tool for crisis decision making. Each of the presidents studied in this project adapted the mechanisms for routine decision making to his own wishes during foreign policy crises.

One of the recurring themes in the case studies concerning the (non)use of the NSC, though use of the people who are part of the NSC, is the interest by presidents to be able to draw on input from others without yielding any power in the process. From Truman through Bush we see presidents as positional guardians, carefully retaining agenda and decision power to themselves. This is an interesting trend, especially when coupled with the inherent powers for the president that reside in foreign, as opposed to domestic, policy. Foreign policy is a place where presidents are less constrained, and operating outside the confines of the formal NSC seems to be seen by presidents as another way to escape institutional constraint. As we see most clearly in the Bush case, secrecy is another way for the president to retain power (DeFrank and McDaniel 1990; Hoffman 1990). This issue, the flip side of which is accountability, takes particular prominence in the wake of the cold war and raises a number of questions about democratic theory and accountability that go far beyond this study.

About the Relative Merits of Organizational Forms

The evidence from these nine crises indicates some very preliminary lessons about the organizational models used by Truman, Eisenhower, Johnson, Nixon, and Bush. First, it is important to note that these presidents each used some variant of the formalistic model. That should not be surprising. Richard Johnson (1974) shows that Presidents Truman, Eisenhower, Johnson, and Nixon all used a formalistic approach to manage the White House generally, and George (1980) argues that they all used that model to organize routine foreign policy-making. The formalistic model was a baseline approach to the management of decision making for each of them. Bush's preference for formalism is perhaps less well known and easily disguised because of his collegial personal style. While these presidents shared some of this formalism, when a crisis began, each president responded in different ways. Truman maintained the formalism and grafted it onto ad hoc decision groups. Eisenhower constructed an ultimate decision unit at the top that included many competitive characteristics. Johnson used a collegial group at the top of the formalistic structures. Nixon and Kissinger decreased the size of the decision unit, ultimately to the two of them, and forced a greater volume of information through the existing structures and demanded an increased analytic capacity from those structures. Bush maintained his formalism but maintained a personal level of collegiality to engender teamwork among his advisers, while retaining great authority to himself.

It is also understandable that a formalistic approach would undergird any variations the presidents would use because of the nature of policy-making in Washington since the end of World War II. The traditional foreign policy bureaucracy (e.g., the State Department and the Defense Department) has grown tremendously. The number of agencies responsible for foreign policy has also proliferated. Only the National Security Council, as it is prescribed by statute, remains relatively small in size. Presidents cannot ignore this large, formal, bureaucracy. They can, however, find ways to mold decision-making arrangements across these agencies so as to maximize leverage over decision making. Ultimately, presidents may be forced to accept some formalistic component in their decision-making apparatus and construct variations on that base model, as did Eisenhower, Johnson, and Bush.

As for how the advisory structures performed in the crises, it is possible to say that the Johnson model generally performed less well than the other models, though the Truman model had some real weaknesses too. This finding may have something to do with the nature of the collegial model—which is what distinguishes the Johnson framework particularly from Eisenhower's and Nixon's. The collegial model has many strengths, but unique weaknesses as well. It may have a tendency to break down into a mutual-support group where initial assumptions and bad ideas are not challenged so as not to upset the balance and collegiality of the group. That happened to some extent in the Johnson cases. But it is not inevitable that that will happen. The collegial-formalistic model did correct itself after the Tet Offensive and became open to outside, discrepant information. Furthermore, the collegialism that was blended into Bush's formalism suffered some of the same weaknesses but not all of them. It avoided the failure to plan but fell victim to the failure to explore fully U.S. objectives and alternatives.

Perhaps a more satisfying reason for why the Johnson group performed less effectively than did the Eisenhower or Nixon groups, or why the Bush group failed to vigilantly perform part of its tasks and the Truman group others of its, focuses on presidential attention to management and process. The evidence of the Eisenhower crises show a president who was engaged and concerned with how the process of decision making was executed. The evidence of the Dien Bien Phu crisis indicates a president who was concerned that the process was not working properly and so created new structures to operate at the same time as the existing structures. This attention may serve to facilitate vigilant decision making, or the effective performance of the six generic decision-making tasks. That is evident too in the Nixon crises, though the attention was not always from Nixon himself. In the 1970 and 1973 crises, the case studies show a decision-making apparatus that was carefully managed, prodded, and driven. While it was often Kissinger who played the most active role in inspiring the bureaucracy and other decision makers, they were nevertheless urged to process information and provide analysis and advice in a thorough manner.

In the middle on this count, in the Bush case there were people responsible for contingency planning and for thinking through costs and risks. It was perhaps not so much the structure that failed to examine U.S. objectives and alternatives thoroughly in the crisis, but Bush who failed to do so, as that fell within his prescribed purview. So too for Truman. He retained to himself the job of defining objectives and may have failed to do so vigilantly. But his structures did not produce the attention to implementation plans that the Bush group did. It was perhaps never clear whose job that was in the Truman cases.

The case studies of the Johnson crises show little attention to managing the process of decision making. They portray a top decision-making group that had already decided what it wished to do. The group did not place a premium on fresh and perhaps challenging analysis. Only after the performance failure at Tet did Johnson reinvigorate his decision-making framework and did it begin to function properly.

In short, the record shows high attention to crisis decision-making management by Eisenhower and a generally effective process of decision making, and at least some attention to it in the Truman cases—this in the age supposedly before the "birth" of crisis decision-making management. The record also shows high attention to crisis management in the Nixon cases and a generally effective record of procedural performance. The record from the Bush case shows substantial attention to delegation of the tasks of developing contingencies. The evidence does not show such careful attention by Johnson until the Clifford group provided it. Indeed, the case studies show generally poor decision making until the Clifford group began its review after Tet. Future research will need to address this question of organizational form versus attention to organizational management, and the quality of decision-making processes.

About Learning During Crises

The evidence of presidential management discussed in chapter 3 provides some insights into how presidents learn from their past experiences in crisis decision making and from each other's experiences. Following Lovell's use (1984, 1987), I refer to organizational learning as a process of organizational change in response to some event. Instances of an advisory structure being changed by the president, especially when its purpose is to change the procedures of decision making with reference to some past experience, is conceptualized as learning in this project. The concept of crisis decision-making management implies an attempt to structure and control a process and to iteratively refine the structure-process "fit" over time (cf. Hayes, Wheelwright, and Clark 1988). In this section I discuss some examples of how Truman, Eisenhower, Johnson, Nixon, and Bush learned about managing crisis policy-making structures from their own past and from each other.

Perlmutter argues that crisis decision-making management was first institutionalized in the Kennedy-Johnson NSC system but that Kissinger replaced this institutionalized structure with his own personal diplomacy (1975, 317). Lord (1988, 101) notes that crisis planning was firmly established for the first time during the Reagan administration in the Crisis Management Center (CMC) in 1983. The CMC worked out of the Old Executive Office Building and reported to the national security adviser. The CMC operated with its own staff. Also at this time there was a Crisis Pre-Planning Group chaired by the deputy national security assistant (Lord 1988, 101).

This set of structures for crisis management did not emerge from nowhere. Presidents have been paying attention to these issues for some time. Stephen Hess argues that presidents mostly learn about organizing the presidency as a response to the perceived weaknesses of their predecessor but that there are times when important lessons are learned along the way (1988). Kennedy, for example, learned a great deal about how to handle a crisis from the performance failure at the Bay of Pigs, and he put those lessons to work during the Cuban missile crisis (see Hess 1988, 81–82).

President Truman
There is little evidence of on-the-job learning in the two Truman crises studied here. Still, it is clear from the case studies that Truman thought in managerial terms about crisis decision-making management. He liked for-

malism and found ways to adapt his crisis machinery to his style. He relied on jurisdictions, channels, and expertise in both the Berlin and Korean crises. He used ad hoc forums extensively in both crises as a way to get information and advice and still retain decision-making authority to himself. The National Security Council was used more in the Korean case than the Berlin crisis, but in both crises the NSC was used more as a briefing body than as a decision-making body. Truman seemed satisfied with the results of the Berlin crisis and the process that attended it and sought to structure the process in the Korean crisis in a similar manner, since the cases seemed analogous to him as tests of U.S. resolve (Truman 1956, 131; Paige 1968, 170; Bernstein 1977b, 8; Donovan 1982, 204). While there were some personnel changes between the 1948 and 1950 crises, there was little other change.

President Eisenhower

There are no clear references to Eisenhower learning about crisis management in the case studies of Dien Bien Phu or Suez, which—as with Truman—is not to say that Eisenhower paid no attention to such things. "Eisenhower brought with him to the White House very definite ideas of how staffs should be constructed and should work" (Hess 1988, 63). Eisenhower had a keen sense of the importance of organization and the effect of organization on the ways groups do their work from his experience in the military. The identification of such management savvy is usually reserved for President Kennedy's performance during the Cuban missile crisis. Nevertheless, it is clearly evident even before Kennedy.

Andrew Goodpaster, Eisenhower's staff assistant, quoted one of Eisenhower's philosophies of decision making as the warning, "Now boys, let's not make our mistakes in a hurry" (Kernell and Popkin 1986, 43). Eisenhower brought with him an appreciation of patience, deliberation, and thoroughness, and he enforced these qualities on his staff. Eisenhower set up formal, largely hierarchical structures, whose job it was to methodically sift through information and provide analysis. He was also concerned that too closed a structure would choke off debate. He liked competition and debate, so he found ways to build it into the way that advisory groups operated, even during crises. While none of the case studies links these philosophies to a specific experience of Eisenhower as president, they were clearly lessons that Eisenhower had learned and brought with him to the White House.

President Johnson

Lyndon Johnson was a participant in decision making for the Bay of Pigs and the Cuban missile crisis. These events, and Kennedy's handling of them, deeply shaped his own philosophy of crisis management. Johnson also appreciated the structure and control of the Eisenhower model. He therefore sought to build a crisis management system that was smaller and more collegial than Eisenhower's advisory groups, but which was also smaller and more formal than Kennedy's. Johnson avoided the full National Security Council as much as possible. He did not trust the "experts" (note their performance at the Bay of Pigs, for example). Nor was he comfortable with all the members of the full NSC (Austin 1971, 32; Halberstam 1972; Prados 1991). Johnson relied instead on the Tuesday lunch group, a subgroup of the NSC. This group usually included Rusk, McNamara, Bundy, and Wheeler (and Clifford on occasion). This group operated informally and collegially, though it reflected a formal organizational structure as well.

The most interesting instance of Johnson learning about his own crisis management approach occurred during and after the 1968 Tet Offensive. The shock that Tet provided made Johnson look again at how he was being advised about the war. Johnson set up the Clifford Task Force to provide a full review of U.S. policy in Vietnam in the wake of Tet—the first open examination of American policy in the region since at least NSAM 288 in 1964. Furthermore, Johnson agreed to meet again with the Wise Men. Clifford knew that the group had come full circle since the beginning of the war and that now its members were largely opposed to the U.S. policy in Southeast Asia. Johnson listened to this group as well.

Johnson's shake-up of the advisory process in the aftermath of Tet led to the first proper examination of U.S. policy since the war began. Underlying assumptions could be examined; a full range of alternatives could be discussed. "After Tet 1968 the decision-making process functioned properly for the first time" (Schandler 1977, 338). It did so in large part because Johnson allowed it to do so by incorporating new structures into decision making. He learned that the old decision-making routines had failed him.

President Nixon

In a similar pattern, there is little evidence of on-the-job learning about crisis management by Richard Nixon. That is not to say, however, that he had not learned a great deal about how to manage decision making and had not developed clear ideas about how to run the White House before he came into office. Hess argues that "Nixon was clearly a management-conscious president who was seriously concerned with the way the White House would be organized" (1988, 104). Nixon set up a foreign policy-making system that was highly centralized and that afforded a large measure of presidential control. The evidence shows that Nixon and Kissinger operated nearly as a dyad at the top of a very hierarchical information-processing system during crises. Nixon's preference in a crisis was to "speed up" the process, force more information and analysis through the structure to the top (Dowty 1984, 187). While there was much reorganization in the Nixon White House (see George 1980, chap. 10; cf. Hess 1988, chap. 8), there was remarkably little change in the structure of crisis decision making between 1970 and 1973.

President Bush

It is hard to discern organizational learning in the Bush administration because only one crisis from it was studied here. Still we do see in the Bush case references to lessons learned from past experience. Most generally, Bush had been a part of the Reagan administration and was thus concerned about its past (not to mention his own) with Noriega and Panama, as well as other events. Kempe reports that Bush wished to avoid the errors of Iran-Contra and Grenada in particular (1990, 12). More specifically, the missed opportunity of the failed coup in October led to an increase in the intensity and tempo with which the Bush crisis team worked on a range of intervention angles, from the operation itself to the publicity and legality of it (Woodward 1991, 100–101; Kempe 1990, 11; Flanagan 1993, 30). Bush wanted more interagency coordination as well as more planning, and he increased the flow of activity and importance of the Deputies' Committee to that effect (Baker 1995, 186). Furthermore, though less rooted in a systematic survey, the reports by Woodward (1991), Baker (1995), and Powell (1995) all indicate that the experience of the Panama crisis was a key learning experience that set the stage for how the Bush team would handle the crisis that would soon emerge in the Persian Gulf, and that the management strategy for the Persian Gulf crisis would be largely identical to the one followed from October through December 1989 (cf. Crabb and Mulcahy 1995).

At first glance, the aggregated evidence from the case studies would seem to show that while presidents do learn from their personal history and from the lessons they draw from past presidents' performance, they seem to learn little from their own experience in office. The small amount of variation in organizational form from one crisis to another for each president would seem to indicate this. But upon closer review, it is more correct to say that presidents learn positive and negative lessons from their own experiences in crises. If a positive lesson is learned in a crisis, that is, if the president learns that the structure used for crisis decision-making produced a process that was acceptable, then no reason exists to change the structure in the future. Time and attentions are scarce resources for presidents; they perhaps do not have time to adjust already working machinery.

After the Tet Offensive, President Johnson was forced to learn a negative lesson. Johnson was forced to see that the apparatus he had established for decision making was broken and had to be repaired. The negative feedback from the environment demonstrated to Johnson that his advisory structure had to be changed. Johnson changed it. Those changes made a difference, as the advisory process began to work properly again. Furthermore, it is interesting to note that Johnson did not make personnel changes after the Tet Offensive decision-making performance failure, but rather, he made organizational and structural changes (which stands in contrast with Kennedy's handling of the Bay of Pigs fiasco). No heads rolled. Instead, the same people who had been around Johnson all along were put into new roles, and new procedural patterns emerged. From this example and others, it is reasonable to at least tentatively conclude that presidents draw positive and negative lessons from their performance and the performance of their advisory structures during crises. Positive lessons are not likely to lead to organizational change. Negative lessons are more likely to lead to such change.

The clearest examples of on-the-job learning in the crises studied here are from the Johnson and Bush administrations, and each is related to a significant performance failure. The Johnson group's failure during the Tet crisis and the Bush group's failure to be prepared and coordinated during the October 1989 coup in Panama seemed to reflect a deficient decision-making process. Each focused the president's attention on the need for structural and management change and invigoration. This finding makes some theoretical sense as well as reflecting empirical facts. Performance failures provide strong feedback from the environment that something is wrong and needs attention. The only lesson to learn in lieu of that negative feedback is that things are working properly and that no modification is necessary. I would suggest that presidents generally think things that "ain't broke" do not need fixing.

Conclusions about Presidential Management

The record of crisis decision-making structures and processes that is presented in this and the preceding chapters shows that presidents do, in fact, pay attention to crisis decision-making management, and they have done so for a long time. The evidence also shows that crisis decision-making groups can perform the tasks of decision making quite well. Post–World War II American foreign policy is not one long record of decision-making debacles. Indeed, the tasks of making decisions in a crisis were accomplished in a generally effective manner in seven or eight of the ten opportunities for decision making examined in this project.

The record also indicates that presidents respond to the onset of a crisis with a variety of organizational configurations for their advisory groups. Presidents Truman, Eisenhower, Johnson, Nixon, and Bush all used some variation of a formalistic approach to advisory group management. These presidents were similar with respect to how they preferred to manage the White House and foreign policy-making during routine periods. However, they set up quite different advisory structures for crisis decision making. Truman retained a high degree of formalism in ad hoc settings. Eisenhower used competitive components to complement his formalistic style. Johnson created a collegial-formalistic hybrid. Nixon retained much of his routine structure that was very formalistic in nature. Nixon relied extensively on Henry Kissinger in a way that Eisenhower and Johnson did not rely on another single individual. Bush used collegialism to complement his formalism and do-it-yourself approach. In general, the Eisenhower and Nixon groups performed the tasks of providing information, advice, and analysis to the president more effectively than did the Johnson group.

The evidence from this project suggests that presidents do learn from their own experiences in crisis decision making. Negative lessons (i.e., lessons that emerge from a performance failure and negative feedback from the environment) are more likely to lead to organizational change. The evidence shows a stable pattern of personnel within each administration. That may not be surprising for Eisenhower and Nixon since their advisory groups generally performed well in these crises. But it may be so for Johnson, whose advisory group had largely failed to adequately perform the tasks of decision making in the Vietnam crises. Johnson responded to this failure by changing the way decision making took place in his administration, rather than changing who was making decisions in his administration. This action speaks to presidents' attention to the structure, as opposed to the composition, of advisory groups.

It is not fair to say that the performance of the Eisenhower group may have differed because of the allied relationships involved their crises. First, the crises did not involve allies in a way that was unique from the other crises. Both of the Truman crises involved allied relationships, as did the Nixon crises. Indeed, Nixon and Kissinger had to deal with more allies and opponents in the 1970 and 1973 crises than did Eisenhower in 1954 or 1956. If anything, we might expect the Nixon structure to be more fractured and open than the Eisenhower structure, but such was not the case. It is unlikely that the nature of the crises in the Eisenhower administration led to its advisory structure. Furthermore, the case studies demonstrate clearly (especially Burke and Greenstein 1989) that dealing with allies was a part of the structure of decision making for Eisenhower, but not the determining factor of that structure. Eisenhower had to communicate with the French in 1954 and with Britain, France, and Israel in 1956. But the competitive/formalistic structure had little to do with the allied relationships. It had everything to do with how Eisenhower managed a group of advisers to help him sort through information and provide analysis and advice. Similarly, Nixon and Kissinger had to deal with myriad allies and opponents in 1970 and 1973, but their decision-making structure was determined by how Nixon wanted a decision-making group to work, rather than by how he needed to communicate with allies.

It may be the case, however, that the Johnson pattern of decision making was unique to Vietnam decision making. There are a couple of avenues out of this problem. First, Eisenhower also had to deal with a Vietnam crisis. We can juxtapose Eisenhower's management and Johnson's to see that "Vietnam" did not lead to a specific organizational response. Second (and more satisfying), future research should include non-Vietnam cases for Johnson to see how he managed advisory structures and decision making in those crises. As for Nixon's crises both dealing with the Middle East, the record of organizational response in the crises is similar to Nixon's routine pattern of decision-making management. I would not expect this management structure to be altered in other crises.[4] But that is an empirical question. Future research should include crises in regions other than the Middle East for the Nixon administration, as well as crises other than Vietnam for the Johnson administration. In the concluding sections that follow, I discuss some other findings from this research that point to other directions worthy of further investigation and some additional concluding items.

Lessons for Future Research

A number of issues emerged during this study that were not a part of the original design of the study and that therefore did not receive adequate attention. It is perhaps instructive to discuss here some of these issues as they were discovered and as topics for future research on presidential management and crisis decision making.

Allies in Crisis

The crises in the Truman, Eisenhower, and Nixon administrations included some degree of dealing with allied nations as well as opponents. This aspect was not fully explored here as it was outside the goals of this project, but it points to the potential importance of the presence or absence of allies in a crisis. While the presence of allies may be only a complicating factor for national decision making, this is an empirical question that future research should explore. Decision-making structures and processes may differ because allies need to be consulted and actions may need to be coordinated. Truman, Eisenhower, and Nixon had perhaps as many allies to deal with as opponents, and we might wish to know more about what difference for organization and decision making it might make if allies are part of decision making in a crisis.

A dichotomy of "allied crisis" and "nonallied crisis" may not be tenable. As was the case with the Truman, Eisenhower, and Nixon administrations, dealing with allies may simply be a part of dealing with crises in general and may have no particular impact on decision makers except as a complicating factor and coordination problem. Conversely, the presence of allies could serve as a benefit by enabling the sharing of costs in the crisis. The evidence from the cases included in this project suggests that allies provide only a complicating factor in a crisis, though it was an ally, Mayor Ernst Reuter of Berlin, who suggested the airlift to General Clay. Allies may make crises more complicated, rather than fundamentally changing the nature of the crisis. But this is an empirical question that could be answered in a more satisfactory way by increasing the number of cases included in a study and by incorporating allied and nonallied crises in the investigation. Cases can also be reexamined with a question set focused on interallied relations. In these ways, findings could be distinguished by the presence or absence of an ally.

The Object of Threat

The crises examined here show some variation in the object of threat. American troops were threatened in the Gulf of Tonkin and the Tet Offensive, but French troops were threatened at Dien Bien Phu, and Israel was threatened in the Middle East crises. American interests were threatened in Berlin and Korea (and maybe Panama, though that is more of a stretch), but not Americans per se (although some Americans were abused and one killed in Panama). Thus, crisis decision-making management and decision-making processes may differ because of the different object of threat in a crisis. This can be a simple dichotomy, noting whether the object of threat in the crisis is American territory or troops, or other objects, such as U.S. allies or interests. The suggestion here would be that crisis organization and dynamics may differ because American troops, as opposed to someone else's, are the object of threat. For example, did Eisenhower's decision-making group behave differently in the Dien Bien Phu crisis than Johnson's did in the Tonkin Gulf crisis because French troops and interests were in danger at Dien Bien Phu, while in the Gulf of Tonkin American troops and interests were in danger?

This project did not address this issue, but it suggests that this may not be an important factor, since Eisenhower's decision-making apparatus seemed to respond with more diligence when an ally was threatened than did Johnson's when the United States's own troops were threatened. This is a counterintuitive finding. One would expect American decision makers to respond with more diligence and to organize with more care when their own troops were in danger. But perhaps not. The findings in this project cannot determine the ultimate importance of the differing objects of threat for decision making, and a simple dichotomy for the object of threat (U.S. or non-U.S.) may not be theoretically tenable. In the age of nuclear weapons and cold war tensions that future projects will likely continue to explore even now that the cold war has ended, threats in even distant places do have implications for American security. President Eisenhower was certainly concerned that the Suez crisis could escalate to general war, as was Truman, and Nixon was definitely concerned that the Middle East crises might lead to general war. But while difficult, future research should try to account for this concern by including cases where the object of threat varies with a sufficient number of cases of each type to provide for useful comparison.

Presidential Elections

The results of this project point to the potential importance of American presidential elections for decision-making behavior during crises. A clear example of this finding can be seen in the aftermath of the Tet Offensive when President Johnson decided not to seek reelection in 1968. Other research has shown that the use of force may help the president's public popularity (e.g., Brody 1991; Jentleson 1992; Mueller 1974; Ostrom and Job 1986; Russett 1990). We have little systematic evidence about how elections may affect the behavior of American presidents and advisory groups in crises. Truman's attention was on the 1948 election during the Berlin crisis. Eisenhower was certainly concerned about the 1956 election during the Suez crisis; the "protector of the peace" cannot very well go to war on the eve of an election. Nixon argues in his memoirs that "if the Suez crisis had not arisen during the heat of a presidential election campaign a different decision would have been made" (1978, 179). While Eisenhower continued to maintain that he had made the proper decision in 1956 (thus disagreeing with Nixon's claim), this does point to the possibility that the presence of an election could have an effect on how presidents respond to crises. Moïse argues that the 1964 presidential election created tremendous pressures on Johnson to strike North Vietnam (1996, 211). The crises studies here, in combination with the literature of presidential popularity and the use of force, suggest that the presence of presidential elections may be an important factor in crisis decision making. Future research should address this issue by including more cases of election-year and nonelection-year crises so that their behavior can be compared.

Simultaneous Crises

The crises studied here at least suggest the potential importance of simultaneous crises, or a "compound crisis" (Williams 1976, 197), as a special class of crises. In 1956, the Soviet invasion of Hungary was ongoing as the Suez crisis began. In 1964, civil rights workers were murdered in Mississippi while Johnson waited for the retaliatory strike against North Vietnam. In 1970, the crisis over the invasion of Cambodia and the potential crisis over Soviet submarine bases at Cienfuegos, Cuba, sparked during the same time period as the crisis over Jordan's civil war. And in 1973, the Watergate domestic crisis came to a head in the Saturday Night Massacre at the same time that Kissinger was in Moscow trying to negotiate a ceasefire in the October War. The structure of crisis management and the dynamics of crisis behavior may be different when more than one crisis occurs at the same time.

Future research should address this question by including an increased number of cases that allow the analyst to sort crises by whether or not other crises are ongoing. That will, however, be a difficult task. It will be difficult theoretically, let alone empirically, to disentangle crises that occur simultaneously. Nevertheless, our knowledge of foreign policy crises should include a better understanding of the dynamics of singular and compound crises.

Protracted Crises

There may be an important distinction to be made between protracted crises and short-term crises. In a protracted crisis, such as in Vietnam or the war in Korea, there are distinct opportunities for choice that may require an immediate response. So in the war in Korea we can separate out the decision to intervene or the decision to cross the Thirty-eighth Parallel. The environment of protracted crisis, however, may affect the process of decision making when a discrete opportunity presents itself. Was decision making during Tet different from other crises because Tet happened during a protracted crisis period? The crises in the Middle East may also be special cases of a protracted crisis in that region. These questions might be addressed in future research by including cases of crisis that differ in this respect and by comparing their dynamics. Foreign policy research has perhaps not taken adequate account of the distinction between crises and protracted conflicts (cf. Brecher 1984). An examination of the nature of protracted crises may also illuminate some of the middle ground between crisis and routine policy-making.

Utility of the Research Design

Before presenting some concluding observations about the research presented here, I should comment on the adequacy of the method used to pursue the questions that preoccupy this project. The coding form used in this investigation (see appendix) was useful in two ways. First, the questions that the coding form asks should correspond with the issues that the project's underlying theory indicates as important. The coding form does so. Indeed, the items in question set 1, which attempt to identify what organizational model was in use during the crises, almost exactly copy the items identified by George (1980) and R. Johnson (1974) as the most important characteristics of each model. The items in question set 2 also capture the essence of the decision-making tasks that are identified in the theory of decision making drawn upon in this project. Beyond that, the coding form produced readily interpretable results.

Second, the coding form included open-ended items and items that went beyond the bare minimum of factors that theory indicated should be on such a form. Such inclusions allowed for the discovery of facts, processes, and lessons well beyond the immediate goals of this project. These other items, for example, suggested the potential importance of presidential elections and led to evidence of the nature of the relationship between Nixon and Kissinger, about the role of the Wise Men for Johnson, and ultimately about the political nature of foreign policy crises. The form kept the investigator "close" to the case studies and therefore kept the project open to the uniqueness of each event. At the same time it focused the project on the similarities of each crisis.

The use of the case studies was a sound strategy, if labor-intensive. It is a strategy that does not denigrate original case studies. Quite to the contrary, it relies and depends on in-depth, original case studies. The endeavor is to use existing case materials as a "data set," to synthesize this knowledge and put it to use to address questions that are more general in nature than those that a single case study might address. Ultimately, the findings of the case-survey method are only as good as the case studies that it draws upon. On the whole, the case studies used in this project were of high quality. While no single study told the whole story of a crisis, a relatively complete picture could be gathered by drawing on all of the case studies of a crisis.

The crises were generally well covered by case studies. The evidence was most slim in the Suez crisis, as no definitive decision analysis exists for this crisis, and perhaps least reliable for the Panama crisis. However, even in these cases, the material was sufficient to identify the nature of the advisory models used and the characteristics of the decision-making processes they produced. The case studies of the crisis at Dien Bien Phu are particularly helpful, mostly due to the recent research by scholars on newly declassified records at the Eisenhower archives. The case studies of the Nixon crises are fewer in number, perhaps, but very detailed and based upon—in William Quandt's case—inside knowledge of the decision-making process.

By drawing on existing case studies, the project draws on a full picture of decision making in the nine crises. As such, it contributes not only to our knowledge of these crises, but also to the methodology of investigation. The project stands as an example of the case-survey method in the analysis of foreign policy and the study of the presidency. It demonstrates another way that researchers can use evidence to address empirical and theoretical questions. However, this method cannot proceed without a body of thorough case studies of decision making in the crises to be studied. The few case studies of U.S. decision making in the 1967 war in the Middle East, for example, would make it difficult to apply this approach to that case without augmenting the evidence with primary materials.

The utility of the generic management models is a less straightforward issue than determining the utility of the coding form or the usefulness of the original case studies. In one sense, the use of these ideal models was very helpful. They provide an order for inquiry, a place to start. They focus attention on characteristics of decision-making structures that exist in the White House during crises. But only in the Truman and Nixon cases do we find the generic model being approximated in practice, and the formalistic model they both shared had many significant differences. In each of the other cases, hybrids of these ideal types were used. This is not necessarily a shortcoming of the models. After all, these models, and the frame of inquiry that they provide, did allow for the discovery of these hybrid forms. The project did not force an idealized vision on the empirical evidence because of these three models. The coding form, and the case-survey method, recognized variations of these ideal models. That is an asset.

But it is also the case that an exclusive reliance on these ideal models may not get us very far. The empirical world is not as neat as the theoretical world. The evidence indicates that presidents use variations of these hybrid models. Thus, our theorizing about management models needs to be broadened. More attention should also focus on the consequences of "mixing" these ideal types. In this area, the research design and findings make a substantive contribution to the study of foreign policy-making. Future research should continue to pursue this issue by exploring what other types of arrangements presidents construct for decision making during crises and the consequences of other variations on these ideal types.

Moreover, further attention should be paid to the logic behind these organization models. What are the incentives and constraints in each model that should produce certain behaviors or processes? Just as Bendor and Hammond (1992) demonstrate that Allison's models are not well specified, such an examination may reveal that further logical specification of the management models used here is in order (cf. Hermann and Preston 1993; Orbovich and Molnar 1992; Pika 1988; Walcott and Hult 1995). It may also be true that there are some underlying dimensions that are important for future research to explore. Role specification and monitoring provisions are two examples of dimensions that may meaningfully distinguish presidents' management configurations.

The design of the project, bolstered by its findings, also contributes to our understanding of the process of decision making. The project recasts questions about decision-making processes from the usual preoccupation with malfunctions to a focus on analytically distinct tasks that may be performed well or poorly. The findings show a wide diversity in the performance of these tasks, ranging from great vigilance to outright neglect. But the findings also show that it is important to think not only about what goes wrong in decision making, but also about what goes right. Theory that aspires to be policy-relevant must address both sides of this equation by striving to develop theories of success as well as failure.

Conclusion

Beyond the immediate and middle-range lessons that were discussed in this chapter, this project has shed light on a number of other broader issues. Perhaps the most important of these broader issues concerns the very nature of foreign policy crises. It is undoubtedly true that some crises are external shocks to routine situations that require a response within a certain amount of time. It is also true that there is a measure of subjectivity to crises. In an effort to treat crises systematically, we have tended to view crises as objective situations that afford use-of-force options that are characterized by different levels of threat, time to respond, and surprise (Brecher 1978; Hermann 1969). This project has worked from that tradition. Yet Halper has reminded us that decision makers tend to define situations as crises that they see as important, and presidents enjoy some latitude in this regard (1971, 207). Crises may be a real boon to presidential power, too, and may therefore be tempting to construct, as criticism may be able to be muted in a crisis (Halper 1971, 227). While Truman certainly did not enjoy any muting of criticism in his crises, Halper's point is an important one, and it is bolstered by the crises studied here. There would appear to be some degree of latitude within which presidents may define or construct situations as crises.

There was no "crisis" for the United States in the Gulf of Tonkin in 1964, yet a crisis emerged. In 1949 it was not apparent that an invasion of South Korea by North Korea would lead to a crisis for the United States, yet it did. The end of the cold war, the drug war, and George Bush's image and personal history with Manuel Noriega may have conspired to create a crisis when it did not "objectively" exist in Panama. Contrariwise, during the crisis over the civil war in Jordan, the Nixon administration learned that the Soviets were building a submarine base at Cienfuegos, Cuba, capable of servicing Soviet nuclear-armed submarines. This construction was a violation of the agreements that followed the Cuban missile crisis and provided at least as much threat to the United States as did the original Cuban crisis. Yet no "crisis" emerged. All this suggests that we have not paid sufficient attention to the political process by which situations come to be defined by decision makers as crises (see Haney 1995b). Such an analysis might proceed along the lines of a traditional decision analysis, a study of ontologies and problem representations (Sylvan and Thorson 1992), or a critical "constructivist" analysis (Weldes 1992). Whatever the form, we should return some of our attention to the subjective, constructed, political, definitional nature of foreign policy crises. Crises are more than exogenous shocks; there are important endogenous components of crises.

In an important article, Roxanne Doty (1993) argues that foreign policy is a product of social construction. Analyses of foreign policy-making often focus on the "why" questions—for example, why did the United States not intervene in Indochina in 1954? Doty reminds us that there are important "how" questions that must be addressed. How is it possible that policymakers came to see a situation as a crisis in the first place, for example, that must be responded to in some way? How are the stakes constructed? How are subjects and objects and appropriate means defined? These questions are beyond this study, though the research presented herein suggests their importance, perhaps especially pertaining to how crises come to be defined as such. But while these questions are beyond the scope of this study, they should not be beyond the scope of our field of study. Future research must also focus on the "how possible" questions.

The evidence presented here also suggests that future crisis research may need to distinguish between types of crises in a more expansive way than the threat-time-surprise conceptualization (or threat–time–use-of-force options in Brecher 1978). Other factors may make them able to be distinguished analytically, if not empirically. These factors include the presence or absence of allies, presidential elections, and simultaneous crises, as well as the difference in crises because of the object of threat. These factors combine with the aforementioned point about the constructed nature of crises to speak to the need for broader theorizing and research into the nature of international crises.

The present study has sought to synthesize case-study research of nine foreign policy crises across five presidential administrations. In the process, it has tried to increase our understanding of the decision-making structures and processes that emerged in these crises by applying the case-survey approach to the analysis of U.S. foreign policy. There are five points that emerge from this project that should be stressed.

First, the evidence shows the presidency to be an institution that is intimately linked with its inhabitant, but an institution that can be studied in systematic and comparative ways. The number of post–World War II presidents is small, but there are ways to overcome this small N in future research by focusing on other independent variables. The project points to some of these avenues.

Second, the project highlights the constructed nature of foreign policy crises. The evidence indicates that crises are political and subjective processes, not just external shocks. Future research should follow this lead, as it suggests that previous theorizing about crises may be inadequate.

Third, the project has sought to add to our substantive understanding of the nature and structure of decision making during crises. It has substantively explored the relationship among the structures that presidents employ, the attention they give to managing those structures in a crisis, and the way that the advisory groups perform the tasks of crisis decision making. Decision making is a structured process with behavioral, though not predictable, consequences. Decision making does not occur magically. It happens within the confines of a structure set up by the president. Such structures are intended to increase the likelihood that the advisory group will adequately perform the tasks of decision making, but there are no guarantees (Hammond 1992, 170). These structures can be identified and studied to explore how the structure and management of decision-making groups affect the processes of decision making. While the findings of this project do not allow for firm conclusions about the systematic impact of different structures on decision-making processes, they suggest that this link may exist, they give us some initial insights in this regard, and they suggest that further exploration of this link would be beneficial.

Fourth, the project begins to address the relative importance of structure and composition in decision making. The people from whom presidents draw advice matter, but so too do the roles they play. This project did not explore the "formal" decision-making groups presidents use, nor did it focus exclusively on "informal" networks. Rather, the effort was to identify, characterize, and study the advisory networks that presidents actually employed, regardless of whether their members had a government job. I have focused on the decision-making groups in use during crises and explored how the groups performed their work. It is undeniably true that presidents must be surrounded with good people, but that is not enough. The findings from this study reveal the importance of structure and management, not just composition. Johnson was surrounded by good people; it made little difference for the quality of decision making in the Tonkin Gulf crisis and the period leading up to Tet in 1968. Good people are important; effective structures and attention to their management would seem to be equally vital.

Finally, the evidence clearly demonstrates that presidents do pay attention to the management of decision-making groups during crises. The evidence indicates a strong record of crisis decision-making management before the alleged birth thereof in the Kennedy administration. Presidents do try to organize and manage decision-making groups during crises. The record shows that they do so in a variety of different ways, and with different results. A truly policy-relevant theory (George 1992) must address questions policymakers have about different approaches to management, different ways to execute decision making, and the likely effects of the former on the latter. This preliminary investigation cannot provide solid answers to the last question, but it does provide some initial evidence for the first two. The evidence would suggest that a future president should think hard, and ahead of time, about how decision making will be managed in a crisis. The tasks of decision making are not self-executing; people need to be arranged around information and each other. The evidence would also suggest that advisers need to have a sense of responsibility for the process. Engendering this sense of responsibility through task assignment is important. And the evidence would indicate that groups often fall short in follow-through. A president would be well advised to both "think again" before deciding and to "think about after" before deciding. In short, a policy-relevant theory of crisis decision making is possible. But to construct it, further attention must be made to the development of behavioral theories of decision making and institutions and to the production of theories of success and failure. The evidence is out there in case studies and archives. We must find creative ways to sift through that evidence and from it construct theory.

Coding Form

Crisis:

Case Study Source:

Question Set 1: What organizational model for decision making is used by the president?

Are the channels of communication:

_____ multiple and open (collegial, competitive)?

_____ clearly defined and hierarchical (formalistic)?

_____ NC [not coded]

Confidence: Low   Medium   High

Is the group characterized by

_____ a structured staff system with assigned functional specialists who brief the president in an authoritative manner (formalistic)?

_____ organizational ambiguity (collegial, competitive)?

_____ NC

Confidence: Low   Medium   High

Do the members of the group have assigned or recognized jurisdictions?

_____ yes (formalistic)   _____ no (competitive, collegial)   _____ NC

Confidence: Low   Medium   High

Concerning responsibility for the decisions made,

_____ does the group stress shared responsibility for decision making (collegial)?

_____ does the president assume responsibility for making decisions (competitive, formalistic)?

_____ NC

Confidence: Low   Medium   High

Where is the president in the group?
_____ at the top (competitive, formalistic)
_____ at the center of a decision-making team (collegial)?
_____ NC

Confidence: Low   Medium   High

Are the group's procedures and routines
_____ characterized by informal procedures (collegial)?
_____ clear, formal, and structured (competitive, formalistic)?
_____ NC

Confidence: Low   Medium   High

Does the president encourage debate and conflict?
_____ yes (collegial, competitive)   _____ no (formalistic)   _____ NC

Confidence: Low   Medium   High

Does the president "reach down" for information and advice?
_____ yes (collegial, competitive)   _____ no (formalistic)   _____ NC

Confidence: Low   Medium   High

Is there explicit attention to issues of structuring an advisory process?
_____ yes   _____ no   _____ NC

Confidence: Low   Medium   High

Examples:

Is there explicit attention to changing the structure of the process in
response to some event or experience?
_____ yes   _____ no   _____ NC

Confidence: Low   Medium   High

Examples:

Is expertise salient in the decision-making group?
_____ yes   _____ no   _____ NC

Confidence: Low   Medium   High

Is a figure influential despite a lack of expertise?

____ yes   ____ no   ____ NC

Confidence: Low   Medium   High

Who?

Does the president indicate a preference

____ early in the process?   ____ late in the process?

____ only at the end of the process?   ____ NC

Confidence: Low   Medium   High

Does the president's preference change over time?

____ yes   ____ no   ____ NC

Confidence: Low   Medium   High

Indicate a typology of the participants and their positions in the group
and policy preferences:

Confidence: Low   Medium   High

Which institutional model best characterizes the essential features of the
decision-making group in the case?

____ formalistic   ____ competitive   ____ collegial   ____ hybrid model

____ NC

Confidence: Low   Medium   High

What variations on the ideal model does the president employ?

What other information was useful for determining the model used by
the president?

Identify the independent variables that may serve as competing
explanations or confounding effects—those variables that are to be held
as constant across cases as possible.

What decision, or policy alternative, is agreed upon by the group? What
actions are taken following the selection of that policy alternative?

Question Set 2: How are the decision-making tasks performed in the case?

1. Survey objectives to be fulfilled by policy response

____ −2 ____ −1 ____ 0 ____ 1 ____ 2 ____ NC

Confidence: Low Medium High

2. Canvass alternative policy responses

____ −2 ____ −1 ____ 0 ____ 1 ____ 2 ____ NC

Confidence: Low Medium High

3. Search for information

____ −2 ____ −1 ____ 0 ____ 1 ____ 2 ____ NC

Confidence: Low Medium High

4. Assimilate and process new (and perhaps discrepant) information

____ −2 ____ −1 ____ 0 ____ 1 ____ 2 ____ NC

Confidence: Low Medium High

5. Evaluate the costs, risks, and implications of the preferred choice

____ −2 ____ −1 ____ 0 ____ 1 ____ 2 ____ NC

Confidence: Low Medium High

6. Develop implementation, monitoring, and contingency plans

____ −2 ____ −1 ____ 0 ____ 1 ____ 2 ____ NC

Confidence: Low Medium High

Notes

Chapter 1

1. Applications include Greenwood's (1975) study of the American decision to use MIRV missile technology in its nuclear arsenal, Maoz's (1981) study of the Israeli raid on the Entebbe airport, and Vandenbroucke's (1984) study of the 1961 failure at the Bay of Pigs. Levy (1986) explores how organizational routines may contribute to the onset of war, Sigal (1970) uses the perspective to study the Formosa Straits crisis, and Vertzberger (1990) explores the importance of organizational routines in developing countries. Dawisha (1980) discusses the appropriateness and problems of applications of this approach to the Soviet context. Weil (1975) applies the paradigm to decision making in North Vietnam during the war in Vietnam, and Kasza (1987) studies policy-making in Japan, Peru, and Egypt with this approach. Further applications include Achen 1988; Bendor 1988; A. Downs 1967; Moe 1989; and Tullock 1987 on bureaucratic behavior. Lincoln (1982) discusses network analysis of interorganizational relations, and McGinnis (1988) discusses various ways to conceptualize foreign policy and domestic political competition. Others have sought to extend and supplement this approach. Steinbruner (1974) presents a cybernetic view of decision making to stand with the rational, cognitive, and bureaucratic models. C. Ostrom (1977) empirically tests the predictive capacity of different models of decision making, finding little difference between a Richardsonian arms race model and an organizational politics model (cf. Marra 1985). For critiques of the bureaucratic politics approach, see especially Bendor and Hammond 1992; Welch 1992; Art 1973; Krasner 1971; Nathan and Oliver 1978; Perlmutter 1974; and Steiner 1977.

2. Problems with groupthink have been discussed in a variety of places (e.g., Longley and Pruitt 1980; Ripley 1988; 't Hart 1990; Whyte 1989), and a more full evaluation of these issues is beyond the scope of this project.

3. See also Welch's (1989) criticism of the Herek, Janis, and Huth treatment of the Cuban missile crisis case and the rebuttal by Herek, Janis, and Huth (1989); and Haney's (1994a) largely confirming note on the Herek, Janis, and Huth process codings of five of their original nineteen cases.

Chapter 2

1. Haas (1986) and Tanter (1978) review much of this widely divergent literature. See also Brecher 1978; Brewer 1972; Holsti 1979; Roberts 1988; and Robinson

1972. For examples of different perspectives on studying crises, see Bobrow, Chan, and Kringen 1977 on Chinese crisis decision making, Wagner 1974 on Israeli crisis decision making, and Wilkenfeld 1991 on trigger-response mechanisms.

2. I conceptualize these as intervening variables in much the same way as Krasner (1983) sees regimes as intervening variables in state behavior.

3. Copies of the coding forms are available from the author.

4. I wish to thank David Perry and Lewis Bateman at the University of North Carolina Press for rushing me an advance copy of the excellent new study by Moïse (1996).

Chapter 3

1. The "Saturday Night Massacre" occurred while Kissinger was negotiating a peace plan in Moscow on October 20, 1973. It centered on Nixon's attempt to fire Watergate Special Prosecutor Archibald Cox. The massacre's victims included Attorney General Elliot Richardson, who resigned his post rather than heed White House Chief of Staff Alaxander Haig's order from Nixon to fire Cox. Deputy Attorney General William Ruckelshaus succeeded Richardson and promptly resigned for the same reason. He, however, was fired in lieu of the president accepting his resignation. Finally, Solicitor General Robert Bork (next in line) was named acting attorney general and fired Cox.

2. When Kissinger called the White House to check in with Chief of Staff Haig and report his difficulties in dealing with the Soviets, Haig too complained. Upon asking Haig what could possibly be going wrong in Washington, D.C., on an autumn night, Haig told Kissinger about the ongoing "Saturday Night Massacre" (Kissinger 1982, 552).

3. Only one case was used for the Bush administration due to time constraints and because the likely second case, the Persian Gulf War, would have to draw on the same types of evidence as the Panama case. It is the opinion of the author that, based upon a quick reading of some of the Persian Gulf case studies, the Bush management style was consistent across these two cases.

Chapter 4

1. This code of "well" was assigned, rather than "very well," because while the group did vigilantly perform this task, and it did so on more than one occasion, it did not do so (according to the case studies) four or more times—the requirement for the score of "very well." (This same reasoning applies in the codings that follow for other tasks and other crises.) Perhaps this distinction is not important. It may be just as theoretically interesting and not as methodologically complicating to assign a single code for the effective or not effective (or neutral) performance of a decision-making task. One can extract such single codes from tables 4 or 5 by collapsing the "well" and "very well" scores into one score and by collapsing the "poorly" and "very poorly" scores into another score. I have not pursued this route because I have tried to use the coding rules in Herek, Janis, and Huth 1987

and the theory that underlies that and other crisis decision-making analyses (e.g., Janis 1982, 1989). The approach used here does place an emphasis on the continued performance of a task, as opposed to a one-time performance of a task, albeit an effective performance.

2. This task was scored "well," as opposed to "very well," for the same reasons as in the Dien Bien Phu case. While the decision-making group performed this task effectively, it did not do so on more than three occasions, according to the case studies.

3. I suspect that Herek, Janis, and Huth (1987) took this report as an indication that no malfunction on this criterion was present in their study.

4. The similarities in leadership styles between Nixon and Kissinger that allowed both to be comfortable with these decision-making structures and procedures no doubt allowed Kissinger to fill in more easily than might have otherwise been the case. But that was the point in the Nixon White House, after all—to construct management structures that could be jointly managed (see George 1980; Haney 1995a; Hess 1988).

5. This is not unlike the problem in survey research of obtaining different results when the measures of questions asked of respondents differ slightly from one data set to another or from one year to another.

Chapter 5

1. For a different approach to studying the Eisenhower management style, see Orbovich and Molnar 1992 and Walcott and Hult 1995.

2. My thanks to a reviewer for pushing for more clarification here.

3. My thanks to Jerel Rosati for helping me clarify this point.

4. Nixon also dealt with Vietnam crises, such as the invasion of Cambodia. Initially, the Cambodian invasion, rather than the Jordanian civil war, was included in the set of Nixon crises. I ultimately used the Jordan crisis rather than the Cambodian crisis largely because the Cambodian case is a very unusual instance of crisis, if it is an instance of crisis at all. However, I had coded enough case studies of the Cambodian "crisis" to have identified the Nixon management model in that crisis as "formalistic."

References

Achen, Christopher H. 1988. "A State with Bureaucratic Politics is Representable as a Unitary Rational Actor." Paper presented at the annual meeting of the American Political Science Association, Washington, DC.

Achen, Christopher H., and Duncan Snidal. 1989. "Rational Deterrence Theory and Comparative Case Studies." *World Politics* 41:143–69.

Allison, Graham T. 1971. *Essence of Decision.* Boston: Little, Brown.

Allison, Graham T. 1979. "Public and Private Management: Are They Fundamentally Alike in All Unimportant Respects?" In *Public Management,* ed. James L. Perry and Kenneth L. Kraemer. Palo Alto, CA: Mayfield.

Allison, Graham T., and Morton H. Halperin. 1972. "Bureaucratic Politics: A Paradigm and Some Policy Implications." *World Politics* 24 (supplement): 40–79.

Allison, Graham T., and Peter L. Szanton. 1976. *Remaking Foreign Policy: The Organizational Connection.* New York: Basic Books.

Ambrose, Stephen E. 1984. *Eisenhower.* Vol. 2. New York: Simon and Schuster.

Ambrose, Stephen E. 1991. *Nixon.* Vol. 3, *Ruin and Recovery.* New York: Simon and Schuster.

Anderson, Paul A. 1983. "Decision Making by Objection and the Cuban Missile Crisis." *Administrative Science Quarterly* 28:201–222.

Anderson, Paul A. 1987. "What Do Decision Makers Do When They Make a Foreign Policy Decision?" In *New Directions in the Study of Foreign Policy,* ed. Charles F. Hermann, Charles W. Kegley, and James N. Rosenau. Boston: Unwin Hyman.

Argyris, Chris. 1967. "Some Causes of Organizational Ineffectiveness within the Department of State." Washington, DC: Center for International Systems Research, Occasional Paper No. 2. U.S. Department of State, Publication No. 8180, January.

Art, Robert J. 1968. *The TFX Decision: McNamara and the Military.* Boston: Little, Brown.

Art, Robert J. 1973. "Bureaucratic Politics and American Foreign Policy: A Critique." *Policy Sciences* 4:467–90.

Austin, Anthony. 1971. *The President's War.* Philadelphia: Lippincott.

Bacharach, Samuel B. 1989. "Organizational Theories: Some Criteria for Evaluation." *Academy of Management Review* 14:496–515.

Baker, James A. III. 1995. *The Politics of Diplomacy.* New York: Putnam.

Barilleaux, Ryan J. 1988. "Presidential Conduct of Foreign Policy." *Congress and the Presidency* 15:1–23.

Barnet, Richard J. 1971. *The Roots of War.* Baltimore, MD: Pelican Books.

Barrett, David M. 1988. "The Mythology Surrounding Lyndon Johnson, His Advisers, and the 1965 Decision to Escalate the Vietnam War." *Political Science Quarterly* 103:637–63.

Barrett, David M. 1993. *Uncertain Warriors.* Lawrence: University Press of Kansas.

Bendor, Jonathan. 1988. "Review Article: Formal Models of Bureaucracy." *British Journal of Political Science* 18:353–95.

Bendor, Jonathan, and Thomas H. Hammond. 1992. "Rethinking Allison's Models." *American Political Science Review* 86:301–22.

Benveniste, Guy. 1977. *The Politics of Expertise.* 2d ed. San Francisco: Boyd and Fraser.

Berman, Larry. 1989. *Lyndon Johnson's War.* New York: W. W. Norton.

Bernstein, Barton J. 1977a. "The Week We Went to War: American Intervention in the Korean Civil War, I." *Foreign Service Journal* 54, no. 1: 6–9, 33–35.

Bernstein, Barton J. 1977b. "The Week We Went to War: American Intervention in the Korean Civil War, II." *Foreign Service Journal* 54, no. 2: 8–11, 33–34.

Bernstein, Barton J. 1989. "The Truman Administration and the Korean War." In *The Truman Presidency,* ed. Michael J. Lacey. Cambridge: Cambridge University Press and the Woodrow Wilson International Center for Scholars.

Best, James J. 1988a. "Presidential Learning." *Congress and the Presidency* 15:25–48.

Best, James J. 1988b. "Who Talked to the President When? A Study of Lyndon B. Johnson." *Political Science Quarterly* 103:531–45.

Best, James J., and Kim DesRoches. 1991. "Learning from Crises: An Empirical Analysis of Crisis Situations in the Kennedy and Johnson Administrations." Paper presented at the annual meeting of the Midwest Political Science Association, Chicago.

Bloomfield, L. P. 1974. *The Foreign Policy Process: Making Theory Relevant.* Professional Paper No. 28. Beverly Hills, CA: Sage.

Boardman, Anthony E., and Aidan R. Vining. 1989. "Ownership and Performance in Competitive Environments." *Journal of Law and Economics* 32:1–33.

Bobrow, Davis B., Steve Chan, and James A. Kringen. 1977. "Understanding How Others Treat Crisis." *International Studies Quarterly* 21:199–223.

Bowie, Robert. 1974. *Suez 1956.* New York: Oxford University Press.

Bozeman, Barry. 1987. *All Organizations Are Public.* San Francisco: Jossey-Bass.

Brecher, Michael. 1978. "A Theoretical Approach to International Crisis Behavior." *Jerusalem Journal of International Relations* 3, no. 2–3: 5–24.

Brecher, Michael. 1980. *Decisions in Crisis.* Berkeley: University of California Press.

Brecher, Michael. 1984. "International Crises and Protracted Conflicts." *International Interactions* 11:237–97.

Brecher, Michael, and Jonathan Wilkenfeld. 1989. *Crisis, Conflict, and Instability.* New York: Pergamon.

Brewer, Thomas L. 1972. *Foreign Policy Situations.* International Studies Series. Beverly Hills, CA: Sage.

Brody, Richard. 1991. *Assessing the President.* Stanford, CA: Stanford University Press.

Buckley, Kevin. 1991. *Panama: The Whole Story.* New York: Simon and Schuster.

Bueno de Mesquita, Bruce. 1990. "Big Wars, Little Wars: Avoiding Selection Bias." *International Interactions* 16:159–69.

Bundy, McGeorge. 1988. *Danger and Survival.* New York: Random House.

Burke, John P. 1984. "Responsibilities of Presidents and Advisers." *Journal of Politics* 46:818–45.

Burke, John P. 1992. *The Institutional Presidency.* Baltimore, MD: Johns Hopkins University Press.

Burke, John P., and Fred I. Greenstein, with Larry Berman and Richard Immerman. 1989. *How Presidents Test Reality.* New York: Russell Sage Foundation.

Caldwell, Dan. 1977. "Bureaucratic Foreign Policy-Making." *American Behavioral Scientist* 21:87–110.

Campbell, Colin. 1986. *Managing the Presidency: Carter, Reagan, and the Search for Executive Harmony.* Pittsburgh: University of Pittsburgh Press.

Campbell, Colin. 1993. "Political Executives and Their Officials." In *Political Science: The State of the Discipline II,* ed. Ada W. Finifter. Washington, DC: American Political Science Association.

Campbell, Donald T. 1975. "'Degrees of Freedom' and the Case Study." *Comparative Political Studies* 8:178–93.

Campbell, Donald T., and Julian C. Stanley. 1963. *Experimental and Quasi-experimental Designs.* Chicago: Rand McNally.

Caporaso, James A. 1973. "Quasi-Experimental Approaches to the Social Sciences." In *Quasi-Experimental Approaches,* ed. James A. Caporaso and Leslie L. Roos. Evanston, IL: Northwestern University Press.

Chandler, Alfred D. 1962. *Strategy and Structure.* Cambridge: MIT Press.

Chubb, John E., and Terry M. Moe. 1990. *Politics, Markets, and America's Schools.* Washington, DC: Brookings Institution.

Clifford, Clark. 1991. *Counsel to the President.* New York: Random House.

Cohen, Bernard C., and Scott A. Harris. 1975. "Foreign Policy." In *Handbook of Political Science.* Vol. 6. Ed. Fred I. Greenstein and Nelson W. Polsby. Reading, MA: Addison-Wesley.

Cohen, Eliot A. 1986. "Why We Should Stop Studying the Cuban Missile Crisis." *National Interest* 6:3–13.

Crabb, Cecil V., and Kevin V. Mulcahy. 1995. "George Bush's Management Style and Operation Desert Storm." *Presidential Studies Quarterly* 25:251–65.

Crawford, Sue E. S., and Elinor Ostrom. 1995. "A Grammar of Institutions." *American Political Science Review* 89:582–600.

Cronin, Thomas E., and Sanford D. Greenberg, eds. 1969. *The Presidential Advisory System.* New York: Harper and Row.

Davison, W. Phillips. 1958. *The Berlin Blockade.* Princeton, NJ: Princeton University Press.

Dawisha, Karen. 1980. "The Limits of the Bureaucratic Politics Model: Observations on the Soviet Case." *Studies in Comparative Communism* 13:300–346.

DeFelice, E. Gene. 1986. "Causal Inference and Comparative Methods." *Comparative Political Studies* 19:415–37.

DeFrank, Thomas M., and Ann McDaniel. 1990. "Bush: The Secret Presidency." *Newsweek* 115, no. 1 (January 1).

De Rivera, Joseph H. 1968. *The Psychological Dimension of Foreign Policy.* Columbus, OH: Charles E. Merrill Publishing.

Destler, I. M. 1972. *Presidents, Bureaucrats, and Foreign Policy.* Princeton, NJ: Princeton University Press.

Destler, I. M., Leslie Gelb, and Anthony Lake. 1984. *Our Own Worst Enemy.* New York: Simon and Schuster.

Dilulio, John J. 1989. "Recovering the Public Management Variable: Lessons From Schools, Prisons, and Armies." *Public Administration Review* 49: 127–33.

DiMaggio, Paul J., and Walter W. Powell. 1991. Introduction to *The New Institutionalism in Organizational Analysis,* by Walter W. Powell and Paul J. DiMaggio, eds. Chicago: University of Chicago Press.

Dinges, John. 1990. *Our Man in Panama.* New York: Random House.

Donahue, John D. 1989. *The Privatization Decision.* New York: Basic Books.

Donnelly, Thomas, Margaret Roth, and Caleb Baker. 1991. *Operation Just Cause.* New York: Lexington Books.

Donovan, Robert J. 1982. *Tumultuous Years.* New York: W. W. Norton.

Doty, Roxanne Lynn. 1993. "Foreign Policy as Social Construction: A Post-Positivist Analysis of U.S. Counterinsurgency Policy in the Philippines." *International Studies Quarterly* 37:297–320.

Downs, Anthony. 1967. *Inside Bureaucracy.* Glenview, IL: Scott, Foresman.

Downs, George W. 1989. "The Rational Deterrence Debate." *World Politics* 41:225–37.

Dowty, Alan. 1978. "The U.S. and the Syria-Jordan Confrontation, 1970." *Jerusalem Journal of International Relations* 3, no. 2–3: 172–96.

Dowty, Alan. 1984. *Middle East Crisis.* Berkeley: University of California Press.

Eckstein, Harry. 1975. "Case Study and Theory in Political Science." In *Handbook of Political Science.* Vol. 7. Ed. Fred I. Greenstein and Nelson W. Polsby. Reading, MA: Addison-Wesley.

Edwards, George C. 1989. *At the Margins.* New Haven, CT: Yale University Press.

Eisenhardt, Kathleen M. 1989a. "Agency Theory: An Assessment and Review." *Academy of Management Review* 14:57–74.

Eisenhardt, Kathleen M. 1989b. "Building Theories from Case Study Research." *Academy of Management Review* 14:532–50.

Emmert, Mark A., and Michael M. Crow. 1988. "Public, Private and Hybrid Organizations." *Administration and Society* 20:216–44.

Etheredge, Lloyd S. 1978. "Personality Effects on American Foreign Policy, 1898–1968." *American Political Science Review* 72:434–51.

Etheredge, Lloyd S. 1985. *Can Governments Learn?* New York: Pergamon.

Eulau, Heinz. 1962. "Comparative Political Analysis: A Methodological Note." *Midwest Journal of Political Science* 6:397–407.

Evans, Rowland, and Robert D. Novak 1971. *Nixon in the White House.* New York: Random House.

Fearon, James D. 1991. "Counterfactuals and Hypothesis Testing in Political Science." *World Politics* 43:169–95.

Feldman, Martha S. 1993. "Organizational Theory and the Presidency." In *Researching the Presidency,* ed. George C. Edwards, John H. Kessel, and Bert A. Rockman. Pittsburgh: University of Pittsburgh Press.

Ferejohn, John A. 1987. "The Structure of Agency Decision Processes." In *Congress: Structure and Process,* ed. Mathew D. McCubbins and Terry Sullivan. Cambridge: Cambridge University Press.

Finer, Harold. 1964. *Dulles Over Suez.* Chicago: Quadrangle Books.

Flanagan, Edward M., Jr. 1993. *Battle for Panama.* Washington, DC: Brassey's.

Foyle, Douglas C. 1996. "Choices Under Pressure: Public Opinion and Decision Maker Responses to Threatening Events." Paper presented at the annual meeting of the International Studies Association, San Diego.

Frankel, Joseph. 1963. *The Making of Foreign Policy.* London: Oxford University Press.

Fredrickson, James W. 1986. "The Strategic Decision Process and Organizational Structure." *Academy of Management Review* 11:280–97.

Freedman, Lawrence. 1976. "Logic, Politics and Foreign Policy Processes: A Critique of the Bureaucratic Politics Model." *International Affairs* 52:434–49.

Frendreis, John P. 1983. "Explanation of Variation and Detection of Covariation." *Comparative Political Studies* 16:255–72.

Gaddis, John Lewis. 1988. "Expanding the Data Base: Historians, Political Scientists, and the Enrichment of Security Studies." *International Security* 12, no. 1: 3–21.

Gaddis, John Lewis. 1992. "The Unexpected John Foster Dulles." In *The United States and the End of the Cold War,* ed. John Lewis Gaddis. New York: Oxford University Press.

Gaenslen, Fritz. 1992. "Decision-Making Groups." In *Political Psychology and Foreign Policy,* ed. Eric Singer and Valerie Hudson. Boulder, CO: Westview Press.

Galloway, James. 1970. *The Tonkin Gulf Resolution.* Rutherford, NJ: Fairleigh Dickinson University Press.

Garthoff, Raymond L. 1994. *Detente and Confrontation.* Rev. ed. Washington, DC: Brookings Institution.

Geddes, Barbara. 1992. "The Use of Case Studies in Path Dependent Arguments." Paper presented at the annual meeting of the American Political Science Association, Chicago.

Gelb, Leslie H., and Richard K. Betts. 1979. *The Irony of Vietnam.* Washington, DC: Brookings Institution.

George, Alexander L. 1956. "American Policy-Making and the North Korean Aggression." *World Politics* 7:209–32.

George, Alexander L. 1969. "The Operational Code: A Neglected Approach to the

Study of Political Leaders and Decision-Making." *International Studies Quarterly* 13:190–222.

George, Alexander L. 1972. "The Case for Multiple Advocacy in Making Foreign Policy." *American Political Science Review* 66:751–95.

George, Alexander L. 1979. "Case Studies and Theory Development: The Method of Structured, Focused Comparison." In *Diplomacy,* ed. Paul Lauren. New York: Free Press.

George, Alexander L. 1980. *Presidential Decisionmaking in Foreign Policy: The Effective Use of Information and Advice.* Boulder, CO: Westview Press.

George, Alexander L. 1982. "Case Studies and Theory Development." Paper presented at the Second Annual Symposium on Information Processing in Organizations, Carnegie-Mellon University.

George, Alexander L. 1991. *Forceful Persuasion.* Washington, DC: U.S. Institute for Peace Press.

George, Alexander L. 1992. *Bridging the Gap: Theory and Practice in Foreign Policy.* Washington, DC: U.S. Institute of Peace Press.

George, Alexander L., ed. 1990. *Avoiding War.* Boulder, CO: Westview Press.

George, Alexander L., David K. Hall, and William E. Simons. 1971. *The Limits of Coercive Diplomacy: Laos, Cuba, Vietnam.* Boston: Little, Brown.

George, Alexander L., and Timothy J. McKeown. 1985. "Case Studies and Theories of Organizational Decision Making. In *Advances in Information Processing in Organizations.* Vol. 2. Ed. Richard F. Coulam and Robert A. Smith. Greenwich, CT: JAI Press.

George, Alexander L., and Richard Smoke. 1974. *Deterrence in American Foreign Policy.* New York: Columbia University Press.

George, Alexander L., and Richard Smoke. 1989. "Deterrence and Foreign Policy." *World Politics* 41:170–82.

George, Alexander L., and William E. Simons, eds. 1994. *The Limits of Coercive Diplomacy.* 2d ed. Boulder, CO: Westview Press.

Gerson, Louis J. 1967. *John Foster Dulles.* New York: Cooper Square.

Gilbert, Arthur N., and Paul G. Lauren. 1980. "Crisis Management: An Assessment and Critique." *Journal of Conflict Resolution* 24:641–64.

Gilboa, Eytan. 1995–96. "The Panama Invasion Revisited: Lessons for the Use of Force in the Post Cold War Era." *Political Science Quarterly* 110:539–62.

Gosnell, Harold F. 1980. *A Political Biography of Harry S. Truman.* Westport, CT: Greenwood Press.

Gould, Stephen J. 1989. *Wonderful Life.* New York: W. W. Norton.

Goulden, Joseph C. 1969. *Truth is the First Casualty.* Chicago: Rand-McNally.

Gravel, Michael. 1971. *The Pentagon Papers.* 5 vols. Boston: Beacon Press.

Greenstein, Fred I. 1982. *The Hidden-Hand Presidency.* New York: Basic Books.

Greenwood, Ted. 1975. *Making the MIRV: A Study of Defense Decision Making.* Cambridge, MA: Ballinger.

Guhin, Michael A. 1972. *John Foster Dulles.* New York: Columbia University Press.

Gurtov, Melvin. 1967. *The First Vietnam Crisis.* New York: Columbia University Press.

Haas, Michael. 1962. "Comparative Analysis." *Western Political Quarterly* 15:294–303.

Haas, Michael. 1986. "Research on International Crisis: Obsolescence of an Approach?" *International Interactions* 13:23–58.

Hagan, Joe D., Charles F. Hermann, and Margaret G. Hermann, eds. Forthcoming. *Leaders, Groups, and Coalitions: How Decision Units Shape Foreign Policy.*

Halberstam, David. 1972. *The Best and The Brightest.* New York: Random House.

Halper, Thomas. 1971. *Foreign Policy Crises: Appearance and Reality in Decision Making.* Columbus, OH: Charles S. Merrill Publishing Co.

Halperin, Morton H. 1974. *Bureaucratic Politics and Foreign Policy.* Washington, DC: Brookings Institution.

Hammond, Paul Y. 1992. *LBJ and the Presidential Management of Foreign Relations.* Austin: University of Texas Press.

Haney, Patrick J. 1991. "Case Studies and Theory Development in the Analysis of Foreign Policy." Paper presented at the annual meeting of the Midwest Political Science Association, Chicago.

Haney, Patrick J. 1992. "Organizing for Foreign Policy: Presidents, Advisers, and Crisis Decision-Making." Ph.D. diss., Indiana University.

Haney, Patrick J. 1994a. "Decision-Making During International Crises: A Reexamination." *International Interactions* 19:177–91.

Haney, Patrick J. 1994b. "The Nixon Administration and Middle East Crises: Theory and Evidence of Presidential Management of Foreign Policy Decision-Making." *Political Research Quarterly* 48:939–59.

Haney, Patrick J. 1995a. "Structure and Process in the Analysis of Foreign Policy Crises." In *Foreign Policy Analysis,* ed. Laura Neack, Jeanne A. K. Hey, and Patrick J. Haney. Englewood Cliffs, NJ: Prentice-Hall.

Haney, Patrick J. 1995b. "Defining Foreign Policy Crises." Paper presented at the annual meeting of the International Studies Association, Chicago.

Haney, Patrick J., Roberta Q. Herzberg, and Rick K. Wilson. 1992. "Advice and Consent: Unitary Actors, Advisory Models, and Experimental Tests." *Journal of Conflict Resolution* 36:603–33.

Hart, Paul 't. 1990. *Groupthink in Government: A Study of Small Groups and Policy Failure.* Amsterdam: Swetz and Zeitlinger.

Hayes, Robert H., Steven C. Wheelwright, and Kim B. Clark. 1988. *Dynamic Manufacturing.* New York: Free Press.

Henderson, Phillip G. 1988. *Managing the Presidency: The Eisenhower Legacy.* Boulder, CO: Westview Press.

Herek, Gregory M., Irving L. Janis, and Paul Huth. 1987. "Decision Making During International Crisis." *Journal of Conflict Resolution* 31:203–26.

Herek, Gregory M., Irving L. Janis, and Paul Huth. 1989. "Quality of U.S. Decision-Making During the Cuban Missile Crisis: Major Errors in Welch's Reassessment." *Journal of Conflict Resolution* 33:446–59.

Herken, Gregg. 1992. *Cardinal Choices: Presidential Science Advising from the Atomic Bomb to SDI.* New York: Oxford University Press.

Hermann, Charles F. 1969. *Crises in Foreign Policy.* Indianapolis: Bobbs-Merrill.

Hermann, Charles F. 1978. "Decision Structure and Process Influences on Foreign Policy." In *Why Nations Act,* ed. Maurice A. East, Stephen A. Salmore, and Charles F. Hermann. Beverly Hills, CA: Sage.

Hermann, Charles F., ed. 1972. *International Crises.* New York: Free Press.

Hermann, Margaret G. 1980. "Explaining Foreign Policy Behavior Using the Personal Characteristics of Political Leaders." *International Studies Quarterly* 24:7–46.

Hermann, Margaret G., and Charles F. Hermann. 1989. "Who Makes Foreign Policy Decisions and How? An Empirical Inquiry." *International Studies Quarterly* 33:361–87.

Hermann, Margaret G., Charles F. Hermann, and Joe D. Hagan. 1987. "How Decision Units Shape Foreign Policy Behavior." In *New Directions in the Study of Foreign Policy,* ed. Charles F. Hermann, Charles W. Kegley, and James N. Rosenau. Boston: Unwin Hyman.

Hermann, Margaret G., and Thomas Preston. 1994. "Presidents, Advisers, and Foreign Policy: The Effect of Leadership Style on Executive Arrangements." *Political Psychology* 15:75–96.

Herrmann, Richard K. 1988. "The Empirical Challenge of the Cognitive Revolution: A Strategy for Drawing Inferences about Perceptions." *International Studies Quarterly* 32:175–203.

Hess, Stephen. 1988. *Organizing the Presidency.* 2d ed. Washington, DC: Brookings Institution.

Hill, Dilys M., and Phil Williams. 1994. "Introduction: The Bush Administration—An Overview." In *The Bush Presidency: Triumphs and Adversities,* ed. Dilys M. Hill and Phil Williams. New York: St. Martin's Press.

Hilsman, Roger. 1967. *To Move a Nation.* New York: Dell.

Hoffman, David. 1990. "Zip My Lips: Bush's Secret Conduct of U.S. Policy." *Washington Post,* January 7.

Hogarth, Robin M., and Melvin W. Reder, eds. 1987. *Rational Choice.* Chicago: University of Chicago Press.

Holsti, Ole R. 1962. "The Belief System and National Images: A Case Study." *Journal of Conflict Resolution* 6:244–52.

Holsti, Ole R. 1972. *Crisis, Escalation, War.* Montreal: McGraw-Queens University Press.

Holsti, Ole R. 1979. "Theories of Crisis Decision Making." In *Diplomacy,* ed. Paul Lauren. New York: Free Press.

Holsti, Ole R. 1980. "Historians, Social Scientists, and Crisis Management: An Alternative View." *Journal of Conflict Resolution* 24:665–82.

Holsti, Ole R. 1989. "Crisis Decision Making." In *Behavior, Society, and Nuclear War.* Vol. 1. Ed. Philip E. Tetlock, Charles Tilly, Robert Jervis, Jo L. Husbands, and Paul C. Stern. New York: Oxford University Press.

Hoopes, Townsend. 1969. *The Limits of Intervention.* New York: McKay.

Hoopes, Townsend. 1973. *The Devil and John Foster Dulles.* Boston: Little, Brown.

Hult, Karen M. 1993. "Advising the President." In *Researching the Presidency,* ed.

George C. Edwards, John H. Kessel, and Bert A. Rockman. Pittsburgh: University of Pittsburgh Press.

Hunter, Robert E. 1988. *Organizing for National Security.* Washington, DC: Center for Strategic and International Studies.

Huth, Paul, and Bruce Russett. 1990. "Testing Deterrence Theory: Rigor Makes a Difference." *World Politics* 42:466–501.

Ikenberry, G. John. 1988. "An Institutionalist Approach to American Foreign Economic Policy." *International Organization* 42:219–43.

Immerman, Richard H. 1989. "Between the Unattainable and the Unacceptable." In *Reevaluating Eisenhower,* ed. Richard Melanson and David Mayers. Urbana: University of Illinois Press.

Isaacson, Walter, and Evan Thomas. 1986. *The Wise Men.* New York: Simon and Schuster.

Jackson, Henry, ed. 1965. *The National Security Council.* New York: Praeger.

James, Patrick. 1988. *Crisis and War.* Kingston and Montreal: McGill-Queens University Press.

Janis, Irving L. 1982. *Groupthink.* 2d ed. Boston: Houghton Mifflin.

Janis, Irving L. 1985. "Sources of Error in Strategic Decision Making." In *Organizational Strategy and Change,* ed. J. M. Pennings et al. San Francisco: Jossey-Bass.

Janis, Irving L. 1989. *Crucial Decisions.* New York: Free Press.

Janis, Irving L., and Leon Mann. 1977. *Decisionmaking.* New York: Free Press.

Jentleson, Bruce. 1992. "The Pretty Prudent Public." *International Studies Quarterly* 36:49–73.

Jervis, Robert. 1988. "War and Misperception." *Journal of Interdisciplinary History* 18:675–700.

Jervis, Robert. 1989. "Rational Deterrence: Theory and Evidence." *World Politics* 41:183–207.

Johnson, Lyndon B. 1971. *The Vantage Point.* New York: Holt, Rinehart, and Winston.

Johnson, Richard T. 1974. *Managing the White House.* New York: Harper and Row.

Kaarbo, Juliet, Ryan Beasley, and Margaret G. Hermann. 1990. "Comparative Case Analysis and Theory-Building." Paper presented at the annual meeting of the International Studies Association, Washington, DC.

Kalicki, J. H. 1975. *The Pattern of Sino-American Crises.* New York: Cambridge University Press.

Kasza, Gregory J. 1987. "Bureaucratic Politics in Radical Military Regimes." *American Political Science Review* 81:851–72.

Kearns, Doris. 1976. *Lyndon Johnson and the American Dream.* New York: Harper and Row.

Kempe, Frederick. 1990. *Divorcing the Dictator.* New York: Putnam.

Keohane, Robert O. 1988. "International Institutions: Two Approaches." *International Studies Quarterly* 32:379–96.

Keohane, Robert O. 1989. "Neoliberal Institutionalism." In *International Institutions and State Power.* Boulder, CO: Westview Press.

Kernell, Samuel. 1986. *Going Public.* Washington, DC: CQ Press.

Kernell, Samuel, and Samuel L. Popkin, eds. 1986. *Chief of Staff.* Berkeley: University of California Press.

Kessel, John H. 1983. "The Structures of the Carter White House." *American Journal of Political Science* 27:431–63.

Kessel, John H. 1984. "The Structures of the Reagan White House." *American Journal of Political Science* 28:231–58.

Kinder, Donald R., and Janet A. Weiss. 1978. "In Lieu of Rationality." *Journal of Conflict Resolution* 22:707–35.

King, Gary, Robert O. Keohane, and Sidney Verba. 1994. *Designing Social Inquiry.* Princeton, NJ: Princeton University Press.

Kingseed, Cole C. 1995. *Eisenhower and the Suez Crisis of 1956.* Baton Rouge: Louisiana State University Press.

Kiser, Larry L., and Elinor Ostrom. 1982. "The Three Worlds of Action." In *Strategies of Political Inquiry,* ed. Elinor Ostrom. Beverly Hills, CA: Sage.

Kissinger, Henry A. 1979. *The White House Years.* Boston: Little, Brown.

Kissinger, Henry A. 1982. *Years of Upheaval.* Boston: Little, Brown.

Krasner, Stephen D. 1971. "Are Bureaucracies Important? (Or Allison Wonderland)." *Foreign Policy* 7:159–79.

Krasner, Stephen D. 1984. "Approaches to the State: Alternative Conceptions and Historical Dynamics." *Comparative Politics* 16:223–46.

Krasner, Stephen D. 1988. "Sovereignty: An Institutional Perspective." *Comparative Political Studies* 21:66–94.

Krasner, Stephen D., ed. 1983. *International Regimes.* Ithaca: Cornell University Press.

Krehbiel, Keith, Kenneth A. Shepsle, and Barry M. Weingast. 1987. "Why are Congressional Committees Powerful?" *American Political Science Review* 81:929–45.

Kunz, Diane B. 1991. *The Economic Diplomacy of the Suez Crisis.* Chapel Hill: University of North Carolina Press.

Kyle, Keith. 1991. *Suez.* New York: St. Martin's Press.

Larson, Deborah Welch. 1985. *Origins of Containment.* Princeton, NJ: Princeton University Press.

Lebow, Richard Ned. 1981. *Between Peace and War.* Baltimore: Johns Hopkins University Press.

Lebow, Richard Ned. 1983. "The Cuban Missile Crisis: Reading the Lessons Correctly." *Political Science Quarterly* 98:431–58.

Lebow, Richard Ned, and Janice Gross Stein. 1989. "Rational Deterrence Theory: I Think, Therefore I Deter." *World Politics* 41:208–224.

Lebow, Richard Ned, and Janice Gross Stein. 1990. "Deterrence: The Elusive Dependent Variable." *World Politics* 42:336–69.

Lebow, Richard Ned, and Janice Gross Stein. 1994. *We All Lost the Cold War.* Princeton, NJ: Princeton University Press.

Levitt, Barbara, and James G. March. 1988. "Organizational learning." *Annual*

Review of Sociology 14:319–40.

Levy, Jack S. 1986. "Organizational Routines and the Causes of War." *International Studies Quarterly* 30:193–222.

Lieberson, Stanley. 1992. "Small N's and Big Conclusions: An Examination of the Reasoning in Comparative Studies Based on a Small Number of Cases." In *What is a Case?,* ed. Charles C. Ragin and Howard S. Becker. New York: Cambridge University Press.

Light, Paul C. 1982. *The President's Agenda.* Baltimore: Johns Hopkins University Press.

Lijphart, Arend. 1971. "Comparative Politics and the Comparative Method." *American Political Science Review* 65:682–93.

Lijphart, Arend. 1975. "The Comparable Cases Strategy in Comparative Research." *Comparative Political Studies* 8:158–77.

Lincoln, James R. 1982. "Intra- (and Inter-) Organizational Networks." In *Research in the Sociology of Organizations.* Vol. 2. Ed. Samuel B. Bacharach. Greenwich, CT: JAI Press.

Longley, Jeanne, and Dean G. Pruitt. 1980. "Groupthink: A Critique of Janis's Theory." *Review of Personality and Social Psychology* 1:74–93.

Lord, Carnes. 1988. *The Presidency and the Management of National Security.* New York: Free Press.

Love, Kenneth. 1969. *Suez: The Twice Fought War.* New York: McGraw-Hill.

Lovell, John P. 1966. "The Study of the Military in Developing Nations: Designing Meaningful and Manageable Research Strategies." Carnegie Seminar on Political and Administrative Development.

Lovell, John P. 1984. "Lessons of U.S. Military Involvement: Preliminary Conceptualization." In *Foreign Policy Decision-Making,* ed. Donald A. Sylvan and Steve Chan. New York: Praeger.

Lovell, John P. 1987. "Vietnam and the U.S. Army: Learning to Cope with Failure." In *Democracy, Strategy, and Vietnam,* ed. George K. Osborn et al. Lexington, MA: Lexington Books.

Mandel, Robert. 1986. "Psychological Approaches to International Relations." In *Political Psychology,* ed. Margaret G. Hermann. San Francisco: Jossey-Bass.

Maoz, Zeev. 1981. "The Decision to Raid Entebbe: Decision Analysis Applied to Crisis Behavior." *Journal of Conflict Resolution* 25:677–707.

Maoz, Zeev. 1990. "Framing the National Interest: The Manipulation of Foreign Policy Decisions in Group Settings." *World Politics* 43:77–110.

March, James G., and Johan P. Olsen. 1989. *Rediscovering Institutions.* New York: Free Press.

March, James G., and Herbert A. Simon. 1958. *Organizations.* New York: Wiley.

Marra, Robin F. 1985. "A Cybernetic Model of U.S. Defense Expenditure Policymaking Process." *International Studies Quarterly* 29:357–84.

Martin, Fenton. 1989. *Common Pool Resources and Collective Action: A Bibliography.* Workshop in Political Theory and Policy Analysis, Bloomington, Indiana.

Mastanduno, Michael, David A. Lake, and G. John Ikenberry. 1989. "Toward a Realist Theory of State Action." *International Studies Quarterly* 33:457–74.

Maynard-Moody, Steven. 1989. "Beyond Implementation: Developing an Institutional Theory of Administrative Policy-making." *Public Administration Review* 49:137–42.

Mayr, Ernst. 1982. *The Growth of Biological Thought.* Cambridge: Harvard University Press, Belknap Press.

McCalla, Robert B. 1992. *Uncertain Perceptions.* Ann Arbor: University of Michigan Press.

McCamy, James L. 1964. *Conduct of the New Diplomacy.* New York: Harper and Row.

McCullough, David. 1992. *Truman.* New York: Simon and Schuster.

McGinnis, Michael D. 1988. "Domestic Political Competition and the Unitary Rational Actor Assumption." Paper presented at the annual meeting of the International Studies Association, St. Louis, Missouri.

McGregor, Eugene B. 1981. "Administration's Many Instruments: Mining, Refining, and Applying Charles Lindblom's *Politics and Markets.*" *Administration and Society* 13:347–75.

Mefford, Dwain. 1987. "Analogical Reasoning and the Definition of the Situation." In *New Directions in the Study of Foreign Policy,* ed. Charles F. Hermann, Charles W. Kegley, and James N. Rosenau. Boston: Unwin Hyman.

Melan, Eugene H. 1989. "Process Management: A Unifying Framework for Improvement." *National Productivity Review* 8:395–406.

Melanson, Richard, and David Mayers, eds. 1989. *Reevaluating Eisenhower.* Urbana: University of Illinois Press.

Meltsner, Arnold J. 1990. *Rules for Rulers.* Philadelphia: Temple University Press.

Milburn, Thomas W. 1972. "The Management of Crises." In *International Crises,* ed. Charles F. Hermann. New York: Free Press.

Mill, John Stuart. [1843] 1967. *A System of Logic.* Reprint, Toronto: University of Toronto Press.

Mintzberg, Henry, Duru Raisinghani, and Andre Theoret. 1976. "The Structure of 'Unstructured' Decision Processes." *Administrative Science Quarterly* 21:246–75.

Moe, Terry M. 1989. "The Politics of Bureaucratic Structure." In *Can the Government Govern?,* ed. John E. Chubb and Paul E. Peterson. Washington, DC: Brookings Institution.

Moens, Alexander. 1991. "President Carter's Advisers and the Fall of the Shah." *Political Science Quarterly* 106:211–37.

Mohr, Lawrence B. 1985. "The Reliability of the Case Study as a Source of Information." In *Advances in Information Processing in Organizations.* Vol. 2, Ed. Richard F. Coulam and Robert A. Smith. Greenwich, CT: JAI Press.

Moïse, Edwin E. 1996. *Tonkin Gulf and the Escalation of the Vietnam War.* Chapel Hill: University of North Carolina Press.

Morgan, T. Cliff, and Sally Howard Campbell. 1991. "Domestic Structure, Decisional Constraints, and War." *Journal of Conflict Resolution* 35:187–211.

Morris, Roger. 1977. *Uncertain Greatness.* New York: Harper and Row.

Most, Benjamin A., and Harvey Starr. 1989. *Inquiry, Logic and International Politics.* Columbia: University of South Carolina Press.

Mueller, John E. 1974. *War, Presidents, and Public Opinion.* New York: Wiley.

Mulcahy, Kevin V. 1995. "Rethinking Groupthink: Walt Rostow and the National Security Advisory Process in the Johnson Administration." *Presidential Studies Quarterly* 25:237–50.

Mullins, Kerry, and Aaron Wildavsky. 1992. "The Procedural Presidency of George Bush." *Political Science Quarterly* 107:31–62.

Nathan, James A. 1975. "The Missile Crisis: His Finest Hour Now." *World Politics* 27:256–81.

Nathan, James A., and James K. Oliver. 1978. "Bureaucratic Politics: Academic Windfalls and Intellectual Pitfalls." *Journal of Political and Military Sociology* 6:81–91.

Neff, Donald. 1981. *Warriors at Suez.* New York: Linden Press/Simon and Schuster.

Nelson, Richard R. 1977. *The Moon and the Ghetto.* New York: W. W. Norton.

Netting, Robert McC. 1972. "Sacred Power and Centralization: Aspects of Political Adaption in Africa." In *Population and Growth,* ed. Brian Spooner. Cambridge: MIT Press.

Neustadt, Richard E. 1970. *Alliance Politics.* New York: Columbia University Press.

Neustadt, Richard E. 1990. *Presidential Power and the Modern Presidents.* New York: Free Press.

Neustadt, Richard E., and Ernest R. May. 1986. *Thinking in Time.* New York: Free Press.

Nichols, Elizabeth. 1986. "Skocpol and Revolution: Comparative Analysis vs. Historical Conjuncture." *Comparative Social Research* 9:163–86.

Nitze, Paul H. 1989. *From Hiroshima to Glasnost.* New York: Weidenfeld and Nicholson.

Nixon, Richard M. 1978. *RN: The Memoirs of Richard Nixon.* New York: Grosset and Dunlap.

North, Douglass C. 1990. "A Transaction Cost Theory of Politics." *Journal of Theoretical Politics* 2:355–67.

Oakerson, Ronald. 1987. *The Organization of Local Public Economies.* Washington, DC: Advisory Commission on Intergovernmental Relations.

Oberdorfer, Don. 1971. *Tet!* Garden City, NJ: Doubleday and Company.

Oneal, James R. 1982. *Foreign Policy Making in Times of Crisis.* Columbus: Ohio State University Press.

Orbovich, Cynthia B., and Richard K. Molnar. 1992. "Modeling Foreign Policy Advisory Processes." In *Political Psychology and Foreign Policy,* ed. Eric Singer and Valerie Hudson. Boulder, CO: Westview Press.

Osigweh, C. A. B. 1989. "Concept Fallibility in Organizational Science." *Academy of Management Review* 14:579–94.

Ostrom, Charles W. 1977. "Evaluating Alternative Foreign Policy Decision-Making Models." *Journal of Conflict Resolution* 21:235–66.

Ostrom, Charles W., and Brian L. Job. 1986. "The President and the Political Use of Force." *American Political Science Review* 80:541–66.

Ostrom, Elinor. 1986. "An Agenda for the Study of Institutions." *Public Choice* 48:3–25.

Ostrom, Elinor. 1990. *Governing the Commons.* Cambridge: Cambridge University Press.

Ostrom, Elinor. 1991. "Rational-Choice Theory and Institutional Analysis: Towards Complementarity." *American Political Science Review* 85:237–43.

Ostrom, Elinor. 1995. "New Horizons in Institutional Analysis." *American Political Science Review* 89:174–78.

Ostrom, Vincent. 1991. *The Meaning of American Federalism.* San Francisco: Institute for Contemporary Studies Press.

Ostrom, Vincent, and Elinor Ostrom. 1971. "Public Choice: A Different Approach to the Study of Public Administration." *Public Administration Review* 31:203–216.

Ostrom, Vincent, Charles M. Tiebout, and Robert Warren. 1961. "The Organization of Government in Metropolitan Areas: A Theoretical Inquiry." *American Political Science Review* 55:831–42.

Paige, Glenn D. 1968. *The Korean Decision.* New York: Free Press.

Paige, Glenn D. 1972. "Comparative Case Analysis of Crisis Decisions: Korea and Cuba." In *International Crises,* ed. Charles F. Hermann. New York: Free Press.

Palumbo, Dennis J. 1975. "Organization Theory and Political Science." In *The Handbook of Political Science.* Vol. 2. Ed. Fred I. Greenstein and Nelson W. Polsby. Reading, MA: Addison-Wesley.

Parks, Roger B. 1982. "How to Study the Effects of Structure." Working paper W82–13, Workshop in Political Theory and Policy Analysis, Indiana University.

Parmet, Herbert S. 1972. *Eisenhower and the American Crusades.* New York: Macmillan.

Pennings, Johannes M., and Paul S. Goodman. 1977. "Organizational Effectiveness: Toward a Workable Framework." In *New Perspectives on Organizational Effectiveness,* ed. Paul S. Goodman and Johannes M. Pennings. San Francisco: Jossey-Bass.

Perlmutter, Amos. 1974. "The Presidential Center and Foreign Policy: A Critique of the Revisionist and Bureaucratic-Political Orientations." *World Politics* 27:87–106.

Perlmutter, Amos. 1975. "Crisis Management." *International Studies Quarterly* 19:316–43.

Perry, James L. 1990. *The Organizational Consequences of Whistle-Blowing.* Washington, DC: Fund for Research on Dispute Resolution.

Perry, James L., and Hal G. Rainey. 1988. "The Public-Private Distinction in Organization Theory." *Academy of Management Review* 13:182–201.

Pika, Joseph A. 1981–82. "Moving Beyond the White House: Problems in Studying the Presidency." *Congress and the Presidency* 9:17–36.

Pika, Joseph A. 1988. "Management Style and the Organizational Matrix: Studying White House Operations." *Administration and Society* 20:3–29.

Pika, Joseph A., and Norman C. Thomas. 1991. "The Turn of the Century Presidency." Paper presented at the annual meeting of the Midwest Political Science Association, Chicago.

Plowden, William, ed. 1987. *Advising the Rulers.* Oxford: Basil Blackwell.

Porter, Roger B. 1980. *Presidential Decision-Making: The Economic Policy Board.* New York: Cambridge University Press.

Powell, Colin L. 1995. *My American Journey.* New York: Random House.

Prados, John. 1991. *Keepers of the Keys: A History of the National Security Council from Truman to Bush.* New York: Morrow.

Przeworski, Adam, and Henry Teune. 1970. *The Logic of Comparative Social Inquiry.* New York: Wiley.

Quandt, William B. 1977. *Decade of Decisions.* Berkeley: University of California Press.

Quandt, William B. 1978. "Lebanon, 1958, and Jordan, 1970." In *Force Without War,* ed. Barry Blechman and Morton Kaplan. Washington, DC: Brookings Institution.

Quandt, William B. 1993. *Peace Process.* Washington, DC: Brookings Institution; Berkeley: University of California Press.

Ragin, Charles C. 1987. *The Comparative Method.* Berkeley: University of California Press.

Ragin, Charles C. 1992. "'casing' and the Process of Social Inquiry." In *What is a Case?* ed. Charles C. Ragin and Howard S. Becker. New York: Cambridge University Press.

Ragin, Charles C., and Howard S. Becker, eds. 1992. *What Is a Case?* New York: Cambridge University Press.

Rainey, Hal G. 1984. "Organization Theory and Political Science." *Policy Studies Journal* 13:5–22.

Rainey, Hal G., Robert W. Backoff, and Charles H. Levine. 1976. "Comparing Public and Private Organizations." *Public Administration Review* 36:233–44.

Randle, Robert F. 1969. *Geneva 1954.* Princeton, NJ: Princeton University Press.

Ravenal, Earl C. 1978. *Never Again.* Philadelphia: Temple University Press.

Report of the Commission on the Organization of the Government for the Conduct of Foreign Policy. 1975. Washington, DC: U.S. Government Printing Office.

Ripley, Brian. 1988. "Rethinking Groupthink: Methods and Evidence." Paper presented at the annual meeting of the International Studies Association—Midwest, Columbus, OH.

Ripley, Brian. 1995. "Cognition, Culture, and Bureaucratic Politics." In *Foreign Policy Analysis,* ed. Laura Neack, Jeanne A. K. Hey, and Patrick J. Haney. Englewood Cliffs, NJ: Prentice-Hall.

Roberts, Jonathan M. 1988. *Decision-Making During International Crises.* New York: St. Martin's Press.

Robinson, James A. 1972. "Crisis: An Appraisal of Concepts and Theories." In *International Crises,* ed. Charles F. Hermann. New York: Free Press.

Robinson, James A., and Roger Majak. 1967. "The Theory of Decision-Making." In *Contemporary Political Analysis,* ed. James C. Charlesworth. New York: Free Press.

Robinson, James A., and Richard C. Snyder. 1965. "Decision-Making in International Politics." In *International Behavior,* ed. Herbert C. Kelman. New York: Holt, Rinehart, and Winston.

Rockman, Bert A. 1984. *The Leadership Question.* New York: Praeger.

Rockman, Bert A. 1986. "Presidential and Executive Studies: The One, the Few, and the Many." In *Political Science: The Science of Politics,* ed. Herbert F. Weisberg. New York: Agathon Press.

Rockman, Bert A. 1991. "The Leadership Style of George Bush." In *The Bush Presidency: First Appraisals,* ed. Colin Campbell and Bert A. Rockman. Chatham, NJ: Chatham House Publishers.

Rosati, Jerel A. 1981. "Developing a Systemic Decision-Making Framework: Bureaucratic Politics in Perspective." *World Politics* 33:234–52.

Rosenau, James N. 1966. "Pre-Theories and Theories of Foreign Policy." In *Approaches to Comparative and International Politics,* ed. R. Barry Farrell. Evanston, IL: Northwestern University Press.

Rosenau, James N. 1980. "Thinking Theory Thoroughly" (revised). In *The Scientific Study of Foreign Policy,* ed. James N. Rosenau. London: Frances Pinter.

Rosenthal, Robert. 1991. *Meta-Analytic Procedures for Social Research.* Rev. ed. Beverly Hills, CA: Sage.

Ross, Stephen A. 1973. "The Economic Theory of Agency: The Principal's Problem." *American Economic Review* 63:134–39.

Russett, Bruce M. 1970. "International Behavior Research: Case Studies and Cumulation." In *Approaches to the Study of Political Science,* ed. Michael Haas and Henry S. Kariel. Scranton, PA: Chandler Publishing.

Russett, Bruce M. 1990. *Controlling the Sword.* Cambridge: Harvard University Press.

Sagan, Scott D. 1979. "Lessons of the Yom Kippur Alert." *Foreign Policy* 36:160–77.

Sagan, Scott D. 1985. "Nuclear Alerts and Crisis Management." *International Security* 9 (spring): 99–139.

Savas, E. E. 1987. *Privatization.* Chatham, NJ: Chatham House.

Schandler, Herbert Y. 1977. *The Unmaking of a President.* Princeton, NJ: Princeton University Press.

Schilling, Warner R. 1962. "Scientists, Foreign Policy, and Politics." *American Political Science Review* 56: 287–300.

Schwenk, Charles. 1988. *The Essence of Strategic Decision Making.* Lexington, MA: Lexington Books.

Scott, Andrew M. 1969. "The Department of State: Formal Organization and Informal Culture." *International Studies Quarterly* 13:1–18.

Scott, Andrew M. 1970. "Environmental Change and Organizational Adaption: The Problem of the State Department." *International Studies Quarterly* 14:85–94.

Scott, W. Richard. 1987. "The Adolescence of Institutional Theory." *Administrative Science Quarterly* 32:493–511.

Scranton, Margaret E. 1991. *The Noriega Years.* Boulder, CO: Lynne Reinner Press.

Shafer, D. Michael. 1988. *Deadly Paradigms.* Princeton, NJ: Princeton University Press.

Shangraw, R. F., and Michael M. Crow. 1989. "Public Administration as a Design Science." *Public Administration Review* 49:153–58.

Shapiro, Michael J., and G. Matthew Bonham. 1973. "Cognitive Processes and Foreign Policy Decision-Making." *International Studies Quarterly* 17:147–74.

Shepsle, Kenneth A. 1979. "Institutional Arrangements and Equilibrium in Multidimensional Voting Models." *American Journal of Political Science* 23:27–60.

Shepsle, Kenneth A. 1989. "Studying Institutions: Some Lessons from the Rational Choice Approach." *Journal of Theoretical Politics* 1:131–47.

Shlaim, Avi. 1983. *The United States and the Berlin Blockade, 1948–1949.* Berkeley: University of California Press.

Shlaim, Avi, and Richard Tanter. 1978. "Decision Process, Choice, and Consequences." *World Politics* 30:483–516.

Shull, Steven A. 1989. "Presidential Influence Versus Bureaucratic Discretion: President-Agency Relations." *American Review of Public Administration* 19:197–215.

Sickels, Robert J. 1974. *Presidential Transactions.* Englewood Cliffs, NJ: Prentice-Hall.

Sigal, Leon V. 1970. "The Rational Policy Model and the Formosa Straits Crisis." *International Studies Quarterly* 14:121–56.

Sigelman, Lee, and Dixie Mercer McNeil. 1980. "White House Decision-Making Under Stress." *American Journal of Political Science* 24:652–73.

Simon, Herbert A. 1981. *The Sciences of the Artificial.* 2d ed. Cambridge: MIT Press.

Singer, J. David. 1977. "The Historical Experiment as a Research Strategy in the Study of World Politics." *Social Science History* 2:1–22.

Small, Melvin. 1979. "The Quantification of Diplomatic History." In *Diplomacy,* ed. Paul Lauren. New York: Free Press.

Smelser, Neil J. 1976. *Comparative Methods in the Social Sciences.* Englewood Cliffs, NJ: Prentice-Hall.

Smith, Jean Edward. 1963. *The Defense of Berlin.* Baltimore: Johns Hopkins University Press.

Snyder, Glenn H., and Paul Diesing. 1977. *Conflict Among Nations.* Princeton, NJ: Princeton University Press.

Snyder, Richard C., H. W. Bruck, and Burton Sapin, eds. 1962. *Foreign Policy Decision-Making.* New York: Free Press.

Spann, Robert M. 1977. "Public Versus Private Provision of Governmental Services." In *Public Management,* ed. James L. Perry and Kenneth L. Kraemer. Palo Alto, CA: Mayfield.

Starbuck, William H., and Paul C. Nystrom. 1981. *Handbook of Organizational Design.* New York: Oxford University Press.

Steinbruner, John D. 1974. *The Cybernetic Theory of Decision.* Princeton, NJ: Princeton University Press.

Steiner, Miriam. 1977. "The Elusive Essence of Decision." *International Studies Quarterly* 21:389–422.

Stern, Eric, and Bengt Sundelius. 1992. "Managing Asymmetrical Crisis." *International Studies Quarterly* 36:213–39.

Stuart, Philip D., Margaret G. Hermann, and Charles F. Hermann. 1989. "Modeling the 1973 Soviet Decision to Support Egypt." *American Political Science Review* 83:35–59.

Sylvan, Donald A., and Steve Chan, eds. 1984. *Foreign Policy Decision Making: Perception, Cognition and Artificial Intelligence.* New York: Praeger.

Sylvan, Donald A., Ashok Goel, and B. Chandrasekaran. 1990. "Analyzing Political Decision Making from an Information-Processing Perspective: JESSE." *American Journal of Political Science* 34:74–123.

Sylvan, Donald A., and Stuart J. Thorson. 1992. "Ontologies, Problem Representations, and the Cuban Missile Crisis." *Journal of Conflict Resolution* 36:709–32.

Tanter, Raymond. 1978. "International Crisis Behavior: An Appraisal of the Literature." *Jerusalem Journal of International Relations* 3, no. 2–3: 340–74.

Thomas, Hugh. 1970. *The Suez Affair.* 2d ed. Middlesex, England: Penguin.

Truman, Harry S. 1956. *Memoirs.* Vol. 2. Garden City, NY: Doubleday.

Tullock, Gordon. 1981. "Why So Much Stability?" *Public Choice* 37:189–205.

Tullock, Gordon. 1987. *The Politics of Bureaucracy.* Lanham, MD: University Press of America.

Vandenbroucke, Lucien S. 1984. "Anatomy of a Failure: The Decision to Land at the Bay of Pigs." *Political Science Quarterly* 99:471–91.

Vaughan, Diane. 1990. "Autonomy, Interdependence, and Social Control: NASA and the Space Shuttle *Challenger.*" *Administrative Science Quarterly* 35:225–57.

Ventriss, Curtis, and Jeff Luke. 1988. "Organizational Learning and Public Policy." *American Review of Public Administration* 18:337–57.

Verba, Sidney. 1967. "Some Dilemmas of Comparative Research." *World Politics* 20:117–27.

Vertzberger, Yaacov Y. I. 1990. *The World in Their Minds.* Stanford, CA: Stanford University Press.

Wachter, Kenneth W., and Miron L. Straf, eds. 1990. *The Future of Meta-Analysis.* New York: Russell Sage.

Wagner, Abraham R. 1974. *Crisis Decision-Making.* New York: Praeger.

Walcott, Charles E., and Karen M. Hult. 1995. *Governing the White House: From Hoover through LBJ.* Lawrence: University Press of Kansas.

Walker, Stephen G. 1977. "The Interface Between Beliefs and Behavior: Henry Kissinger's Operational Code and the Vietnam War." *Journal of Conflict Resolution* 21:129–68.

Walker, Stephen G. 1987. "Role Theory and the Origins of Foreign Policy." In *New Directions in the Study of Foreign Policy,* ed. Charles F. Hermann, Charles W. Kegley, and James N. Rosenau. Boston: Unwin Hyman.

Weil, Herman M. 1975. "Can Bureaucracies be Rational Actors?" *International Studies Quarterly* 19:432–68.

Welch, David A. 1989. "Crisis Decision Making Reconsidered." *Journal of Conflict Resolution* 33:430–45.

Welch, David A. 1992. "The Organizational Process and Bureaucratic Politics Paradigm: Retrospect and Prospect." *International Security* 17, no. 2: 112–46.

Weldes, Jutta. 1992. "Constructing a Nuclear Crisis: The Cuban Missile Crisis and U.S. National Interests." Paper presented at the annual meeting of the International Studies Association, Atlanta.

Whyte, Glen. 1989. "Groupthink Reconsidered." *Academy of Management Review* 14:40–56.

Wilkenfeld, Jonathan. 1991. "Trigger-Response Transitions in Foreign Policy Crises, 1929–1985." *Journal of Conflict Resolution* 35:143–69.

Williams, Phil. 1976. *Crisis Management.* New York: Wiley.

Williamson, Oliver E. 1975. *Markets and Hierarchies.* New York: Free Press.

Williamson, Oliver E. 1981. "The Economics of Organization: The Transaction Cost Approach." *American Journal of Sociology* 87:548–77.

Williamson, Samuel R. 1979. "Theories of Organizational Process and Foreign Policy Outcomes." In *Diplomacy,* ed. Paul Lauren. New York: Free Press.

Wilson, James Q. 1989. *Bureaucracy.* New York: Basic Books.

Windchy, Eugene G. 1971. *Tonkin Gulf.* Garden City, NJ: Doubleday.

Wise, Charles R. 1990. "Public Service Configurations and Public Organizations." *Public Administration Review* 50:141–55.

Wolf, Patrick J. 1995. *What History Advises About Reinventing Government: A Case Meta-Analysis of Bureaucratic Effectiveness in U.S. Federal Agencies.* Unpublished Ph.D. dissertation, Department of Government, Harvard University, Cambridge, MA.

Woodward, Bob. 1991. *The Commanders.* New York: Pocket Star Books.

Yin, Robert K. 1981. "The Case Study Crisis." *Administrative Science Quarterly* 26:58–65.

Yin, Robert K. 1984. *Case Study Research.* Beverly Hills, CA: Sage.

Yin, Robert K., and Karen A. Heald. 1975. "Using the Case Survey Method to Analyze Policy Studies." *Administrative Science Quarterly* 20:371–80.

Young, Oran. 1986. "International Regimes." *World Politics* 39:104–122.

Zinnes, Dina A. 1976. "The Problem of Cumulation." In *In Search of Global Patterns,* ed. James N. Rosenau. New York: Free Press.

Zucker, Lynn G. 1983. "Organizations as Institutions." In *Research in the Sociology of Organizations.* Vol. 2. Ed. Samuel B. Bacharach. Greenwich, CT: JAI Press.

Index

petitive-formalistic model, 64–67,
83, 115–16; and Dien Bien Phu,
62–63, 64–66, 90–93; and Eisenhower as active decision maker, 122;
and Erskine Group, 66; and learning
during crises, 132; and performance
of advisory structures, 130; and performance of decision-making tasks
in Dien Bien Phu, 90–93, 115–16;
and performance of decision-making
tasks in Suez crisis, 93–95, 115–16;
and relationship between Eisenhower and Dulles, 122; and Smith
Group, 66; and Suez Crisis, 63–64,
65–67, 93–95; and use of NSC, 12
Erskine, General Graves B., 66
Erskine Group, 66, 92
Eulau, Heinz, 23
Evans, Rowland, 100, 101
Executive Office of the President,
expansion of, 4
Experiments and quasi-experiments,
26–27

Fearon, James D., 27
Finletter, Thomas K., 60
Fitzwater, Marlin, 80
Flanagan, Edward M., Jr., 53, 105, 106
Foreign policy, as social construction,
144–45
Foreign policy bureaucracy, 129
Foreign policy crises. *See* Crises
Foreign policy processes: case studies
in, 13; definition of, 12; malfunc-
tions of, 13–15
Formalistic model: in Bush adminis-
tration, 80–83, 84, 129; in Nixon
administration, 75–79, 83, 129; in
Truman administration, 83, 129;
nature of, 7
Forrestall, James, 58
Fortas, Abe, 72
Foyle, Douglas C., 92
Frankel, Joseph, 3
Frendreis, John P., 26
Future research: allies in crises,

137–38; object of threat, 138–39;
presidential elections, 139–40; protracted crises, 140–41; simultaneous
crises, 140

Gaenslen, Fritz, 15
Galloway, James, 52
Garthoff, Raymond L., 77
Gates, Robert, 80
Geddes, Barbara, 23
Gelb, Leslie H., 5, 52, 64, 95, 122
Geneva Conference, 63
George, Alexander L., 1, 5, 7, 8, 9, 10,
12, 14, 15, 23, 27, 28, 29, 31, 32, 34,
38, 39, 40, 43, 44, 47, 58, 83, 89–90,
113, 117, 119–20, 128, 141, 146
Gilbert, Arthur N., 21
Goel, Ashok, 10
Goldberg, Arthur, 72
Gosnell, Harold F., 89
Gould, Stephen J., 17
Goulden, Joseph C., 52, 95, 96
Government organization, studies on,
3–4
Gravel, Michael, 51
Greenberg, Sanford D., 5
Greenstein, Fred I., 2, 7, 8, 9, 12, 31,
51, 65, 66, 91, 92, 93, 116
Groupthink, 13, 122

Haas, Michael, 21, 25
Haddad, Richard, 79
Hagan, Joe D., 10, 11, 12
Haig, Alexander, 78
Halberstam, David, 96
Halper, Thomas, 144
Halperin, Morton H., 10
Hammond, Paul Y., 4, 19
Hammond, Thomas H., 142
Heald, Karen A., 33, 34, 35
Henderson, Phillip G., 7
Herek, Gregory M., 2, 14–15, 37, 39,
47, 106–10
Herken, Gregg, 5
Hermann, Charles F., 9, 10, 11, 12, 36,
41